MY LIFE, MY WAY

It was a few bars of *Heartbreak Hotel,* heard briefly through the open window of a car, that captured his imagination. The young Cliff Richard and his friends were desperate to find out whose voice they had found so exciting. Once he discovered Elvis Presley, Cliff knew what he wanted to do with his life. This is his story, told by him. A committed Christian, knighted by the Queen for his charity work, it is not the usual rock star's tale – it's a fascinating story of a man who has broken all the rules, and a unique insight into one of the most iconic figures of our time.

MY LIFE, MY WAY

MY LIFE, MY WAY

by

Cliff Richard
with Penny Junor

Magna Large Print Books
Long Preston, North Yorkshire,
BD23 4ND, England.

British Library Cataloguing in Publication Data.

Richard, Cliff with Junor, Penny
    My life, my way.

    A catalogue record of this book is
    available from the British Library

    ISBN   978-0-7505-3085-9

First published in Great Britain in 2008 by Headline Review

Published in Large Print 2009 by arrangement with Headline Publishing Group Ltd.

Magna Large Print is an imprint of Library Magna Books Ltd.

Printed and bound in Great Britain by
T.J. (International) Ltd., Cornwall, PL28 8RW

Unless otherwise indicated,
all photographs are courtesy of
Cliff Richard and his family.

To my mum and dad,
who are now reunited, and who were an
even greater influence on me than Elvis;
and to all my fans, who have stuck
by me through the years.

ACKNOWLEDGEMENTS

My thanks to Penny Junor for spending many hours encouraging me to think back over my life and career. I've so appreciated her patience, her skill, and her ability to wheedle out of me events and experiences that I'd long since forgotten. Thanks, too, to Val Hudson and her team at Headline for surrounding my book with so much commitment and enthusiasm; and, of course, to Bill and Gill at my office for hours of liaison and back-up.

CONTENTS

PREFACE

This is my book, by me – not to be confused with any number of books *about* me. Maybe I'm naïve, but I have always found it very curious that people have been able to write and sell books about me and to make money out of my name without having had so much as the courtesy to ask. I am fcd up with being portrayed by people who assume they know what I feel.

If you want to know what I really feel about things, this is the book to read.

I can't promise that my memory of dates is going to be all that accurate because I have never kept diaries. I don't keep anything much, believe it or not; I don't even have a complete collection of my records. And this is not an encyclopaedic account of every last concert I've played or album I've made. Plenty of other people have already done that, and the internet is teeming with sites that fans have put together. What this is, is an attempt to put the last fifty years into some sort of context, to make sense of some of the extraordinary things that have happened to me and to explain, as best I can, what it has felt like being Cliff Richard.

INTRODUCTION

I was sitting in a scruffy transport café in the depths of the Brazilian countryside. The electric fans whirring overhead did nothing to alleviate the heat. We had stopped for a late lunch – along with most of the flies in South America – and the uncovered tin trays of cooked meats, beans and rice that had obviously been sitting there since mid-morning looked particularly unappetizing. Our guide, a Brazilian charity coordinator named João, had said a prayer when we set out on our journey in the bus from Recife six hours earlier. He had asked God to protect us on the road and make our journey profitable. He had said nothing about lunch, so I was playing safe. While a few of the others round the table flicked flies from their plates and diced with salmonella, I ate a granola bar I had bought passing through Miami and thought wistfully about what I could have been eating at home in Barbados. Some lightly grilled fish, maybe, with a crisp salad and a glass of Vida Nova Rosé, from my vineyard in Portugal...

It has been a long journey from Cheshunt, and the council estate where I lived with my family in the fifties. I don't live in any one place now: I am a gypsy, with homes in England, New York, Portugal – and Barbados, where I spend four months of the year when it's cold everywhere else. Not all of it has been red carpets and Rolls-Royces – although I must admit to having owned a Rolls for a while. I was talked into buying one in the seventies by Bruce Welch, the Shadows' guitarist. 'I can't spend more on a car than my sisters spent on a house,' I protested, but I did it anyway and I can't pretend I didn't enjoy it. Altogether, it has been a wonderful voyage – but one that still, in so many ways, puzzles me.

At seventeen, when it all began, my ambition was to be like Elvis Presley. I wanted to be a rock 'n' roll star, to stand on stage and have girls scream at me. Miraculously, it happened; it happened to this unexceptional teenager from an unexceptional town in Hertfordshire. The question is: How?

I had no background in show business, I'd had no piano lessons, no guitar lessons, no singing lessons and I still can't read music. I just went out there and emulated what I heard Elvis do on the radio; I formed a band and played in pubs and clubs for a year, and at the end of that year – almost to the day – I made my first record. A lot of that was luck.

But the real mystery is how, fifty years later, I am still performing when so many others who did the same thing – some of them truly great musicians – fell by the wayside. I look at other people who frankly could sing me under the table, yet never managed to get their careers off the ground. I have backing vocalists today who individually, and technically, could sing me off the map, but they have never made names for themselves as solo artists. They have tried and they've failed, and it's nothing to do with their talent because they work constantly. I can only conclude that I was lucky enough to have been born with that indefinable X factor. Alternatively, that someone somewhere had a purpose for me.

My father would have liked me to go to college or university. He would say, 'Get an education and then go for it, if singing is what you want to do,' but time goes so quickly and opportunities don't always come again. If I had followed his advice, I might have missed out on the success I've had in show business; so I have no regrets about the path I took.

But I don't doubt that in the 1950s it was an easier path than it is today. At that time the record companies said, 'Please sign here,' and then they would support their artists and help us improve. Bands today might sell ten million CDs but one failure and those same record companies will be debating whether it is worth their while going for another album. I have never sold ten million copies of one album in my life. My first record went to number two in the charts, my second was number seven, the third was number twenty. It was the fifth one, 'Living Doll', that reached number one, but in the meantime the record company was saying, 'Don't panic; we will find the right song for you.' They were supporting me in a way that doesn't seem to happen today. Today it's, 'Wheel them in and wheel them out.' So who knows whether some of the wonderfully talented singer-songwriters who are just starting out will be around in the years to come?

I was thrilled by my success in those early days, but I never expected it to last. I reckoned on five years at the most. Never, in my wildest dreams, did I think that I would still be rocking 'n' rolling, still filling arenas all over the world, and that girls would still be screaming at me, when I was old enough to have a bus pass. I have the odd grey hair – and so do many of the girls who scream – but so what? I have never stopped loving what I do, and while there are people out there who still enjoy listening to my music – no matter what age we all are – I shall continue to sing for them.

People have described me as an enigma,

but when it comes to how I achieved all this I'm as puzzled as anyone. I do have a few theories, however – and I *have* been lucky. I was lucky to have been born into a strong family, who have sustained me through the years and never allowed the fame and fortune to go too seriously to my head. My father, Rodger Webb, died, sadly, when I was twenty and my mother died, after many years of dementia, three days after my sixty-seventh birthday in 2007. But my sisters, Donna, Jacqui and Joan, are very close. They are probably my greatest fans, though they're not afraid to criticise me.

CHAPTER ONE

Back To The Future

We were brought up in a loving but highly disciplined, God-fearing household, with a very strict Victorian father whose word was law; and I guess, subliminally, his values became my values. He believed in hard work, good manners and honesty, and he took great care of the little money we had. 'Look after the pennies,' he would always say, 'and the pounds will look after themselves.' And he needed to look after the pennies. We were impoverished. I am certainly not impoverished today – yet I still can't leave a light on in an empty room, or let air-conditioning blast away when someone's opened a window. I can't bear it; I have to go in and turn it off. He instilled in me that nothing should be wasted.

He was quite aloof; I don't remember many fatherly hugs, but that may have been because I was the eldest – and a son. I was the only surviving boy: I had had a younger brother, Freddie, who was born in India, as I was, but he didn't live for more than a few weeks. I was only about twenty-one months old at the time so don't remember anything about it really, but my parents must have suffered terribly and I have often speculated what it might have been like to have had a brother.

Dad worked as a manager for Kellner's, a big catering business in India that serviced the railways. The job took him all over the country, so he was away for long periods at a time, but we lived very comfortably in a flat provided by the company in Howrah, a town outside Calcutta. We had servants to cook and clean, as most of the British living in India at that time did, and they too were paid for by the company.

I don't have very many memories of India. I remember it could be cold at night in winter, and if it rained, it flooded and we used to go out with our trousers rolled up, thinking: This is wonderful! Knee-high water was fun. The rest of the time it was swelteringly hot. We were not wealthy, but our life there was fantastic compared with what awaited us in England.

We came to England in 1948 when the British all flooded back home after India won its independence. My parents were British, but both of them had been born abroad and neither of them had ever been to England, so they had no 'home' to come to. My father was born in Burma, and my mother, Dorothy Dazely, in India, which is where they met. She came from a military family. My father wanted to take us all to Australia, but my mother's mother had recently gone to England with her second husband and seven children, and Dorothy wanted to follow her. She won the day. So after five weeks at sea we arrived at Tilbury Docks in Essex in September 1948. I was almost eight, Donna was five and Jacqui just ten months old.

My grandmother was living in a three-bedroom, semi-detached house in Carshalton in Surrey, and so it was to Carshalton that we went; but the house was scarcely big enough for my grandmother's family, let alone the five of us as well. Her neighbours agreed to let us rent their small front bedroom until we found a home, and so we slept in the house next door on mattresses on the floor and covered ourselves with blankets in an effort to keep warm.

We were destitute. My father had sold everything he had in India to raise enough money for our passage, but because the flat we lived in belonged to the company, he had very little to sell. We arrived in Britain with £5. That was it. Worse, my father couldn't find work. He was sixteen years older than my mother, so already in his forties; it was just after the War, rationing was still in place and there was very little work to be had, particularly for someone of his age.

Eventually he found a menial job in Essex. It involved a two-hour commute each way with several changes of bus, but he took it rather than accept hand-outs from the government, which he regarded as charity. 'While I can work, I will work,' he would say, and that is the work ethic that he handed down to me. In order to feed the family, my mother also had to find a job, and for a while was working night shifts. She and I shared a pair of shoes. I wore them to school in the day and she wore them at night. She had never worked in India – it would have been out of the question – but in England, as soon as my youngest sister was old enough to be left, it was essential. It was the only way my parents could hope to make ends meet.

Dad was the dominant force in the family. He was the decision-maker, and he was the one who handed out the punishments. I remember coming home from school one day and telling him that I had been caned unfairly. I insisted I had done nothing to deserve it. He picked up a cane and whacked me again on the back of the legs, which hurt even more than the caning I had had from the teacher. His explanation was that I wouldn't have been caned at school for no good reason. I had let the family down, he said. 'Remember, you are my son and they know that you are my son. They are probably thinking, Mr Webb can't bring up his child properly. This is a slur on me.' I'll never forget it. That was the last time I told him when I'd been in trouble at school. Thereafter, I just didn't tell him. But overall, I think he was probably right, and maybe as a society we are suffering today because we have not been strict enough with children and have allowed them to do their own thing too much. He didn't beat me, he hit me – there's a big difference; I was not abused, but what mattered most was that I didn't like incurring his displeasure.

My mother was the opposite. She was the one to whom we would run when Dad had walloped us. She was never disloyal to him; she never tried to score points. She managed to console us without taking sides. She would always ask what we had done to warrant the punishment, and when we protested that it had been nothing serious, she would say, 'Well, you shouldn't have done that. Don't do it again.' Then she would give us a big hug. So she was a perfect balance to him. She wasn't weak – and she had her own opinions about things – but at the same time she was the subservient wife.

I adored my mother and as a child I was closer to her than I was to my father. It wasn't until he became ill in my late teens, shortly before he died, that he and I developed any real relationship. And yet I don't remember ever feeling rebellious or resentful about his heavy-handedness.

My youngest sisters, Jacqui and Joan, have wonderful memories of my father. They remember how funny he was, how quick-witted, and the harshest punishment they remember was being made to sit on a chair for five minutes if they overstepped the mark. I think he had softened by the time they were born. Joan, the youngest of us all, doesn't remember being frightened of my father at all, nor that he was that much of a disciplinarian; but she was only eleven when he died, and as he had been sick for some time before that he had no doubt lost some of his fire. At times, as a kid, I was terrified of him.

One evening Donna and I wanted to go to the pictures. I was mad about the cinema and still am. My father took me aside and said, 'You can go on one condition: you have to look after your sister and you must both be back by ten o'clock.' The film was longer than usual, so we missed the bus and arrived home half an hour late. I shall never forget walking up the road to our house, panic rising as I saw it in darkness. The house was never dark. My father always left lights on. We knocked on the front door: nothing. We tried to look through gaps in the curtains but they were closed tight. We felt our way in the darkness round to the back and looked in through the kitchen window. There was nobody there. It was black inside. They had gone to bed, they couldn't be roused. There was nothing for it but to spend the night in the coal shed.

There wasn't much coal in the shed – there never was, we always had to eke it out – and my Dad had stored a big old-fashioned pram in there. So I put my sister in the pram and I sat in the coal dust by the wheels thinking I was in for a very miserable, cold, uncomfortable night. After what felt like an age, although was probably only ten minutes or so, the door opened and my father stood silhouetted in the doorway. 'Where have you been?' he demanded. I blurted out that we'd missed the bus and had to wait. 'When I say you have to be in at ten you must trust me that that's the right time for you to be home. If you're not back by then, the door will be locked. Now come inside.'

We all went into the kitchen where my mother was waiting; there was much hugging and I think she probably made us some cocoa. They hadn't gone to bed at all. They had watched us and decided to leave us just long enough to teach us a lesson. Years later my mother said, 'I remember that incident, but I don't think you ever realized how much we worried about you. The minute you were not back at the time you said you would be, we started to think of all the worst things that could possibly have happened to you.' My sisters, of course, went through exactly the same thing when they had their children: everything in life repeats itself. But we were never late again – ever; and to this day I am a stickler for being on time.

I learnt a lot from my father, from his approach to life, from the way he disciplined us and from his reasons for doing so. He was old-fashioned in his views about child-rearing – he was, remember, sixteen years older than my mother – and maybe some people would disapprove of the way he treated us: but although he ran our family with a rod of iron, and although this involved corporal punishment, it seems to me, with hindsight, entirely justified. I have no doubt that he loved us all and I think discipline, like criticism, is fine so long as it is done with love. I resented it at the time, of course, but looking back, he was never really wrong. We weren't two or three minutes late that night coming back from the cinema, we were thirty minutes late, so he was entitled to teach us a lesson. On another occasion, I remember being in the middle of a play rehearsal after school when, to my intense embarrassment, my father arrived and announced that he was taking me home. He apologized to the teacher for disrupting her group, but explained that I had been inconsiderate; I had failed to tell my mother that I would be late home.

The electricity in the house was coin-operated, as many domestic supplies were in the 1950s. You fed a meter with shilling coins and the lights and power came on. Sometimes the lights would go off in the middle of the evening and my father would say, 'Well, we're going to bed in a minute, let's not bother now.' So we would go to bed in the dark and wait until the morning before feeding the meter again. Every now and again, the guy from the Electricity Board would come and read the meter and he'd say, 'There's a ten-shilling refund here,' and my father would exclaim, 'Yes! Fantastic!'

Ten shillings was a lot of money for us at that time; it would buy food for at least two days. Three times a week our main meal was two slices of toast each with tea poured over them and sugar sprinkled on top. On the other days we would get rice and occasionally chicken and sometimes vegetables. I don't ever remember eating fish as a child. And we certainly never had sweets or cakes and biscuits; I don't even remember there being much fruit. It was tough but it didn't do us any harm, and if anything I think it had a beneficial effect on me. It made me appreciate that money doesn't buy happiness – although it does make being unhappy a lot more comfortable. I made money quite quickly at the start of my career, when I was still very young, and that can be quite difficult to handle. Many people in my business have gone off the rails for this reason and never really recovered, but I don't think a day goes by when I don't thank God for all that's happened to me and that I had such a close and loving family – also that we're not still on toast and tea!

At the age of eight, soon after we arrived in England from India, I remember my father saying to me, 'If anything happens between your mother and me, you must side with your mother. This is your role in life.' And I thought, All right, I'll do that. When he died in 1961, one could say I did precisely as he had instructed. I was already the bread-winner but I became the head of the family, the capable one, the man about the house and, to some extent, I suppose, the disciplinarian. I certainly kept a protective eye on my little sisters – and although one of them is now a grandmother, I guess I still do.

After just over a year we moved from Surrey to Hertfordshire, where my aunt Dorothy, my father's sister, and her husband had settled after leaving India. She offered us a room. Again it was a very small room, with two sets of bunk beds and mattresses on the floor. My parents slept on one of the bunk beds, two of us on the other and one on the floor, until my little sister Joan was born when there were two of us on the floor. We did everything in that room.

We lived, cooked, ate, drank, slept – there was even a little latrine in one corner And after Joan was born there was a washing line strung across the room with nappies drying. But by good fortune my mother made friends with the neighbour next door, while talking over the fence, and she invited Mum to have coffee with her one day. Then my mother invited her back in return.

'You live in this house?' said the neighbour.

'No,' said my mother. 'We live in this room.'

The neighbour was shocked. She happened to work for the council, so she took our case to the housing officer and persuaded an official to come and visit. He too was shocked, and as a result our application for a council house went to the top of the list. We didn't get one immediately, but within a year we had moved into a three-bedroom council house, 12 Hargreaves Close, in Cheshunt. The luxury. We had been in England for two years and this was the first time that the family had had more than one small room to live in.

We still slept on mattresses on the floor, though, and the first bed we ever had, my father made. He also made the first armchair. Both he built out of wooden packing cases which he bought from Atlas Lamps, where he had finally found a job that was no more than a cycle ride away. The company sold electrical appliances like lamps and television sets, which often arrived from the manufacturers packed in wooden crates that were pulled open and left lying around the yard. They let employees buy them for five shillings each. He must have bought himself some tools, too – although they can't have been very good tools – also some screws, and I remember watching him plane the rough wood to make the armchair.

He was always a great doer; he couldn't delegate. I would be the one who held the screws or the tools while he did the work. Looking back on it, I wish he had sometimes said, 'You do it. I'll watch, and if you get stuck, I'll be here.' I find I am exactly the same as my father was – I don't delegate. I will do jobs myself even though there are people around far better qualified to do them than me.

Atlas Lamps was part of Thorn Electrical Industries and my father worked in the credit control office. My mother had a job on the production line, where she did an eight-hour day before coming home to cook for the family. It was dull, menial work and she was never very happy there. She would stand by a conveyor belt alongside other women, putting filaments into bulbs as they passed. It was hardly taxing work, so to relieve the tedium she started to work faster – but the other women objected. They were being paid for the number of hours they worked, not the efficiency with which they fitted the filaments, and when she refused to slow down, she was sent to Coventry. She came home in tears because no one would speak to her. But it didn't deter her. She felt the other women were cheating the company and she didn't want any part of that.

Slowly, as time went by, we bettered our conditions; but it was tough, and when I think back to what they did, the respect I have for my parents grows ever greater. They suffered great hardship, but they never gave in and they never gave up hope; they did what they believed was right. Ours was the kind of hardship that either draws people more closely together or splits them apart completely; and our family became very close. Also, my parents were among the last of a generation that respected marriage and stuck with it through thick and thin. I think the secret was that they liked each other as much as they loved each other. That's not to say they didn't get annoyed with one another. If she was cross with my father, my mum would say, in front of him, 'Can you ask your father if he'd like a cup of tea?' and he would say, 'Tell your mother, "Yes please." They would laugh about it later – we all did. Nowadays, relationships seem to be dependent on the good things, not founded on the expectation that there might be some tough times to weather; and when things start to go drastically wrong, we tend to think, Why live through this? Life's too short.

I have often said that I would like to 'fall in like'. Falling in love is OK, but the nature of love changes, the passion goes, and unless you have a strong friendship you are left with the things that inevitably annoy you about that person. I've never understood how two people could fall out so badly they had to divorce simply because of the way one of them squeezed the tube of toothpaste – a story I once read somewhere. Having said that, I do get driven demented when guests are staying in my house and they put the loo roll on the holder the wrong way round! Nobody's perfect. But a close friendship is going to survive everything – and even if you do hate the way they eat peas off their knife, there will be so many other things you like about that person that the imperfections don't matter.

My mother and father also balanced each other perfectly. They brought up four children, who were all very different from one another, and despite the poverty, neither I nor my sisters ever remember being unhappy in our childhood.

Occasionally I would complain that our friends got pocket money, and Dad would say, 'We can't afford it'; but the minute he had some money he would give us something. 'OK, here's a shilling,' he would say.

'You may not get any more for a long time but this is your pocket money.'

I remember him winning £50 on the football pools one day. He said to my mother, 'I could put something down on a television set or we could have a radiogram.' We had had to sell the radio we'd had in India. My mother said, 'Radiogram,' so he bought one. It had a radio and a turntable and we loved it. Admittedly that came from winnings rather than earnings, but we were going up in the world; we had a radiogram and a couple of chairs and we were eating better.

Before the radiogram arrived we had a tiny crystal radio set with headphones, and we used to take it in turns to listen to Radio Luxembourg and occasionally the American Forces Network, which used to play all the doo-wop music. We loved messing around with it. Then my father bought a little portable radio, which my mother used to listen to while she was cooking, and I remember her writing down the lyrics of songs. She would have a pad of paper and pencil ready, and when she heard a song she liked, she would scribble away and catch as many words as she could. It usually took two or three playings before she had filled in all the gaps; and then she would sing along when those songs were played on the radio. I used to watch her; I was fascinated that she had the patience to do it. She would listen to people like Johnnie

Ray, Dickie Valentine, Frank Sinatra, Perry Como, Bing Crosby and Dean Martin. Theirs was the kind of music I grew up with, and although I liked some of it – particularly Perry Como's and Bing Crosby's – I didn't identify with any of those singers.

It was when I heard Elvis Presley for the first time that I thought: I can do that – and suddenly I knew what I wanted to do with my life.

CHAPTER TWO

Elvis

If there had been no Elvis, there would have been no Cliff Richard. Elvis changed everything. I hadn't the first idea who he was when I first heard him sing, but I soon found out. I was part of a little gang at school who hung out together. We were wandering around in Waltham Cross one day. My family had moved to Cheshunt, but I still liked to go back to where we'd lived with my aunt, to see my cousins. Meandering down the road we noticed a car, a dark green Citroën parked outside a newsagent's called Asplands. The window was down and the engine was running. A moment later the driver came running out of the shop, and as he did so this amazing music started coming out of the open car window. We heard no more than the opening two lines of it before the guy had jumped into the car and driven away, but it was enough. We stood there dumbfounded and went home determined to listen to every radio station until we heard that intro again and could discover who the singer was. I can't remember which one of us found it, I don't think it was me, but suddenly we knew about Elvis Presley – and were immediate fans. The song was 'Heartbreak Hotel'.

Sometimes on stage I have a kind of running gag with my fans. I tell them that if there had been no Elvis, there would be no Cliff Richard, and they say, 'Oh yes, there would,' in a sing-song pantomime sort of way, and I say, 'Oh no, there wouldn't,' and then the whole audience goes, 'Oh yes, there would!' It's a bit of fun but I don't think they realize quite how serious I am. In Elvis I really found the beginnings of what I wanted.

But without Jay Norris, my English and drama teacher at Cheshunt Secondary Modern School, I would never have known I could sing. Initially I was disappointed at having to go to the secondary modern. I had hoped to get into the grammar school; I was the top boy that year at my primary school and everyone expected me to sail through the eleven-plus, including me, my father and my teachers. It was a real blow when I failed – my father was horrified, and so was I – and from then on I was never really very academic, but in retrospect I was very lucky. The secondary modern had only just been built when I went there in 1952, so everyone was new and enthusiastic, and instead of maybe being at the bottom of the class in the grammar school, I managed to scrape into the top stream right the way through my schooling; and I am sure it was because of Jay's support.

Jay was in her mid-twenties, passionate about poetry and drama, and full of energy and optimism. She pinpointed several people in her English class and told us we had to join the Drama Society, we would enjoy it. She was right: I did enjoy it; we all thoroughly enjoyed it. I loved being on stage – in fact, I loved everything about the theatre. And she was so encouraging. I remember once having to explain my way out of not having done my homework and inevitably turning on the charm. At the end of it she said, 'When you leave school, you really should get a job that involves smiling at women.' I've reminded her of that so often.

When I reached the fifth form, aged about fifteen, Jay cast me as Ratty in a production of *Toad of Toad Hall* and she said, 'You know

Ratty's got to sing?' I was horrified. I enjoyed singing but I had never sung to anyone other than my family, and even then, if relatives or friends came to the house and my parents asked me to sing, I was so shy I'd always refused. I didn't think I would ever be able to stand and sing in front of an audience. I told Jay I couldn't do it, but she said, 'Nonsense. If you won't sing, you can't play Ratty.' So reluctantly I did it, and I found to my surprise that I quite enjoyed it.

Jay was my form teacher that year; the year I was made a prefect. It was also the year that rock 'n' roll hit Britain in the shape of the American artist Bill Haley and the Comets and an unforgettable song called 'Rock Around The Clock'. He took the country by storm, and my friends and I were all desperate to see him. We thought we'd never get tickets unless we went very early on the Monday morning the ticket office opened, so three of us volunteered (although I am not sure that volunteered is actually the right word) to get up at four o'clock in the morning to go to the Regal Cinema in Edmonton, where he was playing, to buy tickets. We had been planning to go back to school for the afternoon – we had got there at six – but the box office didn't open until midday, so we decided it was too late to go in to school and went home instead and started playing records. Unfortunately, someone snitched on us and we were hauled before the head-master. 'This is very disappointing,' he said, as he solemnly stripped us all of our prefects' badges.

Back in the classroom, Jay said the same thing. 'And to think you would do this for something so inconsequential. You won't even remember Bill Haley ten years from now.'

'I bet we do,' I retorted.

Ten years to the day, after I had left school, I knocked on Jay's door with a big box of chocolates and I said, 'You don't owe me anything, but I'm reminding you: Bill Haley.'

It was my first rock concert and it was unbelievably exciting. I am sorry I lost my prefect's badge but I needed to be there – I can remember that feeling. We couldn't afford anything better than balcony seats and we were four or five rows back. He started with 'Razzle Dazzle'. There was no introduction: red velvet curtains opened and we heard, 'On your marks, get set, get ready, go man go!' And we were up on our feet, stomping on the floor, and we stayed on our feet for the whole of the show. I thought the balcony was going to give way – and people have said this when they come to my shows – the whole thing was shaking. Everybody was on their feet, fists in the air. It was a fantastic experience, and I would have gone again, but they never came back. They arrived in an explosion of promotion and publicity, thousands of people were waiting for them in Birmingham and Manchester, the shows were all sold out, everybody loved them, and yet when they left no one knew they had gone. They disappeared without a whimper.

That was my last year at school. I had discovered Elvis, I couldn't get him out of my mind, and academia went down the tubes. I couldn't be bothered with it; I started missing out on homework and had no interest in school life any more. I couldn't wait to leave. I was still terrified of singing in public but I knew that this was what I wanted to do; I wanted to be like Elvis and I practised hard. I played his records and sang along to them, curling my lip, thrusting my hips and combing my hair into a quiff like his. Not surprisingly, when I left school in the summer of 1957, aged not yet seventeen, I had passed just one O Level, in English. My father was very disappointed by my results. I had stayed on at school, along with fifteen others in the top stream, especially to take O Levels when most of our contemporaries had left and gone straight into jobs and apprenticeships; and I had come away a year later with practically nothing to show for it. After a summer job picking tomatoes, I started at Atlas Lamps, where my father had found me a job. By day, I clocked in as a filing clerk, which bored me witless, on £4 a week; by night I played rock 'n' roll in pubs and youth clubs.

Dad had bought me my first guitar for my sixteenth birthday. He had played banjo in a trad jazz band when he was younger and he taught me some useful chord progressions. The guitar cost him £27, and he could never have afforded to pay for it outright. My mother was the one who encouraged me. She would say, 'Let's write off to Hughie Green,' who presented a television programme called *Opportunity Knocks*, or, 'Let's apply for this local talent competition,' and she would come with me, when my father was at work. I wouldn't win, but I might get through a heat to the second or third round and she would be right behind me. My father would say, 'This is good but don't forget, if it doesn't happen, you still have to have a job and a life. Always remember that.' That said, the minute I did make it, he was one hundred per cent behind me – and closely involved in everything I did. In the beginning, I was still a minor: in the fifties you didn't come of age until twenty-one. He managed me, he looked after me and he made sure I wasn't exploited. And he came on the road with me whenever he could.

To begin with I was playing skiffle, a style of music that people like Lonnie Donegan made popular in the fifties. Skiffle originated in New Orleans in the 1900s and was traditionally played on washboards and improvised instruments. It wasn't the sort of music I wanted to be singing at all, but I heard that a skiffle group, led by Dick Teague, was looking for a singer. By sheer good luck I bumped into an old school friend on the bus whose boyfriend was the drummer in the band, so I auditioned. We only played in pubs and village halls, but it was a fantastic opportunity to sing and to perform in front of audiences. As luck would have it, I had a kindred spirit in Terry Smart, the drummer, who shared my enthusiasm for rock 'n' roll, and eventually we left Dick Teague and formed our own band, recruiting Norman Mitham, whom I had known at school, as guitarist. We called ourselves the Drifters and rehearsed every night in the front room at my parents' house in Hargreaves Close. Each week we bought new singles and we worked out the chords while Donna, my eldest sister, wrote out the lyrics for us, just as Mum had always done.

Our lucky break came early in 1958 at a pub called the Five Horseshoes in Hoddesdon, where a guy called John Foster happened to be drinking with his mates at the bar. He asked whether we needed a manager; he could get us a gig at the 2i's. We'd read about the 2i's. It was a coffee bar in Old

Compton Street, in Soho, named after two Iranians who had once owned it. It was the Mecca of British rock 'n' roll and had launched the careers of stars like Tommy Steele and Terry Dene. They had live music in the cellar, and for anyone interested in rock 'n' roll it was the only place to be; the prospect of being able to play there was all we could have wished for. John Foster wasn't all we thought him. The closest he had been to rock 'n' roll, we discovered later, was to have stood next to Terry Dene at the 2i's. John was a lorry driver who had no experience of music management whatsoever – but he loved rock 'n' roll, liked what he heard us doing and knew the man who booked the gigs at the 2i's. We leapt at his offer to steer our careers and agreed to meet him on the Green Line bus to London the following Saturday.

It was a day I shall never forget. I hadn't been to Soho before, had never seen so many strange and exotic people. There were no coffee bars in Cheshunt, with the noise of the Gaggia machines and the pungent smell of freshly made coffee. Coffee bars were a new thing and the 2i's was humming. We auditioned that afternoon and that night we played to our first paying audience. We were not the star act, but we went down well and we were invited back the next night and the one after that. They kept us on for the whole week, playing for peanuts. I think we earned £10 between us. We were convinced we were going to be discovered and our careers would take off – but absolutely nothing happened. We did, however, meet some important people. We met Ian Samwell, who became our lead guitarist and who went on to write the song that turned me into a recording artist and changed my life for ever. He was playing in a skiffle group but, like me, knew his real love was rock 'n' roll, and when he heard the sort of music we were playing he immediately asked whether he could join us.

We also met a girl called Jan Vane, who was there with her sister. She said, 'I think you're fantastic. I'd like to start a fan club.'

We hooted with laughter and said, 'OK, we haven't any fans but, yes, we'll have a fan club!'

The third person we met during that week was a guy called Harry Greatorex, who ran a ballroom in Ripley in Derbyshire. He wanted to book us, but he wanted us to be Harry Webb and the Drifters.

I said, 'No, we're just a band; we're called the Drifters.'

He said, 'No, I need a name at the front.'

I said, 'Well you can't have Harry Webb, that's not on the cards.'

'In that case,' he said, 'we'll have to think of one.'

So we all went off to a pub round the corner in Old Compton Street called the Swiss, sat down with some drinks and went through names. Someone suggested Russ Clifford and I said, 'No thanks.' Then came Cliff Russard. I said, 'Cliff sounds good ... rock face, rock 'n' roll...' Then someone else suggested Richards with an 's' on the end, and Ian Samwell said, 'Wait a minute. Why don't you drop the "s", then you've got two Christian names, Cliff and Richard, which is unusual so people will remember it, and it can also be a tribute to Little Richard.' I thought, Perfect, it's all very rock 'n' roll; and 'Cliff Richard and the Drifters' sounded good.

Why didn't I want to use my real name? It just never felt right; there was no magic in it. It was too ordinary – I wanted something special. We were competing with names like Jerry Lee Lewis, Buddy Holly and Elvis Presley. Harry Webb didn't come close. Also there were songs about like 'That's The Trouble With 'arry', and so people were calling me ''arry boy', which I hated; so I was more than happy to give it up. Even now I hear names in show business and I think: Why didn't you change your name? They are either unspellable or unpronounceable or too commonplace, or the name sounds as though it belongs to an accountant – my apologies to all accountants! Of course, in the end, creatively and artistically it doesn't matter what your name is; but there is an imagery that is part of rock 'n' roll. Clothes are another part of it. I could go out dressed in the clothes I wear every day; it wouldn't make any difference to how I sing or how I perform. And yet in a way it would. When I go out on stage, dressed in the shoes and the clothes I choose to wear, I want the audience to get the impression I may have come from another planet.

Of course, I was emulating Elvis. He had broken the mould. He was the one who started to wear gold lamé and white suits on stage; completely different from singers like Frank Sinatra and Bing Crosby in their traditional dark suits. Having seen what Elvis wore, I wanted to find a look that would set me apart too. I went out and bought a pink jacket. I wore it with fluorescent pink socks, grey suede shoes, black trousers, a black shirt and a pink tie. Immediately I had a look that was entirely my own. All I did after that was change the combination. I wore white, yellow or green with the black, but it was always a black shirt and everything else – jacket, socks, tie – matched. Even today I like to look different.

I had the pink jacket made in Savile Row. I just said, 'I want something bright and colourful, preferably pink; show me some material,' and sure enough they had this pink material. So they made me a square, loose-fitting jacket with a single button. Then I went to Cecil Gee and bought myself some tapered trousers, socks and grey suede shoes, and I found a pink tie, and it kicked off. I was the first bad-taste dresser ever! And of course, once we started appearing on television, it worked there too. On black-and-white television, which is all there was at that time, it became my look. I was instantly recognizable; and it was important for me that I stood out from the crowd. I think it always has been. When I was young at school, all my friends had duffel coats and I begged my parents to get me one. When they finally could afford it, I chose a brown one. All my friends' duffel coats were black or navy blue. Mine was the only brown one I had ever seen, and I was the only one at school wearing a different colour from the rest.

I went home from the 2i's after that week and told my family that I was no longer Harry Webb but in future wanted to be called Cliff Richard. None of the family seemed to mind at all; in fact they seemed rather excited. My mother, Donna and Jacqui took to the new name immediately; my father took rather longer and Joan, who was just seven, kept forgetting and would say 'Ooops' every time she called me Harry.

I felt different with the new name. No one would ever have screamed at Harry, but I knew they could scream at Cliff. It was as though I was becoming a different character – almost like the mild-mannered Clark Kent putting on his blue catsuit and transforming into Superman. The minute I put on the pink jacket, the pink socks and the rest of the kit, I was Cliff Richard; and when I came off stage I went back to being a shy little boy. I learnt how to talk to the press pretty quickly, but I was always nervous – and yet the nerves went away when I went on stage, where I had a role to play.

The event in Ripley was bigger than anything we had done before. It felt like the big time. We arrived at the station in Derby to find posters all over the town announcing: 'Direct from the famous Soho 2i's Coffee Bar – Cliff Richard and the Drifters.' The ballroom was packed and the audience seemed to love us. We missed the last train home and spent the night at the venue, exhausted but elated. Back in London, John Foster booked us into the Gaumont Theatre in Shepherd's Bush for the Saturday morning Gaumont Teenage Show. It was a mixture of film and a talent competition and we were topping the bill – probably because we were free. It was there, for the first time, that girls in the audience suddenly started screaming when we appeared. It seemed that the Elvis impersonation was doing the trick. It was an extraordinary sensation but I found myself lapping it up. From that day onwards, we gauged our success by how deafened we were by the sound of girls screaming.

There were a couple of other coffee bars we played in Soho, one of which was owned by Nancy Whiskey's husband, the pianist Bob Kelly. She was a Scottish folk singer and the bar was named after the skiffle song 'Freight Train', with which she had a huge hit in the fifties. This was John Foster's thank-you letter after the event, written on 17 June 1958.

Dear Mr de Villiers,
Many thanks for giving CLIFF RICHARD AND THE DRIFTERS the opportunity to play at the "Freight Train" last Sunday evening.

Despite the late arrival of your staff they thoroughly enjoyed the evening and were pleased by the most appreciative audience. Unfortunately playing for almost three hours proved rather too strenuous. This was, however, compensated by the addition of eight new members to our "Fan" club.

Should you require our services in the future we shall be pleased to hear from you.

Assuring you of our best intentions at all times.

Yours faithfully
(J. Foster)
Manager

I wish I had kept more letters.

We were invited back to the Gaumont a second time and, hoping that we would get the same kind of enthusiastic response from the audience, John Foster invited an agent to come and hear us. The screams were so loud this time I could hardly hear myself sing, and at the end there must have been three hundred or so screaming girls on the street outside, rattling the locked doors waiting for us to come out. George Ganjou, whose name John had found in a copy of *The Stage*, knew nothing about rock 'n' roll and he wasn't our agent for long, but I do owe a great debt of gratitude to him for taking us on and for introducing us to his friend Norrie Paramor, who was Artiste and Repertoire Manager at EMI's Columbia Records. We had made a demo disc – for £5 at the HMV shop in Oxford Street – and George gave it to Norrie. It had an Elvis number on it and a Jerry Lee Lewis song. Norrie played it to his teenage daughter, who went wild about it; and not long afterwards we were installed in Studio 2 in the EMI recording studios in Abbey Road, making our first record. It was a song called 'Schoolboy Crush', which had been a hit in America, and on the B side we recorded 'Move It', a song that Ian Samwell had written on our way to the audition with Norrie, sitting on the top of a Green Line bus between Cheshunt and Oxford Street in London.

Traditionally the B side of a record was never considered very important, but it was 'Move It' that caught Jack Good's attention and led to us appearing on the new television pop programme *Oh Boy!*, which he produced. That was really the beginning of everything. 'Move It' turned out to be huge, while 'Schoolboy Crush' was unnoticed.

By the end of the week after our second appearance on *Oh Boy!* – 27 September 1958 – 'Move It' was not just in the charts, it had shot to number twelve in *Melody Maker's* top twenty. We were ecstatic. To add to our excitement, George Ganjou announced that he had arranged a tour for us, supporting some American artists called the Kalin Twins, who were in Britain promoting their hit record 'When'. This was to be our first ever full-scale rock show, it was scarily professional, and we realized that we needed a stronger line-up of musicians in the band.

In the weeks between first meeting Jack Good and appearing on *Oh Boy!* we had done a short season at Butlins holiday camp at Clacton-on-Sea. During that time Norman Mitham had decided to leave the Drifters and was replaced by a guitarist we had met there called Ken Pavey. Ken didn't want to do the tour – he had been offered a job elsewhere – which left us with Ian Samwell playing bass, Terry Smart on drums and me singing; I was no longer playing guitar at all. So John Foster went down to the 2i's and found Hank Marvin and his friend Bruce Welch. They were both sixteen, and their backgrounds were very similar to mine. They had left school with no qualifications and a passion for rock 'n' roll, joined a skiffle group, come to London from Newcastle to play in a talent show and changed their names to sound more credible. Bruce had a job in the 2i's coffee bar, and he and Hank were playing with a group called the Chester-nuts. Hank agreed to come on the tour if his friend could come too and so it was that Hank played lead guitar and Bruce rhythm.

The tour opened at the Victoria Hall in Hanley, Staffordshire, on 5 October. We caught a bus by Baker Street station along with other members of the cast. There were about eight acts, all of us building up to the main event which was the Kalin Twins. Our slot was immediately before theirs. At the time of the booking, they were the big stars, over from America; they were the ones with the record at the top of the charts – but in the intervening weeks, 'When' had slipped and 'Move It' had gone to number two. I was still only seventeen – I turned eighteen during this tour – but we were suddenly pretty hot stuff and the teenagers in the audience went wild. I felt very sorry for Hal and Herbie Kalin; they were not to know that my career was about to rocket. According to the press, I was Britain's answer to Elvis, and night after night their music was drowned by the chants of 'We want Cliff!'

The show wasn't working, and the organizers asked whether we would change our position in the running order so that, instead of appearing just before the headline act, we would come on in the first half of the show so that the screaming could be over and done with before the Kalin Twins appeared. I said no. My contract was quite specific about where we played, and I didn't feel *so* sorry for the Kalin Twins that I was prepared to give up the incredible advantage that this piece of luck had landed in our laps.

Over the years I seem to have acquired the image of being a goodie-goodie, squeaky clean, weak Mr Nice Guy – I think it originated with my becoming a Christian – and I would hate to shatter any illusions: but I don't think people get on in this business unless there is a hint of steel somewhere.

I would never behave now as I did towards the Kalins, but in those days I needed to take every advantage that presented itself. In some ways it wouldn't have made any difference where our spot was in the running order – the audience would still have shouted 'We want Cliff!' – but what the positioning did do was attract the attention of the press. They loved it. They made out that the American headliners couldn't get on to the stage because of *our* boy Cliff.

I like to think I made it up to Herbie and Hal, but they did have to wait a while. Thirty-one years later, in 1989, when I did a huge show at Wembley Stadium called *The Event*, I invited the Twins to be part of it. It was spectacular, though I say it myself – the opening section a recreation of that era, with a lot of the stars of the day. We filled the venue for two nights. It held 72,000 people – the largest audience I have ever played to – and when tickets for the first night sold out in the course of a single weekend, the promoter took a gamble on a second night and sold all of those too.

But how could I know all of that lay ahead? In 1958 I was hungry and had to clutch at every straw, every opportunity, every advantage and go for it. I couldn't afford to be sentimental. Even so, some things were easier than others. Telling friends that they weren't good enough musicians to stay with the Drifters was not easy. Jet Harris had been playing for another act during that tour and was clearly streets ahead of Ian Samwell on bass guitar. Having watched us from the wings night after night, he asked whether he could play with us too. He had been in a band called the Vipers with Hank and was a very talented musician. He was older and had more experience than all of us, not just of music but of life. He lived a bohemian lifestyle and was everything I wasn't; he was dangerous and he brought a slightly rebellious edge to the group. At the end of the tour I decided we needed to keep him and Ian had to go. It was particularly difficult because Ian was not just a friend – he had written 'Move It', without which we might never have been heard of. I am ashamed to say I took the coward's way out and left the task of telling him to John Foster. It wasn't my finest hour. Still, Ian Samwell went on to become a very successful songwriter and record producer in America. He died, sadly, in 2003 but we remained friends to the end.

Terry Smart was the next one who had to go, and that again was difficult. He and I had been together since the very beginning and he was the last of the original Drifters; but he just wasn't a good enough drummer, and if Cliff Richard and the Drifters were going to go all the way to the top we couldn't carry him. We invited Tony Meehan, who had also played at the 2i's, to take Terry's place, and Terry went off and joined the Merchant Navy, which had been his original plan anyway.

Ian and Terry were also both to come to *The Event* thirty-one years later. They sat in the audience, but I was so pleased that they accepted my invitation to be there. Norman

Mitham came too, which made it the first time all three of the original Drifters had been together since the fifties – and the first time I had seen any of them in years.

After the Kalin tour, my professional life went crazy. Norrie Paramor told my father that he thought I needed a change of management. George Ganjou stepped aside – with a sigh of relief, I suspect – and John Foster happily became our road manager, leaving the way clear for a professional. The man Norrie recommended as my manager was a Canadian, Franklyn Boyd, who had been a singer himself and a music publisher. By now I was appearing on *Oh Boy!* regularly, I had a bit part in a film called *Serious Charge* and I did a show on Sunday evenings, but Boyd felt I needed more experience on stage and so he cranked up the bookings. By the end of that year I had finished a tour, I was rehearsing *Oh Boy!* during the day, then going on to do two performances in a variety show at the Finsbury Park Empire, and often filming night scenes for *Serious Charge* after that. I had been professional for less than four months and I had just turned eighteen. I was exhausted. The group and I were so busy there was often no time to go home at night, so I rented a flat in Marylebone High Street and everyone dossed down there. All sorts of strange people came to stay – you never knew whose body you would have to clamber over in the morning. It was exciting, of course; but also, as I soon discovered, dangerously exhausting.

One night I was on stage, I opened my mouth to sing and nothing came out; not even the smallest squeak. My voice had completely gone. My father came to the rescue and called a halt to the madness. 'I'm sorry,' I heard him say. 'That's enough. I am pulling my son out of everything. I signed the contract and I am pulling him out.'

I was feeling so sick and unwell that I didn't argue. I didn't resent my father interfering; it never occurred to me to feel anything other than relief that someone had come along and rescued me. I went home to Cheshunt and did nothing for two weeks. Every engagement was cancelled; I saw no one and sang nothing.

Looking back, it's not surprising I collapsed. You can't go into anything physical, however promising or talented you may be, unless you practise and warm up and build up to it gradually. You couldn't go on to a tennis court cold and play for five hours, you wouldn't dream of it. I came in off the streets; I had never toured, I had never made a film, yet now I was doing both, and in addition I was doing concerts every evening. They were all very demanding activities – and my body was eighteen, for crying out loud; it wasn't strong enough for all of this. So it just gave up.

It is a lesson that stayed with me, and I have my father to thank for the fact that I stopped in time. I am obviously stronger now than I was then, but even now I am careful about what I take on and I try to stick to doing one thing at a time. If I am rehearsing a show, for instance, I try to avoid doing interviews. I give myself one hundred per cent to learning the words, learning the dance steps, checking on the music, and I find it really hard to go from that to suddenly being Mr Personality in conversation with a journalist and then switching back to the blinkers again. Of course it's possible, and I can do it if I have to, but I don't like it. I prefer to give each project the respect it deserves.

The bands I work with now are always surprised by the amount of time I spend rehearsing. It's habit. I was taught by real show-business professionals. When I began, singers were encouraged to be all-round entertainers, to do pantomime and variety and films, and so we worked with people like Des O'Connor and Joan Regan – a fantastic English singer – and jugglers and vaudeville people, and they drummed it into us that no matter what you are feeling or how badly hung over you are, the show goes on and it has to be the best show that that audience has ever seen. 'Your audience shouldn't really know your problems,' they used to say. 'You have to give it a hundred per cent every time. You do your act and you smile your way though it. You come off and you can cuss and swear if you like but you don't do it on stage.' And that has stuck with me. Maybe I'm unusual; most groups these days play concerts after a couple of run-throughs, but people pay a lot of money to come to a Cliff Richard concert and I feel I owe it to them to have a polished act.

My part in *Serious Charge* was incidental but it was to have a huge impact on my career. Lionel Bart had written a song called 'Living Doll' for the film that the Drifters and I were subsequently contracted to release as a single. We all hated the way it was arranged in the film; it was sung as a rock 'n' roll number but it really didn't work. Fiddling around on tour in Sheffield one evening, Bruce Welch reworked it as a country song, which was far better, and despite our lingering misgivings we recorded it that way – and it took off. 'Living Doll' went into the charts at number fourteen and rose to number one, where it stayed for six weeks. My first number one! It sold nearly two million copies, and having a country feel, also, incidentally, widened my repertoire. I am sure it was a bonus to be seen as a singer who was not rigidly bound to any one style. 'Living Doll' also put the Drifters well and truly on the map as instrumentalists. Hank Marvin's guitar solo on that record was inspirational. Now they quickly started releasing records on their own, which quite often competed with mine in the charts. We used to pass each other either going up or coming down.

In fact it was after 'Living Doll', when they released their first single, 'Feelin' Fine', in the United States, that they were forced to change their name. Unbeknown to us all there was a well-established group in America also called the Drifters, and now they threatened legal action. The American Drifters had been going for some years, and so Hank, Bruce, Tony and Jet backed down and, after tossing around a number of names, settled on Jet's suggestion that they call themselves the Shadows.

Franklyn Boyd didn't last long as our manager after the night I collapsed with exhaustion. It wasn't obvious to me – I was very fond of Franklyn – but my father and Norrie Paramor both said they didn't think it was working out. Franklyn was fundamentally a music publisher, not a manager, and so after about six months together we parted company. His replacement was a man called Tito Burns, approached on the recommendation of Cherry Wainer, one of the musicians with whom I worked on *Oh Boy!*. I was sorry to see Franklyn go, but we remained good friends. He was a really nice man, with a lovely wife, and I used to stay with them when I was recording or doing other things in London.

Tito managed me for about two years, but again we didn't always agree; and then, during one of my seasons at the London Palladium, I met Peter Gormley, a forty-one-year-old Australian, with whom the Shadows had just signed. He had come to England with Frank Ifield, the country singer, but had previously been a journalist among other things, so knew about publicity as well as film and music. I immediately thought, What a great guy; he was always there for the Shadows, in the theatre night after night, and we talked a lot. Eventually I asked him whether he would consider managing me. His immediate reaction was that I already had a manager. 'Yes,' I said, 'but his contract will be over at the end of the year,' which was true. My contracts were never for longer than a year at a time for just that reason, so that I was never tied down. Peter was scrupulous. He said he wouldn't even talk to me about it until I was free. I told Tito in March 1961, when the contract expired, that I would be going in a different direction in future, but even then Peter refused to take a single penny from me for the first year. 'Everything we are doing now,' he would say, 'is probably based on what your previous manager did.' Do people like Peter still exist today? I do wonder.

He was an exceptional man, with me through thick and thin – although fortunately there were not so many thin times – and I have a lot to thank him for; him and Norrie Paramor. I have had some very special people in my life and been very lucky in the individuals who have looked after me throughout my career. Peter and Norrie are sadly no longer alive but both of them, along with my father, were crucial to my being here today. They viewed me as so much more than a moneymaking machine. I regarded them both as close friends. That's unusual; the music industry doesn't often throw up artists and producers or managements that have that kind of relationship; but these two men were like father figures to me. In fact, when I wanted to buy Charters, the grandest of the houses I ever had in this country, who did I ring? Peter Gormley, even though he was retired.

'It's costing one and a half million,' I said.
'If you can afford it, bloody do it!' he said.
So I did.

CHAPTER THREE

Ambition

I have had the most exciting and rewarding career and it has come as a wonderful surprise, not just to be singing fifty years on, but still to be so fit and to have a voice that is so much better than when I started. I am recognized almost everywhere I go, I have a Bentley (rather than that Rolls-Royce), I have those four houses and – I have worked hard for it – enough money never to need to worry about it again. I have sold over 250 million records and had a number one hit single in every decade; I've starred in films, plays and musicals, and been a guest at Buckingham Palace and 10 Downing Street.

But that has only been half of my life; the more visible half. What I didn't know when I had that dream of being Elvis fifty years ago was how fame in itself would be so superficial and ultimately so unfulfilling. I would need more than rock 'n' roll in my life, and more than money, to make me feel complete. It took several years to discover what was missing; and I was fortunate that I found out before I filled the vacuum like so many others did: by abusing their bodies. It is no coincidence that since the sixties we have habitually talked about sex, drugs and rock 'n' roll in one breath. It was all so easy, it was available, it was mind-blowing and it stopped one thinking too hard about how vacuous, how empty, celebrity can really be.

Was it just luck that I didn't go down that route, or was it because of my family situation? After my father's death, the responsibility of looking after my mother and three younger sisters fell to me. At twenty, I was suddenly the man of the house; I had promised my father I would look after them all and I was determined to fulfil my obligations. So the opportunity to drink too much, be irresponsible and indulge in the sort of hedonistic lifestyle that most of my fellow rock 'n' rollers enjoyed didn't immediately present itself.

As for my sexuality, I am sick to death of the media's constant speculation about it. What business is it of anyone else's what any of us are as individuals? I don't think my fans would care either way. Sex is not one of the things that drives me in the way that it clearly drives a lot of other people. Maybe that's in my physical make-up or maybe it's because of my upbringing. I was a child of the fifties, not the sixties. Free love and the contraceptive pill hadn't yet arrived. In the fifties it was 'sinful' to have sex before marriage, and homosexuality was illegal. There was nothing unusual in having innocent relationships and anything else involved a lot of guilt. To be honest, when I was seventeen I found the idea of girls throwing themselves at me pretty scary, and when I became a Christian, a few years after my father's death, I was taught that sex outside marriage was against the teachings of the Church. Now I am less rigid in my interpretation of Christianity. The world has changed – people don't always marry, many of them have partners. Many of my friends are women, and many of my friends are gay – let's face it, homosexuality has been legal for more than thirty years. For me, the commitment is what counts – and I'll leave the judging to God.

What *was* lucky was that I had always had a real aversion to smoking – my father was a heavy smoker – and I couldn't bear the smell of it. At that time the drug people most commonly used was marijuana, so if a joint was passed round, I never even wanted to try it. When my friends were smoking at school, to be part of the gang I said, 'You all go and smoke and I'll be lookout, I'll tell you when a teacher's coming.' And that way I remained one of the cool kids without having to put a cigarette into my mouth. I hated cigarettes. If I got the smell of one on my hands I had to stop what I was doing and go and wash my hands. I still can't stand the smell of cigarette smoke. When I made a film called *Expresso Bongo* my character was supposed to smoke. I said I couldn't do it.

They said, 'What do you mean? We just need...'

I said, 'I can't. I can't inhale cigarette smoke, I don't even like it going up my nostrils when someone else is smoking.'

So, just before the camera rolled, someone else took a puff of a cigarette and blew the smoke into the camera. I then strolled into the scene stubbing out a cigarette while speaking. The director shouted 'Cut' and I went and washed my hands!

Nerves were a huge problem in those early days. I was still cripplingly shy, but suddenly I'd made a record and I was on tour and singing in front of two thousand people. I thought, I *can* do it. But it did terrify me. When I first toured in America in January 1960, we began in Montreal in Canada before moving on to the United States, and I was so scared I vomited on the side of the stage.

For the first and last time both my parents came on that tour; usually my mother stayed at home with my sisters. She flew to New York separately and met us there. My father travelled with me the whole way – for the last time. After we returned home he became very sick, and I think that the discomfort and cold he experienced on the long journeys between venues may have contributed to his illness. We went everywhere by Greyhound bus and for six weeks we spent hours and hours on the move, anything from eight to sixteen hours at a stretch, freezing cold and uncomfortable, trying desperately to sleep in our seats with nothing more than overcoats to keep us warm. It was a long time to be living like this: do-able for me and the Shadows, who were scarcely out of our teens, but not so sensible for a man in his fifties. He had always been a heavy smoker and during the tour he developed a bad cough which he couldn't shake off. In the end he developed a thrombosis, but I am convinced that the tour was the beginning of the end. He was never well again. Back in England, he became incapacitated quite quickly and we moved his bed downstairs and turned the living room into a bedroom for him.

Our lives changed dramatically with his illness. My mother loved cooking and was an avid watcher of cookery programmes on television. Every evening she would present us with some wonderful new dish that she had seen demonstrated on the TV or found a recipe for in *Woman's Weekly* or some other magazine, and we ate like kings. But when my father became ill, she was so busy looking after him that we ate beans on toast for weeks on end.

One of the problems of my father's illness was that the doctors didn't discover what was wrong with him early enough to intervene, and if it hadn't been for Leslie Grade, the great show-business agent who was acting for me at that time, he would probably not have lasted as long as he did. Leslie took one look at my father and sent his personal physician down to see him. This doctor immediately admitted him to Enfield hospital, where he was put into an oxygen tent. If that had been done sooner and his condition diagnosed earlier, my father might not have died in 1961. But he didn't help himself. He was such a determined and obstinate so-and-so; he found a way of unzipping the oxygen tent from the inside so he could have a cigarette on the quiet. 'What do they know, these doctors?' he would mutter.

One good thing did come out of his illness, however, which was that in the last months of his life he and I became closer than we had ever been. As he became weaker, he became more willing to accept help. Little by little our roles were reversed and we were able to talk properly for the first time in our lives. He leant on me, sometimes physically. The tragedy, of course, is that this new-found relationship, and the pleasure we were able to take in each other's company, ended so soon after it had begun. He missed the best bits of my career and the beautiful houses and holidays and other things that my success brought. That success was already beginning, and the money coming in was making life easier. I had bought a television set with my first cheque, and then after the American tour I bought the family a house – the first my parents had ever owned. It was a four-bedroom semi in Winchmore Hill near Enfield in north London. I also made sure that neither of them had to work any more; and I paid for taxis to take Mum to the hairdresser each week, little things like that.

But my father never came to a film premiere, never saw me fill the Royal Albert Hall, the Birmingham NEC Arena or Wembley Stadium. He wasn't around to hear about my lunches at Buckingham Palace or to come to see me receive the OBE or the knighthood. He didn't see me top the bill at the London Palladium or perform in front of the Queen at the Royal Variety Performance, or sing in the Eurovision Song Contest. He was just fifty-seven when he died and I had only been recording for three years. I think he would have been proud if he had lived to see the rest; and the fact that he missed all of that is my greatest regret. He would have loved sitting on the terrace at my house in Barbados, rum punch in hand, looking out over the sparkling ocean and listening to the chirrup of tree-frogs as the sun set, or wandering round the neat rows of vines at my Quinta in Portugal and tasting the latest vintage – he would have thought, as I do, that he was in paradise.

I don't think we realized he was going to die, and the shock when he did was profound. None of us was there when he actually passed away – it happened during the night of 15 May 1961 in a hospital, the address of which was World's End Road – and oh, how we cried. He had been the whole world for my mother and she was distraught. So were my sisters, and it fell to me to take charge, be strong and cope with everything – and I was ill-equipped for the task. I had no expectation that I would be so upset and it was his death, I am sure, which ultimately drew me towards Christianity.

I felt completely empty. Lost. Numbed. My father had been such a dominant figure in my life. He had been there for every decision, every question, every uncertainty. He controlled everything, he made the rules, set the limits, meted out the punishment; and I had lived under his rule unquestioningly. I knew nothing else and I had wanted nothing else.

He had even controlled my love life. I had a few innocent flirtations with girls in my teens, which my parents and sisters were well aware of, but there was one girl I hadn't told them about for very obvious reasons.

Her name was Carol Costa and she was married at the time to Jet Harris, the Shadows' bass guitarist. Jet had a drink problem and he wasn't a good drunk. Carol, who had a young baby, turned to me for comfort. I have heard other members of the Shadows say that she hit on me and seduced me. I was very young and a complete innocent, but let's just say at the time I was surprised but not unhappy to be seduced. I don't think I was in love with her – although I was certainly infatuated – but I did know that what I was doing was not right. Even if she was unhappy, she was a married woman. My parents found out when she sent me a passionate letter which made it clear we knew each other rather well. Mistaking it for fan mail, my mother opened it.

There ensued a long lecture from my father when I got home from the Palladium that night. It lasted into the small hours. I knew his views on sex – not that it was a subject ever discussed at home. He and my mother were Christians and believed that out of wedlock, anything of a sexual nature was taboo; that sex was something given by God to married couples for the procreation of children. They came from a generation that paid more than lip-service to the Ten Commandments – and my sisters and I had been brought up according to a strict code of behaviour, which I am sure will be with

76

us for ever. We were on the cusp of change; the sixties brought about a revolution, but it hadn't yet happened. Carol's letter made it clear there was something going on. What my father was angry about was the fact that I was having this relationship – any relationship – behind his back. 'Who is she?' he demanded. 'Why have we not met her?' Had he known the full truth he would not have been pleased.

Of course, the reason I hadn't told them about Carol or brought her home to meet them was because I was not comfortable with the relationship. How would I have introduced her to Mum and Dad and my sisters? 'This is Carol, she's married to Jet Harris, a friend of mine.' So Dad was right to have challenged me, and once he had, I realized that I didn't want to carry on with it. Adultery was a cause for serious scandal at that time and if my affair with Carol had become public knowledge, or if she and Jet had divorced and I had rushed off and married her, it would almost certainly have wrecked my career.

I've always been a coward when it comes to telling people things I know they won't want to hear. Even now, if I don't think a dancer in my show is up to scratch, or a gardener's not doing his job properly, I will ask someone else to deal with it. And with Carol, to my shame, I didn't dare tell her myself. I asked Tony Meehan to ring her for me.

Delia Wicks was another girlfriend I know I could have treated better. She was a dancer in one of my shows at the Palladium, and although my family knew about her, no one else did because I swore her to secrecy. I had seen the look on fans' faces when they'd seen me driven away from a venue with a pretty girl on my lap. I'd seen them stamping my programme into the gutter. I didn't want to risk upsetting them any more. Delia was wonderful and we spent a lot of time together, but then I woke up one day and the feeling had gone – as simple as that; so I ended our relationship. But I did it by letter. I was on tour and I told myself it was kinder to let her know immediately than to let her live with false hope, but it was the easy way out. Yet had I faced her she might well have talked me into continuing a relationship that was never going to go anywhere.

I didn't rage against my father for interfering when he took me to task over Carol. I didn't even think that it was none of his business; and I certainly didn't respect him any the less. The dressing-down wasn't fun – I've always hated confrontation – but with hindsight, I think he probably did the right thing. He was looking out for me, he saw me as his child, and he was guiding me to do what was right; and legally, at nineteen, I was still a child. He wasn't against my having a girlfriend, he just didn't like the fact that I was being so secretive about this one, and I am sure he guessed there was a good reason. He was perfectly happy with the other ones he met.

Of all the women I've known there were only two that I have come close to marrying. One was Jackie Irving, another very pretty dancer, whom I had met in Blackpool during a six-week run at the Opera House, a few months after breaking up with Delia. She was utterly beautiful and for a while we were inseparable. She took me to meet her mum, who ran a boarding house in Blackpool, and when she moved down to London I took her home to meet my parents – who welcomed her with open arms. My father loved her; he thought she was 'a real cookie'. He was quite ill at that time, and he and I didn't talk about marriage, but he made it very clear that he strongly approved of her. I did speak to Peter Gormley about marriage, though. I said, 'What do you think? If I marry her will it ruin my career?'

He said, 'You might lose ten per cent of your fans. Do you care? You shouldn't care; you should think about yourself.'

The other girl I came close to asking was Sue Barker, whom I met in 1982, and about whom I went through a similar thought process. There's no doubt that my feelings were strong for Sue, just as they had been for Jackie. I seriously contemplated asking her to marry me; but in the end I realized that I didn't love her quite enough to commit the rest of my life to her – exactly as I'd felt about Jackie. There were no broken hearts; in each case the intensity of feeling – on both sides, I think – faded. In each case we talked it through and we walked away friends. Both of them subsequently got married – Jackie to the pop singer Adam Faith; Sue to Lance Tankard, a policeman.

I was hugely ambitious. I wanted success more than anything else, including sex and marriage. I loved having girls scream when I appeared on stage, I loved hearing my records being played on the radio. I loved what people were writing about me in the newspapers. I loved everything about my rock 'n' roll life. It was exhilarating, thrilling, intoxicating – and frankly at that age I didn't feel the need for any kind of emotional or physical distraction. Sometimes when we were on stage I would turn round to the Shadows and say, 'You fancy a riot?' and wiggle my legs or thrust my hips a bit, and the audience practically stormed the stage. It was an incredible feeling to have that much power.

I was on a roll. After I had appeared on *Oh Boy!* two or three times in the summer of 1958, the world seemed to go crazy. 'Move It' shot up the charts to number two. The press were accusing me of 'the most crude exhibitionism ever seen on British TV'. *New Musical Express* wrote: 'his hip swinging is revolting ... hardly the kind of performance any parent could wish their child to witness'. One paper even asked: 'Is this boy too sexy for TV?' My parents just laughed when they read that. They didn't think I was sexy at all. My Dad said, 'Why can't you be like Marty Wilde?' He was the competition; he was also singing rock 'n' roll and being hailed as an English answer to Elvis, and he looked the part; he was very cool. Dad thought he was the bee's knees as a singer. I guess parents don't ever see their children as sexual beings, and I am not sure that I ever saw myself that way. I always thought I was a sensual performer.

Oh Boy! went out live at six on a Saturday night from the Empire Theatre in Hackney. It was ITV's answer to the *Six-Five Special* on BBC, and quite revolutionary in its time: non-stop rock 'n' roll with a studio audience, most of them girls who screamed solidly for half an hour. It was fast-moving, beautifully lit and incredibly exciting. Jack Good, the producer, worked really hard in creating an image for me: he went through the songs line by line telling me how to stand, how to look, where to look, how to curl my lip and what to do with my hands. Jack turned me into a front man. I was still struggling with shyness and it was fantastic to have him pay me so much attention. I owe him a lot. He made me get rid of the guitar and shave off my sideburns. He didn't want an Elvis impersonator; what he wanted was someone who had the same appeal as Elvis and who would have the same impact. I couldn't see that I was that someone. I could see there were similarities, of course, because I was singing rock 'n' roll, I dressed similarly and I had a predominantly female audience that screamed at me; but Elvis was sultry and had already been doing his thing for about five years. Even now, I still look back and think: Mmmmm; Elvis was streets ahead – how could I think of catching up? But even then I also thought: Mmmmm, I'm going to try!

One newspaper said it was my eyes that gave me my sex appeal. I remember reading that out to the Shadows and they went, 'Wwwaaayhhhheeeyyy, sexy eyes!' From then onwards I did do a *lot* of smouldering – lowering the eyes and looking up from underneath my eyebrows and stuff like that – and it was entirely because of what I had read in the newspapers. I was virtually created by a combination of Jack Good and the press.

I sometimes look back at old photos, and there is one that was used on the back of an album of me aged about nineteen or twenty.

I was taking a bow, and I had one hand in my hair – and I just don't remember having great hair. Now I can look back and see that I was a pretty hot-looking kid, but as I was living through it I didn't think so at all. I have never been confident about how I look. I have never caught sight of myself in the mirror and been satisfied – except maybe when I've been made up for television or something like that. With hindsight, my best period was probably between the ages of thirty and forty: I like how I looked then, even though I didn't at the time. I have never liked my hair. From certain angles I thought it made me look like Dirk Bogarde and that was not what I was after. I wanted to look like Elvis.

It's not just vanity that makes me so aware of my looks and my shape. This business I'm in is highly visual, it's all about image, looks and youthfulness – it's not enough to have a good voice; singers have to be seen as well as heard – and that's a real disadvantage for me in my sixties. I used to be called 'the Peter Pan of Pop' – now *that* was just luck, I didn't do anything to make myself look younger – and even today, I like to think I still don't look my age – at least not from a distance. But now I do work at it. I say to cameramen these days, 'I don't care about art any more. You've just got to make me look good: if I need lights behind me, do it; do whatever it takes.' I don't think the public should see anything less than me at my best. I have a few grey hairs but they don't really show too badly, so I just have a few low-lights put in now and then. My mother went to the hairdresser every week and we knew she used to colour her hair; it wasn't until she had dementia and the colour grew out that any of us realized she was actually as white as snow underneath it all. She probably didn't even know that herself. I'm not that far gone – yet!

As for exercise, performing on stage provides all I need, and I play tennis a couple of times a week on tour. I started doing a bit of gym work once but I pulled a muscle in my shoulder so I had to stop. I started again when I was preparing to play Heathcliff, in the nineties. I wanted to bulk up a bit so I was in the gym every other day for eighteen months, but it was a failure. In the end people were asking me if I'd lost weight. I would say, 'No, I'm nine pounds heavier than I've ever been in my life,' and they would say, 'Well, you don't look it.' I asked my trainer, who said that if I'd been seventeen and done the work I'd done, I would have looked like Arnold Schwarzenegger. 'As it is,' he said, 'you just look like you.' The testosterone doesn't flow so fast at fifty-five.

I've tried Botox and it just didn't work. I really didn't like the feeling and it made my eyebrows droop over my eyes. I went to four different doctors, all of them recommended by friends, but the same thing happened each time. So I don't bother any more. I met some British doctors in the Philippines on my last world tour who were doing corrective surgery on children with cleft palates. For some reason, whether it's poverty or genetics, it's a very common condition in that part of the world. Surgery never fails and it changes their lives completely; but, of course, none of the parents can afford it, so these doctors pay their own way out there and spend a month operating all day, every day, then go back to their normal jobs in the UK. The before-and-after photographs of these children are stunning. I was so impressed by them that I invited the doctors to dinner at the British Ambassador's home. I thought they might meet someone useful who might sponsor them. Over dinner we were talking about facial surgery and I said to one of them, 'I don't even know whether it would be possible, but I'm getting to that stage in my life when I would quite like to get rid of one or two creases and the forehead lines, just get things tweaked a bit.'

He said, 'That would be an interesting challenge' – so I thought one day I might phone him.

Photography is the real hassle. If it wasn't for people wanting to take photos all the time it wouldn't matter how I looked. People's expectations are so high. I have been in the supermarket and heard people discussing me. 'Did you see Cliff?' they'll say. 'He hasn't even shaved. He didn't smile.' So, I haven't shaved for a day; and do they really expect me to smile all the time, even when I'm doing the shopping? Give me a break. That's unrealistic; but when I am on stage or performing I feel I have a duty to look as good as I can and, unfortunately for me, that means looking young. My art form is a young person's; we created it when we were young and that's the image to which we will always be compared. No one ever foresaw that I might be pushing seventy one day and still be able to sing and perform. The frustration is that while I can't look as young as I did in the sixties, I feel the voice and the music are far better than they ever were then. And I know I have more energy. Inside I'm still eighteen!

About twenty years ago, I had a scare with my throat. Two little pink inflammation marks appeared: the specialist said they weren't yet nodules, but if I wasn't careful, that's what they would turn into. He said, 'I want you to stop talking for two weeks,' and put me on to steroids. I started off on day one taking fourteen pills, then thirteen the next day, and so on decreasing for the two weeks. I went on holiday with friends and had to write everything down. It was awful, because by the time I had written down what I wanted to say, they had already moved on to another topic. They'd say, 'Oh yeah,' and ignore me. But I did it, I went through with it all, and at the end of the fortnight my vocal cords were as good as new. After that, I took some lessons in how to warm up my throat, which I had never done before. I didn't want to change my voice in any way and still don't, because it's served me well, but what I am keen to do is improve it and use it more effectively.

Two years ago, Olivia Newton-John, my friend of old, gave me a birthday present of an hour with her singing coach. Olivia never seems to have problems with her throat and she's still singing like a bird. She said, 'Look, you've got to meet this guy,' and it was amazing. I had the lesson at her house: he sat at the piano and went through all these trills that I had to do with my lips, and with my tongue – vocal warm-up exercises – and also things that I should try to do with my voice to increase my range. To my surprise, he said I was a tenor.

I said, 'I thought I was more a baritone.'

He said, 'No, some of the notes you have are definitely a tenor's. You can strengthen those notes.' He made me a CD, which I work with every other day when I'm resting, and if I am touring I'll do the exercises, for twenty-five minutes every day before the show. It is definitely helping my vocal cords. I have really felt the benefit. It's fantastic. I have felt it in my recording voice, and while touring over a six-month period in 2006–2007 my voice was as clean as a whistle all the way through.

I always felt I needed to retain a certain dignity as I grew older, particularly after I became a Christian and had to deal with all that that entails. I thought if I could just be myself and sing and perform, somebody out there would like it. Not everybody would, but not everybody finds the same person attractive anyway. That's human nature. What I've done seems to have worked, and even now I think I can go on stage and still look the part. I am comfortable with who I am. When I look in the mirror I say to myself. 'This is it; this is what you are now, this is what the audience is going to get. Just do the show and enjoy it.' And I do.

I never met Elvis. It is one of the regrets of my life – particularly since I once had the opportunity and I turned it down. That was in 1976 when 'Devil Woman' had reached number four in the American charts. Elton John released it on his Rocket Records label and I went over to do some publicity. One of the journalists interviewing me asked about my early career. I said my usual thing, that if there had been no Elvis there would be no

Cliff Richard, that I didn't want to be like anybody else, and he said, 'I know Elvis. Would you like to meet him?' I leapt at the offer. 'Well, he's in Vegas at the moment. If I can arrange it, can I at least have exclusive rights to the pictures?'

I said, 'Absolutely.' Then I thought about it for a second. 'Hang on,' I said. 'Are we talking about *this* visit? Elvis is about fifteen stone at the moment. I want this photograph for my rogues' gallery. Couldn't we wait until he looks vaguely like the Elvis that was so magnetic? He always looks great when he gets ready for a movie. Let's wait.'

And so I put it off; and shortly afterwards he was dead. I could have kicked myself – what an idiot I was – but I have the next best thing. There is a Spanish artist who paints pop stars; he painted me for a charity auction, and he offered to paint Elvis and me on stage together if I gave him a couple of photographs. I have the painting at home and the funny thing is he has drawn it so that I have the mic in my hands, I'm singing and Elvis looks as though he's just said, 'OK, it's all yours.' Still, I'll always wish I'd had the photo taken!

There was another time when I hoped I might meet Elvis: way back in 1959 in Germany. Some friends and I had gone on holiday to Viareggio in Italy. It was the first holiday I had ever been able to afford and the first time I had ever been abroad since arriving in the UK from India. Four of us went in a Morris Oxford Estate and drove down through Belgium, Germany and Switzerland. On the way back through Germany we took a diversion to Bad Nauheim, where we knew Elvis was posted with the US Army. We had no problem finding the house – the wall was covered in graffiti with messages like 'I love Elvis' – and my friends all said, 'Why don't you go in?' The front door was round the side of the house so, knees knocking, I opened the wooden gate, walked up the path from the road and round the building, and rang the bell. I heard footsteps coming towards me. My heart was in my mouth. I was about to meet The King. Instead, the door was opened by a great big bruiser of a guy. I asked if Elvis was in, and he said, 'I'm afraid not; he's in France at the moment. He won't be back for a week or so.' So I said, 'OK,' and scooted back to the car – and I was glad in a way that he hadn't been there because I was so nervous I probably wouldn't have been able to speak. So I know what some of my fans go through.

I met his manager, Colonel Tom Parker, when I was in New York with my parents at the end of my first American tour, and he invited us to lunch: we accepted, but any notions of fine dining we might have had disappeared when he reached into his desk drawer and came out with a collection of sandwiches. My father used to dine out on that story.

A couple of years later, on our 1962 American tour, Elvis's father was in the audience when the Shadows and I played in Memphis. He came backstage and said, 'You guys are like a vaudeville act.' I remember that night so well. It was the time of the Cuban missile crisis and no one came to see us. In Memphis we had about 150 people in this huge hall. What I don't remember is whether it was Hank or me who went on stage and said, 'Ladies and gentlemen, it's great to be here – but we have a choice; either you can come backstage and have a cup of tea with us or we can do the show,' and they all cheered. Elvis's Dad knew I was a big Elvis fan, so he invited us back to his house, Graceland. Now that was fun: driving through those famous gates and up the drive to the house, which was very Southern with big white columns at the front and a huge rug at the entrance with an effigy of Elvis woven into it. I said I couldn't possibly walk on it, so I edged my way round the side. Elvis wasn't there: it was just his father and his uncle, and they showed us over the place. Elvis's bedroom was incredible; there was a vast round bed in it, and a bathroom with huge mirrors and a special hairdresser's salon chair. Downstairs there was an enormous room with a pool table in the middle, furniture round the edges and the walls entirely covered in gold discs, awards and accolades. They seem to have given Elvis gold discs every time he coughed. We were completely in awe.

His father was a charming man. His mother, who had a very strong hold on Elvis, had died of hepatitis four years before. She was very young, in her early forties. He worshipped his mother – and it was after her death that he began to fall apart and have all the problems, including eating the wrong food, taking uppers and downers and goodness knows what else, that probably killed him. There would have been other factors too, of course, like the fact that he was a twin and his twin died; apparently a twin has great difficulty in coming to terms with the death of their 'other half'. I'm convinced that if his mum had been alive, she would have reined in his excessive behaviour. I heard he sent a plane to Chicago once because he thought that was where the best burgers came from. I don't think he would have done things like that if she'd been around. His father was nice, and I am not suggesting he didn't respect him, but from what I've read she was the controlling influence.

I can identify with that, although in my case it was my father who was the controlling influence: even after his death – even sometimes today, in my sixties – before following a particular course of action, I ask myself, 'What would my parents think? Would Mum and Dad be happy with this?'

It was a tragedy that Elvis died so young. Everything I have, I have because of him, and I am not the only one. He was the inspiration for a whole lot of people who started singing in the late fifties. Frank Sinatra was fantastic but he didn't inspire my generation – although I can't explain the pleasure I felt when I heard one of my records on the radio after the DJ had played one of his. I mean to say, *my* record after Frank Sinatra... And closer to home, Al Saxon and Dickie Valentine – wonderful singers, but at that stage they didn't touch us. Somehow, Elvis came along and knocked us sideways. I'm just glad that he lived long enough to see what an impact he'd had. I am glad I met his father and saw Graceland, but I will always regret not meeting the man himself.

I do know that he was aware of me, though. We had the same publisher in America, who was a great friend of my manager at the time, and he said, 'Oh, Elvis knows all about Cliff's music. He knows exactly what's happening around the world; he keeps in touch with all the opposition.'

Well, it's nice to be thought of as 'the opposition'!

CHAPTER FOUR

Conversion

Five months after my father's death, the Shadows and I went off on a tour of Australia and New Zealand. It was the beginning of a lasting love for that part of the world. I must have been back more than twenty times since then, and I am always knocked out by the warmth of the reception and the general friendliness.

Mum came with me on one of my visits. It was in 1988. She had been dying to see New Zealand and she saw it in style. I have a very special, very loyal fan club there run by Katrina, who lives in Auckland. Whenever I am playing in the city, she opens her house and floor space to fans from all over the country; anyone who wants to come to a Cliff concert is welcome to stay. She's unbelievable. On this occasion she had organized a dinner for me. I couldn't go in the end, but she had invited my mother as well, so I suggested to Mum that she should go and represent me. They were fantastic to her; she came back saying, 'I was treated like the Queen.' They had given her a chair to sit on with 'Producer' written on the back, which slightly puzzled her.

'Mum, you produced me,' I said.

'Oh my goodness, of course.' She was so thrilled.

Roger Bruce, my PA for many years, was on that trip with us. He and Mum had a great relationship. He called her 'Apricot Lil', because she loved apricots, and she called him 'Juicy Brucie'. He was great with her. He took her up in a helicopter in Auckland, and when they touched down after twenty minutes, she said, 'Is that all?' She probably thought she was going to see the whole island. Roger always insisted in hotels that he and I should have rooms next to one another with connecting doors, so that if anything happened he would be able to reach me. In New Zealand we had three rooms in a row, with interconnecting doors: Roger's was between Mum's and mine. At 3 a.m. the fire alarm went off and he swears it was like a Ray Cooney farce, my mother and I remaining sound asleep as he ran between the three rooms, desperately trying to wake us up, while smoke billowed from a fire in the laundry room several floors below.

It was on that trip with Mum that I had a phone call from Jacqui, who was expecting her fifth child, to say that she had had a baby boy, Philip, but he'd arrived two months prematurely and wasn't expected to survive. He was born in Norfolk, where they lived, but was rushed immediately to Great Ormond Street Hospital in London. He remained there in a high-dependency ward for the first two months of his life. It was the most terrible time: there were major complications and the doctors thought it very unlikely that he would pull through.

Jacqui and I had a long chat. She was very upset and didn't know what to say to Mum. I said I would break the news. When I did, Mum immediately wanted to go home. I couldn't leave New Zealand just yet, so I put her on a plane and she made the journey on her own – brave in her late sixties, when she had never travelled alone before. Jacqui and Peter took their other children out of school and went to stay with her in Nazeing so they could be nearer to Great Ormond Street. Mum was a real star during that whole period: she cooked for everyone, looked after everyone and held things together; and all three of them took turns in keeping vigil by the baby's cot side. Today Phil is almost twenty-one, a well-adjusted, lovely guy, and you would never know there'd been anything wrong with him.

I was twenty-one on my first visit to Australia and New Zealand in 1961; in fact, I actually turned twenty-one on the flight over there. Shortly before we left, Bruce Welch and Tony Meehan had a blazing row which ended in Tony leaving the Shadows. Things had been quite fraught between them and he had had enough. We were all working crazy hours, seven days a week, and he had just started a family. His replacement was Brian Bennett, who was an old friend of Hank and Bruce and whom we had all known from the 2i's, where he'd been house drummer. And when, in April the following year, everyone finally got tired of coping with Jet Harris, whose drinking had been causing major problems on tour, it was Brian Bennett who recommended Brian 'Licorice' Locking to replace him as bass guitarist. Today Jet doesn't drink and even does solo gigs. I do wish him well.

Although I had no idea at the time, Brian Locking was a Jehovah's Witness and it was he who set me off on my spiritual quest. We spent a lot of time in those days as a group setting the world to rights. We would sit around in airport lounges or in the hotel bar after a gig and talk endlessly about sex, drugs, rock 'n' roll, politics and religion – all the usual things that young people discuss over a couple of pints. One day I was talking about my father and how I was thinking of consulting a spirit medium to try and get in touch with him, an idea that had first occurred to me in Australia. I had felt very unsettled since his death. He had been too young, and I felt cheated that he had gone and was no longer here to see all the exciting things that were happening. He had seen Bruce Forsyth present me with my first gold disc during *Sunday Night at the London Palladium*, when 'Living Doll' sold a million copies. Nine million people watched that programme. He'd seen me buy my first car – a grey Sunbeam Alpine with red leather seats, of which I was so proud. And he'd seen my appearance in the first couple of films but those were just bit parts. Since his death I had played the lead role in *The Young Ones*, which was a smash hit, and the single of the same name had gone straight into the charts at number one. Our tour of Australia and New Zealand had been hugely successful – just as South Africa had been the year before. He was still alive when we went to South Africa, but had been too ill to travel with us, so never saw for himself the rapturous reception we were given; and I so wish he had.

I loved what was happening. I had the red carpet laid down for me everywhere I went, had to fight my way through crowds of hysterical fans, I was fêted and famous. And yet, and yet... There was something missing. I didn't come off stage at the end of an evening feeling as elated as I should have, as I did at the beginning when my father was alive. I am not sure what I was expecting; but whatever it was, it wasn't happening.

Very often I didn't even want to socialize, and if the Shadows went out with fans and girls in the audience who hung around, I tended to go off to my room and leave them to it. Everything seemed to be falling into my lap and I didn't feel I had earned it. I worked long hours and I worked hard, but I wasn't having fun. I was earning money hand over fist: I changed the Sunbeam for a Thunderbird, a car I loved, I had bought a car for my mother, we had everything we could possibly need and I had more work lined up – recordings, tours and films – than one person could decently do; and yet I felt a great yawning emptiness.

I started thinking about the meaning of life and the futility of it all, wondering if there was anything else, any purpose in it. And death; was it the end? Did all that effort that my father put into living decently and honourably count for nothing? How did Dad's life of hard work and hardship square with mine, which thus far had been so effortless? If there was nothing more, nothing beyond the grave, then what was the point? I had so many questions and so few answers; questions that I had never seriously thought to ask before. My father had had the answer to everything, he'd *been* everything in the Webb household. He had been solid and dependable, he had guided and managed my life, pulled me up when he thought I had gone astray; it had never crossed my mind that he wouldn't always be there, and now that he was gone all the old certainties had gone with him.

I had come across some people on tour who dabbled in spiritualism and played around with a Ouija board. They did it for fun, but firmly believed that it was spirits that made the glass move in response to questions. They were convinced and they were convincing. It was very tempting to give it a go, or to visit a medium and take part in a séance to see whether I could contact my father.

When Licorice Locking heard me say this, the whole tone of the conversation suddenly changed. He was appalled. Did I not realize how dangerous it was to dabble with the occult? It was wrong, it was expressly forbidden in the Bible. I must not do it under any circumstances.

I had never seen him like this; he was deadly serious and genuinely passionate. I told him to show me – I wasn't prepared to take his word for it; so he produced a Bible and read from the Old Testament book of Deuteronomy:

'There should not be found in you anyone who makes his son or his daughter pass through the fire, anyone who employs divination, a practitioner of magic or anyone who looks for omens or a sorcerer, or one who

binds others with a spell or anyone who con-
sults a spirit medium or a professional fore-
teller of events or anyone who inquires of the
dead.'

I was flabbergasted that a guy who played
rock 'n' roll for a living, as he did, should
know the Bible well enough to be able to
find a particular passage just like that –
especially since it was directly related to my
question about whether I should contact my
dad. It wasn't the answer I wanted to hear;
but it was an answer.

So Licorice and I talked about his faith
quite a lot after that, and like all Jehovah's
Witnesses he was keen to tell me – and keen
to recruit me. I had heard about the sect, of
course, because they had come to the door at
home on many occasions, as they do, distri-
buting the *Watchtower* magazine and wanting
to talk about the Bible, but beyond that I
knew nothing. Licorice was quite a recent
recruit. He had become a Witness after meeting Brian Bennett's mother, Hilda. She had
been a devout Witness for years and Brian,
her only child, had been strictly brought up
in the same faith. He had dutifully trailed
from door to door with his mother, forgone
birthdays and Christmas, which Witnesses
don't celebrate, and attended meetings when
all his friends were out having fun, but the
moment he'd left home he had given it all up.

My father had been deeply religious; he

was an Anglican, as my mother was, and I had been brought up in that denomination. He had read the Bible and prayed regularly; I remember I burst into his room once and found him on his hands and knees praying out loud. I guess it was an eastern thing, a leftover from his years in India. He tried to get us to have Bible readings at the week-ends and we often went to church. None of us questioned it until, at the age of fourteen, I found myself in confirmation classes, having been steered there by my parents. One Sunday I realized I didn't understand what I was being taught and couldn't see the need for it. So I went home that day and told my parents that I wasn't going to go again. I was expecting an argument but, to their credit, they said, 'OK.' It was the best possible thing they could have said. Many years passed before I set foot inside a church again. I wasn't a non-believer during those years; I could never have been an atheist, because I cannot believe that this universe happened by accident, but I certainly had no need for organized religion.

I was very taken with a story I once read about a Christian who worked for an atheist. The atheist said, 'I don't believe all this non-sense about the universe being created by God,' so the Christian enlisted the help of a friend who was an engineer and between them they built a model universe, with all the planets in line, all hanging on wires with the sun in the middle and each one revolving round the inner ones and the sun, with nothing touching or colliding. He put it down on his boss's desk and his boss said, 'Where did that come from?' and the employee said, 'I don't know. It was just there.'

The boss said, 'Well, who made it?' and the employee said, 'I don't know who made it; it was just there.'

'Oh, please,' said his boss. 'Come on; something as intricate as this must have been made by somebody.'

I rest my case.

So I didn't stop believing in God; but I couldn't see what part He had to play in my life as a rocker. It didn't seem to fit with any of the things I desired out of life. I wanted to be famous and wealthy, to sing and have people scream at me. Not quite the model of humility that goes with the Christian message. But within a few months of my father's death I felt there was this void, and I couldn't put my finger on what was causing the feeling. It never crossed my mind that maybe I was lacking in spiritual fulfilment. All I could do was ask myself why I was not hysterically happy.

I did a lot of reading and a lot of soul-searching. I looked at Judaism and at Buddhism, but neither seemed distinctive enough, so I sought further. The Jehovah's

Witnesses encouraged me to start reading the Bible again. I met a whole lot of them when we were on tour in America in 1962. Licorice asked if I wanted to go to a meeting with him in Miami, and after the conversations we had had, I was intrigued. So Hank and I joined him and it was an amazing experience. I was stunned by how friendly they all were. They hugged us as we walked in and everyone said, 'Hi' and 'Welcome'. It was a lovely evening. There was a tremendous buzz in that Kingdom Hall that was infectious. What it was, in fact, was charismatic, although I didn't know the term in its religious context at that time. I didn't understand what they were singing, but they were reading from the Bible and I found it so interesting. 'If you want answers to some of these questions that you're asking,' they said, 'read the Bible.'

'But how can the Bible, written centuries ago, be relevant to me and my life as a pop singer?' I protested.

'Read it and see.'

The Witnesses believe the Bible is the word of God – whose name is Jehovah – and much of it they take literally. I was so excited by this meeting that when I arrived home I immediately relayed it all to my mother and sisters, and they were swept up with my enthusiasm. I then discovered that my mother already knew about the Jehovah's Witnesses.

She had been introduced to them by her uncle and aunt, who had been converted by evangelists on their doorstep. Soon she and my sisters Donna and Jacqui were well on the way to their own conversions.

I went to several meetings over the next couple of years, and I did read the Bible, and found it relevant in many ways; but, though I have the Jehovah's Witnesses to thank for bringing me back to it, once I started reading, the last thing I wanted to do was join them. However, the whole experience did make me think that I should take another look at the Church.

In fairness it was probably Jay Norris, my old English and drama teacher at Cheshunt Secondary Modern, who got me back on to the right track. She and I had kept in touch, and years after I had left she invited me back to play in a production of *A Midsummer Night's Dream* with a mixture of current and past pupils and staff, four or five of whom were old classmates whom I hadn't seen since we left. I played Bottom, which was such fun. I was so grateful to Jay; no one in the profession would have dreamt of asking me to play a part like that. I was making more and more films and I had even done some theatre, but in the outside world I was typecast as a rock 'n' roller.

I think Jay felt that I was a bit lost; she knew that I was going to Witness meetings and was horrified, as many people are, by the religion. It is very prescriptive and does require enormous commitment. Licorice even gave up his career for it: he left the Shadows just eighteen months after he joined because the constant touring meant he couldn't fulfil his religious obligations. Anyway, Jay quietly arranged for me to meet a colleague of hers, Bill Latham, the school's new religious instruction teacher, who she hoped would talk some sense into me. Every year, for her birthday in July, she organized a car rally for her friends, who set off into the Hertfordshire countryside armed with a list of cryptic clues set in rhyming couplets by Jay. This year, 1964, she engineered it so that I would share a car with Bill. We argued all night, but her plot worked: we became friends.

Bill was a couple of years older than me, but we came from very similar backgrounds and families with similar attitudes to manners and behaviour – backgrounds where old-fashioned, gentlemanly courtesy was the norm. Beyond that, on the face of it, we had little in common. He was not interested in rock 'n' roll, or even pop music; he dressed and looked like a schoolmaster, with a salary to match. I must have seemed rather flash to him. He knew who I was – he had been a reporter with the local newspaper before he began teaching – but I don't think he particularly liked my records and was certainly not fazed by my fame. All of that was very appealing, as was the way he and his friends talked so easily and conversationally about God and Jesus. I found myself envying them and wondering how they'd reached that state; how they were able to talk about Jesus without feeling embarrassed – and more importantly, how satisfied with life they seemed.

Bill had become a Christian as a teenager, through Crusaders, an evangelical Bible-based youth organization, and twelve years on he was helping to run the group in his spare time. His friends were fellow evangelicals and many were the times we all sat down together and slugged it out. I had so many questions about the Bible and about the teachings of the Jehovah's Witnesses versus the teachings of the orthodox Christian faith, and when they didn't have an answer for me they found someone else who did. This way I met a lot of Christians. I was probably quite argumentative and challenging. I wanted to be sure that I understood what I was hearing. I was intrigued by all that these people stood for and so, hungry to learn more, I found myself going along to Bill's Bible-study classes on Sunday afternoons and sneaking surreptitiously into the back row to listen.

One day it was David Winter's turn. David (who later became Head of Religious

Broadcasting at the BBC) was a friend of Bill who was very good on the three-in-one question – finding a plausible explanation for the Trinity. I simply couldn't understand the business of God and Jesus being the same and yet not the same, and each time this came up everyone said, 'You must talk to David Winter.' So I pumped him with questions, and although he gave me thought-provoking answers, he finally said, 'Look, no one is going to give you perfect answers to any of this stuff because how are we supposed to understand the workings of God when it's hard enough to understand the workings of men? You're going to have to come to your own conclusion based on what you know and what you've read, and what we've understood and explained. And you're going to have to find your own way through that.'

So I did – and in the end I found that it always came back to the character of Jesus, whom the Jehovah's Witnesses don't believe was divine. In my mind there was no doubt that Jesus had existed. So I said to myself, 'OK, this is getting easier. If it's true that Jesus existed, and if He's the one who said, "I stand at your door and I knock. And whoever opens the door, I will come in," then He is the one I should confront.'

I lay on my bed one night with these words going through my head. It was after a particularly heavy session, when I had been asking a lot of probing questions of my friends. The honest fact is, I was trying to prove Christianity wrong so that I could say 'Thank you and goodbye' and dismiss it – as I had all the other faiths I had looked into. I wanted to be free to move on to something else. If I had satisfactorily proved them wrong, I might have found myself where the Beatles ended up, in India with the Maharishi Mahesh Yogi, because we were all chasing a spiritual path. But this one proved hard to dismiss. My friends often talked of this phrase 'knocking and being accepted in', and I thought, That's all it is. Jesus is trying to get into people's lives: but He doesn't force entry, He loves, so He isn't going to come in unless I invite Him to.

And so that night, staying at Bill Latham's house in Finchley, I finally thought, All right, then: I'll say the magic words; and I just lay there and said, 'OK, I believe in you and your claims and I'd like you to come into my life.' And that was it. I was hoping, obviously, that I would experience some spiritual manifestation – the door would rattle, the wind would gust, I would suddenly feel warm or icy cold. There was none of that. Nothing happened. I fell asleep, slept soundly all night and woke in the morning feeling absolutely no different.

It wasn't until I was in Paris, maybe six

months later, that I realized something had taken root. We were sitting outside a little restaurant next door to the Hôtel de Paris, where we used to love staying when we did concerts there. We would come down late in the morning, having been up till all hours, and sit with a cup of coffee and a croissant or a baguette and watch all the beautiful people go by. They are so chic in Paris, aren't they? No matter what time of day it is, the women always look fantastic. I think it is my favourite city in the world. Suddenly someone came up to our table and said, 'Cliff!' It was somebody I had known before I'd been converted – although I didn't think of it as a conversion at that point; I had almost forgotten about that night when I had lain in bed and invited Jesus into my life. My friend came and joined us, and after we'd been talking for about five or ten minutes, he said, 'You've changed.'

I said, 'What do you mean, I've changed?'

'For a start,' he said, 'you haven't used the F word once.'

It was true: I had stopped using it. In fact, I had stopped swearing altogether, and it hadn't been easy. We all used to swear like troopers – it was habit – and I had to get the Shadows to shout at me whenever I lapsed. But that wasn't the only difference my old acquaintance said he noticed. He couldn't put his finger on it, he said, but something about me had definitely changed. I didn't know what he was talking about; but that night in bed – where I do some of my best thinking – I came to the conclusion that the only possible explanation for any change in me was that something had happened that night in Finchley. Without my noticing it, my invitation had obviously been accepted. I decided it was maybe time to make even more changes.

I started to look at the world through new eyes. I thought about charity work. Then an invitation arrived asking whether I would appear as a guest at one of Billy Graham's rallies at Earl's Court, in June 1966. The great American evangelist was embarking on a four-week crusade in London, and somehow his organization had heard about my conversion. I had been a Christian for about eighteen months by then, but I hadn't made any kind of formal announcement, and it was by no means public knowledge. 'Would you be prepared,' they asked, 'to come up onto the platform and tell people that you believe?'

I asked my Christian friends what they thought. 'You need to be absolutely certain that this is what you want to do,' they said. 'It's not the most popular thing to be a Christian, certainly not in England. You have to be prepared that you might lose fans.' So I took that on board, I chewed on it and I thought, Losing fans isn't a good enough reason to say 'No,' because if I believe this, if I really believe that by some miracle I have come into the presence of God, and have a new kind of spiritual life, then nothing else, not even my career, can possibly be as important. And if half my fans go, to heck with it. I don't care. I could probably manage on half my fans. So I took a deep breath, and I wrote back and I said, 'OK, I'll do it.' And it was terrifying.

Of all the nerve-racking experiences I've had in my life, and there have been plenty, that was possibly the most terrifying of all. I stood up there in front of an audience of twenty-five thousand people, with five thousand more outside the main arena, and told the world that I had become a Christian. It was a very hard thing to do. I had no idea what the reception would be, what my fans would think, what the press would make of it. I was on that stage for about ten minutes in all, and having made my statement of faith, I sang 'It Is No Secret (What God Can Do)', a gospel song, written by one of Billy Graham's converts, that Elvis had recorded. When I sat back down I found that I couldn't bend my arms; it was like being paralysed. While I had been singing, I had been gripping the sides of Billy's podium, and it was as though the blood in my arms had congealed. It was obviously just terror –

as it was on the day of my investiture at Buckingham Palace. Jesus perspired blood just before he was crucified, because he was so afraid. My blood just coagulated – that's about as close as I've come to being like Jesus!

The press had a field day. 'Cliff Gets Religion', 'Cliff Becomes A Monk', 'What Game Is He Playing?' screamed the headlines. I hated the derision. On *Top of the Pops* one day a journalist said, 'You do realize people are laughing behind your back?'

Shock, horror! I went home and told some of my Christian friends.

'I suppose he might be right,' I said. 'Maybe people are laughing behind my back.'

'Yes,' they said, 'maybe they are, but just think, if you'd been a Christian two thousand years ago, they would have been laughing at you while lions ripped out your throat.'

CHAPTER FIVE

Filling The Void

What I discovered, in my quest to make sense of the fame and the emptiness I felt after the death of my father, was Christianity, and that is what has sustained me and made my life so worth living all these years. Without sounding too pious about it, after I converted – and it was a major and very serious commitment – my priorities changed. I started to think about others, and how I could use my fame, not only to sell more records or buy bigger houses but to do some good in the world. And, glib as this might sound, once I started to give time and money to people who hadn't had the lucky breaks I'd had, the emptiness and dissatisfaction that was gnawing away at me faded away and I started to wake up in the mornings feeling better about myself – and, come to think of it, I have been feeling ridiculously good ever since.

If you were to ask me which of all the days in these fifty years has been the most thrilling, I would have to say it was the one in May 1995 when a letter from 10 Downing Street arrived at my home in Weybridge. The Prime Minister, it said, intended recommending me to the Queen for a knighthood in the Queen's Birthday Honours. I read it twice; then I read it out to Bill Latham, now one of my management team, who was sharing my house with me at that time. I couldn't believe what I was seeing. 'This couldn't be a joke, could it?' And perhaps the most exciting part of it was that it was not for my career as a singer – I had already been honoured for that. This was for my contribution to charity.

I started to laugh at the sheer implausibility of it; and I laughed and laughed and laughed. I couldn't stop. I was so happy and so completely taken by surprise. I'd had an OBE, for my singing – as you know, OBEs go to people like me – but it had never crossed my mind that I might ever get a knighthood. Businessmen were given knighthoods, civil servants, actors, politicians, important people; but me? It was just out of the question, I had never given it a thought.

I stupidly didn't keep the letter; I should have done but I don't save any sort of paperwork. So I have to paraphrase, but it said that my name was being recommended to the Queen, and if she were to agree, would I accept the honour? If I did, from that moment until it was officially announced I was sworn to secrecy, and if any information was leaked it would be assumed I was the source and the honour would be withdrawn instantly.

Would I accept it? What a question. Paper burned with the speed at which I put my pen to it: 'Yes please!' I was so thrilled, and actually very emotional; just knowing that the Queen along with the Prime Minister and thousands of members of the British public had thought me worthy of this honour – because my understanding is that you only get an honour like that these days if people badger the Prime Minister's office on your behalf. I had to pinch myself; it truly was the most exciting thing that's ever happened to me, and such a boost to my self-esteem.

The difficult part was having to keep it a secret. I wanted to shout it from the rooftops, but I was terrified of having it withdrawn. Neither Bill nor I breathed a word to anyone; no one in the office knew before the Queen's birthday, when the list was published in the newspapers; I didn't even tell my family. The list was published shortly before the start of Wimbledon, and I was coming back from Portugal for the tournament: it's one of the high spots of the year for me and I try to be there on most of the days. I landed at Gatwick to find dozens of press photographers awaiting my arrival – that's when I knew that it wasn't a dream – and that night I celebrated with a huge party at home for all my family and friends.

A workman was the first person who called me 'Sir'. I couldn't imagine how I was going to deal with being addressed so formally – I was 'Cliff' – but the next day when I went to Wimbledon to collect my tickets I walked past a guy sitting on the grass with a bottle of beer and a sandwich. He was one of the contractors erecting all the tents and paraphernalia for the hospitality area.

'Morning, Sir Cliff,' he said. 'All right?'

I replied, 'Yeah, thanks!'

And you know what? It felt great.

It still does. I don't need everyone to go around calling me 'Sir Cliff' all the time, but it is quite nice if people say it when they first meet me. In fact it sounds strange to me when I'm referred to as 'Mr'; there is no 'Mr' on my passport or credit cards.

I was allowed three guests at the investiture so I took my three sisters, Donna, Jacqui and Joan. My mother had come when I collected the OBE in 1980 but the girls had never been inside Buckingham Palace, so I asked Mum whether she minded if I took them instead. She was just beginning to get forgetful at that stage. 'No, of course you take them,' she said, and before she could say another word I said, 'OK,' and asked the girls.

It was a happy day. When we arrived at the palace – in all our finery – my sisters and I had to part company. They were ushered straight into the Ballroom, which is where the investiture takes place, and were given seats plum in the middle. I was taken to wait with all the other recipients in the Green Drawing Room, hung with priceless masterpieces. When we were all assembled, all feeling horribly nervous, the Comptroller of the Household, in full dress uniform, introduced himself and went through what each of us was to do when our turn came to receive our award. 'When you go to the podium,' he said, 'there will be this kneeler.' It was just a soft leather thing about two feet high, with a knee rest and a handle on the top. 'I would suggest that you do hold the handle,' he said firmly. 'People have fallen off this. You put your right knee, here, like this, put your head forward and say nothing. Please, say nothing until Her Majesty says something to you. This is the procedure: she will come to you, she will touch both your shoulders with the ceremonial sword, then you will stand up.'

I was so disappointed. I said, 'You mean she doesn't say "Arise, Sir Cliff"?'

He said, 'No. She touches your shoulders, you stand up, you lean forward, she puts the award around your neck, you then face her and she may or may not speak to you. But she always does.'

In my case she said, 'I do believe this has been a long time coming.' And I kind of babbled. I said to my sisters afterwards, 'I don't think I said anything.' I was so choked up. What a collection we were: my sisters were crying, and I couldn't speak. Afterwards I said to them, 'I bet the Queen's sitting there now thinking, Why did we choose him? We could have chosen someone who could at least speak English.' I couldn't get anything out; it was like the whole of my throat had closed up. It was a bit like the day when I spoke for the first time at a Billy Graham crusade. I was so scared my arms locked. I couldn't move them; I thought I was paralysed. On this occasion I wasn't scared in that way. I was just terrified I was going to fall off the kneeler, particularly because I'd been warned that some people had. And some older women, he told us, had curtsied so deeply that their knees had locked and they had been unable to get up again. The whole morning was so emotional. I kept thinking: that sword, how many shoulders has it touched in the past? And this time it's mine. Insignificant me.

Afterwards we joined my mother and the rest of the family, and we all went off and celebrated with champagne and a fantastic lunch at the Savoy Grill. My youngest sister, Joan, hadn't been to the Savoy Grill before and didn't realize it was one of the smartest hotel dining rooms in London. She thought I was taking them all out for a burger. She had no class, that girl – but she was a fast learner!

My sisters are all quite different. Donna, the eldest, has my father's build and colouring: small, fine-boned, with dark skin and very dark hair. She is very independent and I see less of her these days than of old. She and her husband, Terry, are so wrapped up in each other that if a bomb dropped on London and the only place still standing was their house at Ware in Hertfordshire, neither of them would notice for about a year. Jacqui also has my father's build and shape of face. She is the brainiest. None of us is highly educated – none of us went to university but she mulls things through while the rest of us plunge in without too much thought. She and her husband, Peter, are Jehovah's Witnesses. They are both involved in the church and Jacqui takes her religion very seriously. Her children have been brought up that way too. Of all my sisters, Joan is most like me; we both have our mother's round face. Joan and her daughter, Linzi, come to just about every concert of mine they can. They laugh a lot and dance a lot, and even with my eyesight I can usually spot them in the crowd.

As children, Donna and I were inseparable; we went out at weekends together, went to the cinema together, and I remember we used to practise jiving together. Mum and Dad loved jiving too – we would all do it, and Mum was always telling me to stop swinging Donna so wildly. She was very petite, not quite five feet tall, and I think my mother was frightened I would break her. There was quite a gap in age between me and Jacqui and Joan, a gap which when we were all young seemed huge but which, of course, vanished as we grew up, and these days I think I probably know Joan best. As the last child, Joan was very spoilt and wanted everything her own way, which I found annoying. I loved her because she was one of the family, but I didn't actually like her very much, and sometimes didn't like what she was doing or saying. All that changed when she married her second husband, David. I don't know what they did to each other but she became much more likeable – and, according to his parents, so did he. After they married I grew closer to Joan. She was always geographically the closest, too, and now she has a house near mine in Portugal; so we see a lot of each other and we talk on the phone as well.

All my sisters have children. Donna adopted a boy and a girl. She had very serious gynaecological problems years ago, which left her unable to have children of her own. We were terrified she might die: she needed a blood transfusion but she, like my mother, was a Jehovah's Witness at that time, and as such was prohibited from receiving a transfusion. My mother made the decision on her behalf and Donna was given the blood she needed. It saved her life, but Mum paid the price – there was an 'inquisition' by the church. Jacqui has two boys and three girls, and Joan has two girls and a boy. They are all fun kids, and some of them have children of their own now. My sisters' children have been so important to me over the years. When they were growing up they didn't have the faintest idea who I was. They loved me for myself, not because I was Cliff Richard. There are not many people I can say that about with hand on heart.

That is one of the downsides to this extraordinary life I've led. I have been in the public eye since I was seventeen and most of the people I meet, even the young ones, know who I am; and so I have no way of knowing whether they like me because I am *me* or because I happen to be famous. With my nephews and nieces I know that they like *me*. Every time I saw them when they were babies they cried and screamed like mad, so we had no real relationship, but from the age of about two or three, once they were past that stage, I became really popular with them. They knew nothing about my fame, they didn't care, and it was fantastic.

One day when Emma, Donna's adopted daughter, was about six or seven she came into the room and she kept looking at me strangely, then looking at the television and then back at me. I asked her what was wrong and she said, 'I think I saw you on TV.' It was like a little awakening. After that, they all slowly became aware that I wasn't quite like everyone else; but it changed nothing between us.

Knowing that they are pleased to see me, as my sisters are, is more important to me than almost anything else, and I have no doubt that having a close family has been crucial in keeping me relatively sane. My sisters all know where I came from, and how and where we lived, and why I behave the way I do and use the expressions I use. So much of it comes from our childhood and our parents – and that's something that no one else, however close, can share.

CHAPTER SIX

Changes

My greatest fear as I stood on the stage at Earl's Court declaring my faith was that I would be committing professional suicide; that the public would turn away in droves. Thank God, my fears were unfounded. Six months later, the Shadows and I performed in pantomime at the London Palladium and it was the most successful the Palladium had staged in eighty years. It was the beginning of a period of change, nonetheless, in both my professional and my private life. Up to this point, in the first eight years, my career had seemed unstoppable. Now it seemed to be levelling out. I hadn't cracked America, which the Beatles, coming five years after me, had done with spectacular success; my new releases had greater competition for the top of the charts; and my third major film, *Wonderful Life* – hot on the heels of two smash hits, *The Young Ones* and *Summer Holiday* – was widely panned, and probably quite rightly.

The Young Ones had been the second biggest box-office hit of 1962, the single by the same name went into the charts at number one and the album of the soundtrack sat at the top of the LP chart for six weeks. It had been fun to make, a great cast – Melvyn Hayes and Teddy Green became friends, and we went on to do *Summer Holiday* together, where Una Stubbs joined us. Una became, and still is, a very good friend; I love her dearly but, despite years of rumour, it was never to be more than that. She and Melvyn and I then went on to do *Wonderful Life*, and of course the Shadows were in all three too. We were like children, out partying until late every night, even though we all had to be up early – some of us at 6.00 a.m. – to be in make-up. We had the most wonderful time – it truly was a Wonderful Life. My only complaint was that I didn't like the look of myself in *The Young Ones:* at 12st 7lb I was too chubby – and it didn't help that a character in *Coronation Street* called me 'that lovely chubby Cliff Richard'. But by the start of *Summer Holiday* I'd managed to get myself down to 11st, which felt a lot better and funnily enough is the weight I am today.

Summer Holiday was more like a holiday than work. I swanned round Greece for six weeks on a red London double-decker bus with a group of good mates and we were all paid for the privilege. My family even came and joined me for a while. Donna was newly married, but my mother and two youngest sisters came out for a holiday. They were so excited to be able to come on set and watch the filming, but the excitement soon wore off when they discovered that filming is the most boring process to watch because each scene is shot over and over again from every angle. The result, though, was fantastically successful – it broke all records for a British film. The soundtrack, most of it written by the Shadows, remained at the top of the LP charts for fourteen weeks, and we had two hit singles from it – the title song, and 'The Next Time/Bachelor Boy' – each of which sold a million, earning me another two gold discs. They are the old numbers I sang on my recent trip to Brazil, and although none of the Brazilians knew who I was, they recognized the songs and screamed with excitement. At my concerts back home, too, audiences always want me to sing songs from that period of my career.

Summer Holiday came out in January 1963, the year in which the Beatles took the country by storm. The premiere was in

Leicester Square and I arrived with my family in a big limo, as we had for *The Young Ones*. Leicester Square was jammed solid. Thousands of people stood outside the cinema, many of them holding placards saying 'Cliff We Love You'. My limo edged slowly towards the entrance but as the driver pulled up and I started to open the door a policeman said, 'On your way, on your way!'

I said, 'I'm Cliff Richard, it's my film, it's my premiere.'

He wasn't interested. 'You can't stop here,' he said, and so we didn't. I missed it. I watched the premiere from my manager's apartment in Maida Vale. A year later the Beatles had the same experience, and the press were saying they had never seen anything like it here in London. Oh yes, they had. How soon they forget!

The Beatles were absolutely great. They took pop music to a whole new level and I often think of the Shadows and me as the bridge between the old and the new. With the experience and confidence of having played in Hamburg, they had the nerve to tell management that they were a pop group and didn't want to be all-round entertainers. They wrote their own songs, to which they insisted upon keeping the copyright – they were the first group to do that – and they called the shots. I wasn't mad about being squeezed out of the number one position by their records, but the Shadows and I managed to hold our own during the years of Beatlemania, and had number ones of our own. The Beatles sold a phenomenal number of records; at that time we didn't sell as many as they did but we were still selling as many as we had before they appeared and we still sold out our concerts. We had plenty of hit songs during that period – I think it's true to say that between 1962 and 1970, when the Beatles disbanded, we had about thirty records in the Top Twenty while they had twenty-three. They were geniuses, though; I loved their music and their songwriting, and their whole approach shook up the industry in a way that was good for everyone. They arrived at a time when a number of artists were renegotiating with the record companies and because they were selling so many records they could afford to up the ante. Peter Gormley never liked to push for too much. He was always very fair as a negotiator and thought that some people at that time were asking for more than they deserved. 'I am going to ask for what I think is right,' he would say, 'and that leaves us room to go up.' So we always went up, pennies at a time.

In the beginning it had been one old penny per record sold. That meant I had to sell two hundred and forty records to earn one pound. Admittedly we did sell a lot of records at that time. Nowadays, recording artists sell nothing by comparison. You hear people talk about a band that's been number one in the States and they've sold 120,000 copies. My singles were selling over a million – in a country that's a fraction of the size. But I wouldn't have changed a thing, even if I could have. It meant a huge amount to me that so many people wanted to buy my records – I like knowing that a large part of the population of the world has something of mine – but, of course, if I had been on a realistic royalty, my wealth would have been in another stratosphere. I equate it to tennis. If you talk to the older players, they'll tell you that they earned peanuts compared with today's professionals. One veteran told me that she had been runner-up in a tournament at Wimbledon and her prize was a £10 voucher that she had to spend in the Wimbledon shop. It was a different world. Today even the runners-up go home with hundreds of thousands of pounds. Heigh-ho – that's life.

These days I sometimes get stopped by people in the street, and it always brings me right down to earth when they recognize me instantly and say, 'Oh Cliff, I was a big fan of yours. Are you still recording?' Who can blame them for not knowing? Unless the radio is constantly playing your new material, no one knows it's there, and for the last five or ten years now my records just haven't been played. Some stations have said, 'We don't play Cliff'; one actually declared itself a 'Cliff-free zone'. Even when 'Millennium Prayer' had been at number one for three weeks and had sold over a million copies, it was rarely heard on radio.

Some stations won't even take advertisements for my shows. That completely stunned me. Malcolm Smith, my business manager, decided to give one final boost to sales of the last tickets for the 2006–2007 tour and was told by several radio stations that they wouldn't carry the ad. 'I am a paying customer,' Malcolm said. 'What do you mean, you won't take our advert?'

They said, 'We don't play Cliff Richard so we don't want his advert.'

I can't believe they have the right to do that. I was really angry – but it was also really hurtful. The problem for me is, where other advertisers might be selling baked beans, I am selling myself, so the rejection is always going to be personal.

In the mid-nineties I was invited to speak at the BAFTA annual radio conference. They asked if I had anything to talk about. 'I sure have,' I said emphatically. I told them how important radio was in my business and how the relationship between radio stations and recording artists has changed. When I had finished I was given the longest standing ovation of my life.

I explained that in the past we were so close to radio that I had once phoned Roger Scott at Capital Radio from the recording studio. He had the afternoon show, and I said, 'We have a problem: we're mixing a new track here and we can't tell why it doesn't sound quite right. Would you play it for us?'

He said, 'You're kidding! When can I play it?'

I said, 'We'll send it to you by courier; it will be with you in half an hour.'

Meanwhile we were listening to the show, and he was saying, 'Cliff Richard and Bruce Welch [who was producing) have just called me and they're going to send me a track from their new album. You, listeners, are going to be the first people to hear it.'

Half an hour later he played it for us and sure enough, there was nowhere near enough bass. It was immediately obvious – but you really did have to hear it on the radio, on a regular car radio, to work out what was wrong. So we took it back and pumped up the bass, and there was our record. I can no longer remember what song it was – but that was the sort of relationship we had with the radio stations.

Radio is still the best way for people to hear your music. If I'm on a television show the viewers only hear the song once; an A-list record on the radio would be played five to seven times a day, so if someone's listening all day, by mid-afternoon they know there's a new Cliff Richard record out, have recognized it a couple of times, decided they like it and made up their mind to buy it (or not). That was the usual pattern. Not many records are instant hits, as 'Living Doll', 'We Don't Talk Anymore', 'Dreamin'' and 'Millennium Prayer' were. Those all shot to the top of the charts quite quickly – but most records creep there, and they get there because they are being played and heard over and over again.

I had a song called 'What Car' in the charts in 2005. It was from an album I made in Nashville called *Something's Goin' On*. The single didn't make it to the A-list but it did get on to the B-list at Radio 2, so it was played about three times a week while sales gradually built up. At its peak, it was played 350 times in one week. I was ecstatic until I discovered that that same week the number one song on the playlist had 2,500 plays. How can I possibly compete? I understand if a DJ doesn't like the record himself, or doesn't like me, but what I don't understand is why, if the record has made it to the charts – which must mean a percentage of the audience likes it – a DJ will continue to refuse to play it to his listeners. All answers to your local radio stations please.

So we have radio stations, happy with half

a million listeners. Please! What kind of a business venture that *could* have four million is happy with half a million? It's nonsense. If I had a radio station I would say, 'Play anything that is number one. Play anything that is in the top twenty. If it goes up, keep playing it, if it starts to drop, slowly take it out.' That, to me, makes total sense; you will be playing records that people must want to hear, otherwise those records wouldn't be in the charts. Conversely, if a record does not make the top twenty, then obviously no one is buying it, and therefore no one wants to hear it. Play what people want to hear and your radio station will get a bigger cross-section of listeners. That's what broadcasting is about. Nowadays they narrowcast. They aim at, say, a group aged between five and ten years old. Hello? How many of them have any money? OK, they get Mum and Dad to buy the records for them, but it's still a small group. The largest group of people who listen to records on the radio are probably between the ages of thirty and sixty, and most of them listen to Radio 2 because Radio 2 plays just about everything.

It's not just radio, of course, that's to blame for the fall in record sales. The beginning of the end was when they first brought out blank cassettes. I had a friend who used to teach and he said that one kid would buy an album and record it on to a blank tape, then come into school and all his friends would use the cassette to make their own copies. Now it's the internet. People can download single tracks from iTunes for peanuts and put them on to their digital machines, from which they can make perfect CDs. They can be copied over and over again, and the quality is fantastic. But the fact remains that people are not going to download something unless they know it exists, unless they've heard it – and that still means radio.

Radio and rock 'n' roll were made for each other. The problems start when you get power-crazed people who want to fragment the art form and say, 'We only do country,' or 'We only play rap,' and 'We won't play this or that.' Do that and you have broken down the heart of rock 'n' roll, which is a huge umbrella encompassing all of those things – everything from Des O'Connor on one side, who had some pop ballad hits and was huge, to Led Zeppelin and heavy metal on the other side, and me dabbling around in the middle somewhere. The radio tsars have changed how radio sees popular music – and of course, it's their right to change it – but in doing that they've done our industry absolutely no favours. In sales terms we are at the lowest ebb ever; and it has happened in the last few years. It's just gone right down. I can talk about it philosophically now, and I don't feel any pain, but the frustration for me is that I still think of myself as a recording artist. I have never thought of myself as a performer. I sometimes write on those forms you have to fill in on the aeroplane 'Entertainer' – or sometimes just 'Singer' – but I still see myself as a recording artist. That is slowly being eroded, and there will come a time, I know, when I won't be able to write that any more.

I was so angry about all of this, I became a complete bore, mumbling and moaning at everyone in the office. They kept telling me to stop whingeing – but I felt I was fighting for my livelihood, for something that had been part of my life for fifty years, and I was not going to give it up lightly. I think many of the people running radio stations are totally wrong – and it's not just me losing out, the public are losing out because they are not getting the choice they should have. I am not alone in this. A lot of older artists are in the same boat. Status Quo even tried to sue Radio 1. I didn't think that was really feasible – you can't sue people for not playing your record, it's not our God-given right to be played – and, not surprisingly, they lost. I'm not angry any more, and I don't think I go on about it as much as I did – unless someone brings up the subject – or I write a book! I am just intensely frustrated; but it seems there is nothing any of us can do, and sadly it means we will record less and less.

In the beginning I only ever recorded in Studio 2 at the EMI studios in Abbey Road. When the Beatles came along, they loved that place as well, and we had big fights about who would get it. I met Paul McCartney some years later, and he said to me, 'It was just favouritism.' I said, 'What do you mean?' and he said, 'Well, whenever we phoned up for Studio 2 they'd say, "Sorry, Cliff's got it."' I said, 'Oh Paul, come on, Bruce Welch used to do our phoning for me and the Shadows, and he used to say, "The Beatles have got it again, shall we go into 3?" And I would say, "No, we'll wait for 2."' We both thought EMI was showing favouritism to the other band because we both loved that studio so much. For them, as for us, it was the birthplace of our recording careers.

The studio would be booked for three hours and we would go in with between three and five songs and be expected to get them done in that period. There was no multi-tracking; we rehearsed the song, then played it through to the producer and the engineers in the sound box; they would say, 'OK, we're ready for a take,' and we would do it as many times as it took to get it right. If it fell apart in the middle, as it often did, we'd start again. We might get it on take five, we might have to go to take nine. I think 'Living Doll' was take seven. As soon as they were happy with one song we went on to the next; and when we left the studio, we had the finished copies in our hands.

I found that incredibly exciting; and recording is still, of all the things I've done in my career, the most exciting, satisfying and creative part of what I do. I love performing and that comes a close second, but going into a recording studio with nothing but the bare bones of a song and coming out with something that is purchasable is incredible. And if you can convince somebody in an audience that you sound like your records, it's a miracle. I get letters from people saying they heard me at Wembley Stadium or wherever and I sounded indistinguishable from the recording. I smile and say, 'Thanks,' but, of course, that's impossible. Nothing can sound like the record because the acoustics will never be perfect in an auditorium – but if I can convince people that it does, I'm thrilled.

Recording has changed as the technology has advanced, and so has the excitement. When I started, it was a case of putting the track straight down and hearing it straight back; there was no chance of changing it. Now you can take your time about recording and it's not even necessary to record with the group. There will be multiple tracks I can use, just for my voice, so I can go into the studio and sing two or three lines at a time, and end up recording the song maybe eight times – and I can still fiddle around with it after that, change notes if I want to – and then the producer will make a composite of the eight versions of the song I have given him. He can take one word from one version and another from the eighth version; and the ninth will be a composite of all the others. That's how they like to do it these days.

The producer is in control because in the end, he's the one who mixes it, blends together what he's selected out of everything that's been recorded, and presents the track you finally hear. But I guess because I've been around for so long producers don't mind my comments or criticism at that crucial stage. I might say to them, 'Do you think you could lift the drum up?' and they might say, 'Oh, that might make it too heavy,' and I'll say, 'Yes, but that's because it's too fat; if we thin it out you get this sound rather than that.' I make the sound for them and they go, 'Oh yeah, I see what you mean.' So you see, it's all part of the process of making it grow. Artists, painters, must feel the same way. When they sell a sculpture or painting I suspect they quite often think, Not sure I like that sky; that cloud could have been lighter. The same thing happens when I hear records of mine. I think, Why didn't I bring the vocal group up, or Why didn't I do another harmony at that point? Given half a chance I would go on for ever, tweaking here and there, seeking perfection – but that way madness lies.

At the end of the session, I ask for what we call a monitor mix – unfinished but audible – and they cut a little CD for me that I can play in the car on the way home. If I think: Oh no, I'll change that when I go back, it's because I know it can be done. Rock 'n' roll is the best and freest art form since painting. There are no rules. It's like putting layers of paint on to a canvas: the artist will put on one colour then smudge right into it, then another and another until he has what he wants. A recording is layer upon layer of sound textures, and sometimes you are not aware of everything on the track, which is why I like to play my music loud so that I can hear that cymbal or triangle which would otherwise be lost. You can even layer your vocals these days so you can be in vocal harmony with yourself– or even sound like a choir if you want to. You can take your time building it up or taking bits away. Phil Spector, the legendary music producer, was a master of filling the track with everything but the kitchen sink – and sometimes even the kitchen sink. It was known as Phil Spector's 'wall of sound' – yet nothing ever got in the way of the lyrics or the singer. No one else did it as brilliantly as he did.

Nowadays, you don't even need a studio.

You can sing in an old shack, it doesn't matter – as long as you have a good producer: that's vital. I've sung in a field, I've sung in a producer's home beside a busy road. We recorded between gaps in the traffic. He'd pull the curtain back and say, 'OK, take one.' I record really close to the microphone, and when I've got my headset on, and my voice goes through all the technology, and comes back in my ears, I'm not aware of anything, the rest of the world might not exist. I love it.

CHAPTER SEVEN

Foreign Fields

My first experience of serious crowds was in southern Africa, where 'Move It' went straight into the charts. The Shadows and I toured there in 1961 and we were completely mobbed. The local press reported that there had never been a reception like it. We landed in Rhodesia, as it then was, and thousands of people were at the airport to greet us. As we set off for the city, they jumped into cars and on to scooters and motorbikes, forming a massive cavalcade that escorted us into the town of Bulawayo,

with everyone waving, shouting and screaming all the way to the hotel. The next night
they were all at the concert, and they were a
fantastic audience – we absolutely stormed
them. It was so exciting; we came off the
stage on a massive high and I said, 'I can't
sleep, I'm not going to go to bed tonight,
I'm going to wait to see what the press has
to say tomorrow.'

How I wish I'd gone to bed. In a nutshell,
the review, written by someone calling himself 'The Thespian', said: 'As talentless as
Cliff Richard is, so the Shadows are
talented' – and that was it. He wrote about
the Shadows and didn't mention me again.
Disaster; I was shocked. But it didn't seem
to make much difference to the bookings.
We played a second concert in Salisbury,
which was another complete sell-out with
another fantastic audience, then flew down
to South Africa. At Johannesburg there were
even more people waiting for us at the
airport. The crowd was unbelievable and I
remember seeing a black-and-white photograph of our arrival. I was standing in the
middle of this crowd, policemen everywhere, people reaching out, and my head
was back and I was just roaring with
laughter. It was unbelievable. I climbed into
the back of a big, red, fancy American car
that Gary Player, the South African golfer,
had lent me – I think I had it to myself and

the Shads were in another car – and I was driven slowly, with the hood back, through the crowds. They were all touching me and screaming and saying they were coming to the show and would see us all tomorrow.

As we drove out of the airport the crowds seemed to disappear; the next minute they were alongside me on scooters and motor-bikes, and we travelled like this all the way to the city centre. The car radio was on and I could hear the commentary – '… and now he's going past the Jan Smuts block…' – and heads would stick out of the windows of the office blocks to either side of us, and there was a lot of waving. We arrived at the hotel in Eloff Street, and there were so many people in the street we could barely get to the entrance. When we finally made it, we had some tea and went upstairs to relax, and the people looking after us said, 'I'm afraid you're going to have to come out. No one's going home.' The room had a little balcony overlooking the street, so the Shadows and I went out on to the balcony and I said: 'Hi, everybody! The Shadows and I are really happy to be here. Thanks so much for coming. We'll see you at the concert.' We turned and went inside and slowly slowly, the crowds began to disperse. I still find it hard to believe that it happened to us – and a couple of years before the Beatles, too.

We were aware of apartheid in South

Africa, but I didn't fully understand what it meant at that time and I was puzzled that there were no black faces at our concerts. On subsequent visits we insisted on going into the black townships to play additional concerts. I remember waiting at Johannesburg airport once in the early seventies, because the tour organizers had forgotten to get a permit to allow me to play to multiracial audiences. I said, 'I'm not leaving here unless you show me the permit.' So I sat at the airport until they finally produced the necessary piece of paper. It took hours. On another occasion the authorities wouldn't allow me to play to a multi-racial audience at a concert in Klerksdorp, so I said, 'In that case, I'm not coming.' The South African press were very brave. I thought they would be gagged by the government, but they said, 'Good on you, well done, Cliff.'

Not many international sportsmen and performers were playing in South Africa in the eighties, because anti-apartheid campaigners had imposed a boycott on the country, and those who did go faced heavy criticism at home. In England many consumers were refusing to buy South African exports and no one was travelling there on holiday. Passions ran high and I was deeply sympathetic with the anti-apartheid campaigners – I found apartheid abhorrent – but I didn't feel that isolating the country was necessarily the only way to deal with it. It didn't solve the problem and it didn't help the black population. My thinking was that if people could accept God into their lives, then they would turn away from apartheid, because as soon as a person's heart is filled with any kind of love, it automatically sees that treating other human beings as second-class citizens and forcing them to live apart in separate areas is outrageous. So I went to the country, unpaid, as a Christian, at the invitation of churches, to present my faith in a series of gospel tours, and the audiences we played to seemed to appreciate it.

Not so the people of Norway. When Shirley Bassey and I were invited to appear on a television show together in Oslo in the mid-eighties, we arrived to find a protest under way outside our hotel. The reason was that we had both played in South Africa. I found it pretty galling, since I had only ever gone at the invitation of the Church there to play for charity. Shirley had sung at Sun City. I don't know whether she had been paid for that, but either way, she was incensed. 'How dare they?' she exclaimed. 'I'm a black person!'

We fought our way to the television studios and half way through the show there was a minor disruption in the crowd. About eight people, out of four or five thousand, stood up and waved anti-apartheid placards, but the producer lost his nerve and pulled the plugs. It caused a major stir and the Norwegian Prime Minister subsequently appeared on television to say how ashamed he was that visitors who had come to the country to provide entertainment should have been treated in such a disgraceful way. As someone said to me afterwards, 'It's crazy; those eight people represented 0.00065 per cent of the crowd.' True; but although few in number, they were jostling outside the studios and cursing and swearing at Shirley and me, and it was a very ugly scene. Back at the hotel, the place was crawling with army personnel and policemen. Apparently my life had been threatened and they were obliged to take the threat seriously. They gave me the whole top floor of the hotel to myself, and I spent a nervous but very heavily guarded night there trying to make light of the situation. I can't pretend it wasn't a relief to be on a plane and flying home the next day.

It transpired that I was on a United Nations apartheid blacklist. I wrote to Harry Belafonte, the Jamaican calypso singer, who was then a goodwill ambassador to UNICEF, and I said, 'I have no idea why I'm on this list. Yes, I do go to South Africa. And this is why I do.' I explained that I went there as a Christian. 'Since the ban came into force I have never been paid for my services. I go there to speak about my faith, I tell them what I think about apartheid, and I try to help change the hearts of people. Should I really be on the blacklist?' I had a nice letter back saying he thought it was a mistake and my name had been removed. I was never bothered by protestors again, but it was a scary experience. Now it is nothing more than a bad memory.

I love South Africa and I have been back many times, sometimes to sing, sometimes privately for holidays. A lot has changed since those days and there have been huge improvements: when I first went there, blacks and whites couldn't swim on the same beaches, travel in the same buses, sit on the same bench or use the same toilet. All of that has gone, thank God; but there are still vast shanty towns, just across the road from where the wealthy white people live, so in some ways nothing has changed. The black and white populations haven't entirely integrated. There are too many people who thought, when Nelson Mandela became President, that they were going to be given jobs and homes instantly, and they still don't have either. And there are other problems. One place I visited has one million refugees living in it, and many of them are from Nigeria. People are flocking to South Africa from other African countries. Heaven alone knows how they're going to deal with that challenge.

For all these reasons, I have never thought of South Africa as a place where I might live. The landscape is beautiful, the weather's good, the scenery's fantastic, and the food is wonderful – but it's a vast country, and unless I devoted myself to tackling some of its problems, I wouldn't feel comfortable living there. Some of my band have said they would, but I wonder whether they could honestly drive past all those people living in cardboard boxes day after day on the way to a show or to the office and then drive back to their lovely homes with swimming pools. I couldn't do that and I don't think they could. It brings me down just thinking about it, because, as I've tried to say in the songs I've written, we can't solve the problems of the world. I feel worse than useless almost a hundred per cent of the time. The thing about Christianity, though, is that it keeps you positive. It reminds you that, 'Regardless of how helpless you feel, you must keep on doing what you do.' I have to believe that in the end God has a master plan for every-thing and each one of us plays a small part in creating the whole.

After I became a Christian in 1966, my horizon changed. I was suddenly conscious that I was wealthy, that I had much that so many people in the world didn't have, and I wanted to give some of it back. Terrible images of starving pot-bellied children, victims of the Biafran civil war, came into our living rooms each night on the news, and I realized that perhaps my family were not the most needy people on earth. There were parts of the world, like Nigeria, where people had no roofs over their heads, no food to feed their children, and no medicines for curable diseases. I had taken care of my own, I had helped my family buy their houses; now I wanted to try to help others. But we had all read about mountains of grain left rotting on quaysides and millions of pounds in aid money disappearing into the pockets of corrupt officials. None of us wants our money to be squandered; I wanted to give it to people I could trust who would use it wisely. And in 1968 I found just the people.

David Winter, the friend who had been involved in the process of my becoming a Christian, told me that a group within the Evangelical Alliance was launching a charity which would use money raised by Christians for disaster relief, funnelling aid directly to the people for whom it was intended. It would work with Christians actually in the disaster areas, so there would be no government involvement and therefore no corruption. It was to be called The Evangelical Alliance Relief Fund, Tearfund for short, and the visionary behind it was a young vicar called the Rev George Hoffman. George and I clicked immediately. He

147

was seven years older than me and one of the most impressive men I've known. He was very emotional, totally committed. Sometimes he would come back from a trip, ashen – he was a pale man to start with – and he would sit down and frantically sign cheques, saying, 'They have to have this money.' I don't think there was a board to control expenditure at that time. Sometimes boards can take the heart out of a charity. Tearfund managed to keep the heart thumping and George was that heart. He was very special, everyone loved him dearly, and we worked together for twenty-one years until he moved on.

The tragedy is that three years later, having travelled all over the world, suffered all kinds of stomach bugs, been shot at by terrorist groups and survived it all, back home in England George was run over by a car and killed on his way to speak at a church gathering. It was horrifying. I was on tour at the time, in Birmingham, and my PA, Roger Bruce, waited until after the show to break the news. He knew that I would never have been able to get through it had he told me any earlier. I was so upset; and I was angry too. Why him? Sometimes I say to God, 'Look, I know we are not able to understand everything, but I really don't get this.' But sometimes that's simply the way it is.

As soon as I met George I started to give

a percentage of my income to Tearfund, and I still do, although I now do it via my own Charitable Trust. I also did gospel concerts for Tearfund. 'Help! Hope! and Hallelujah!' was the first, at the Royal Albert Hall in 1969. I sang with the Settlers, a terrific folk group, and raised £800 for a Land Rover to help missionary agricultural work in Argentina. Concerned that it might be hard to fill the place, someone at Tearfund came up with the idea of having a Land Rover on a pedestal at the Albert Hall, thinking Rover would be only too pleased at the opportunity for publicity. They weren't, but agreed grudgingly – only for the vehicle they sent to break down on the MI! So they had to hire another from a firm in London, and then they discovered that it was impossible to get something the size of a Land Rover into the building.

George thought that with my profile I could also be useful in raising awareness, so I began to take trips to disaster areas, which the press would cover, and which Tearfund would film to show to church audiences in the UK. Since Tearfund is celebrating its fortieth anniversary this year, and I am celebrating my fiftieth, it seemed logical to give them the proceeds from my first concert of my anniversary tour. It has been a very special relationship: over those forty years I've been on many trips to many continents and been through every emotion under the sun.

The first trip was to Bangladesh in 1973. Since the civil war between India and Pakistan in 1971, which killed three million people, hundreds of thousands of refugees had fled to the newly created state of Bangladesh. They escaped persecution, but only to find themselves starving and dying in filthy, overcrowded, disease-ridden camps. It was a major humanitarian crisis and the first time I had witnessed anything like it. I overheard a couple of aid workers discussing me shortly after I arrived. 'We can't take him there. The excreta's so deep he'd need thigh-length boots.' And the other said, 'Well we could take him to that other camp where the stuff's dried out by now.' I felt sick at the thought of what I had let myself in for, and when we arrived at the camp the reality was even worse than I had anticipated. Everywhere, mothers with desperately sick babies were holding them up to these nurses begging, 'Please, take my baby,' knowing that if they did, their baby might stand a chance; but the nurses had to be ruthless, taking only the babies that were most likely to survive. 'We haven't got enough equipment,' they explained; 'so if there are five babies and two of them look strong enough to pull through, those are the ones we have to pick.' Apart from anything else, I felt that those nurses should never have been put in that impossible position.

The hospital itself was surprisingly uplifting, because children are amazing: if they are afflicted by curable diseases – as many of these were – once they are cuddled and loved and have some medicine inside them, they bounce back. We would walk into the ward and the nurses would say, 'Good morning!' and they would all shout 'Good morning!' and be laughing and smiling. It was very infectious, and suddenly, in the midst of all the desperation, I was suddenly laughing and smiling too.

George Hoffman was with me, also Bill Latham and a photographer. Bill by this time had given up teaching and was working for Tearfund as George's deputy director. That brought the full complement of the charity's staff to four – George, Bill, the treasurer, and a secretary who looked after the books. It is amazing how it has grown since then. Now the UK office numbers three hundred and fifty, with a further thousand overseas; and income has ballooned from £26,000 in its first year to over £50 million today.

As soon as it became known that I was raising money for Tearfund, I started to get a lot of letters from other charities and individuals, all wanting financial help. And since Tearfund's work tended to be in the Third World, and there was clearly also great need closer to home, it seemed sensible to

151

set up something in Britain. So it was that, in the late sixties, the Cliff Richard (Charitable Trust) Ltd was born. I started it off with a lump sum; then I began to put the proceeds from one in every ten concerts into it, and whenever I was asked to sing at some event or other I would ask for a donation. Slowly the fund grew. Over the years we have been able to help a lot of people in Britain – mostly the young, the old, the disabled and charities involved in medical research: the sort of things I am personally interested in. I guess we must get around two thousand appeals a year and pay out to several hundred of those, but they have to be registered charities – it's impossible to give to individuals, there are just too many.

We were not making a film on that trip to Bangladesh, merely taking still photographs. I knew the picture they were angling for but I couldn't do it. Those children had scabs all over their heads, their noses dribbled, their eyes were encrusted and there were flies everywhere. There was no way I was going to touch them. I posed kneeling beside one child, not quite touching, and wondering what I was going to do, when Bill – he swears it wasn't him, but I know it was – trod on this child's fingers, and the baby opened its mouth and let out a piercing wail. The same thing had happened with my sisters' children many times, and the response is automatic:

the baby screams and the person nearest grabs the child to comfort it. Now this baby reached up and instinctively I grabbed it – and immediately the wailing stopped and it snuggled into my neck and snuffled. It was the most unbelievable feeling. Suddenly this child was no longer a sickly statistic, but a person. It changed everything for me. The rest of my visit was so much easier, I could touch the children, I was fine. Afterwards, of course, I would shower, wash, and scrub my fingernails, because some of the things these people have to live with would kill us almost instantly – or certainly make us very ill.

I was there for about three days, and every night when we finished we'd go back to the home where the nurses stayed, we'd have a meal together, and then we would sing and talk. On the last night I said to them, 'You know we're going away tomorrow. I really feel I should stay here with you folks.'

One of them said, 'Can you give an injection?'

I said, 'No, I can't.'

She said, 'Then we don't need you here. Why don't you go home and do what you do – tell people about what's happening here, raise money for us to save these children – because we can't do what you do.'

And I realized that, of course, she was right. We each had a role to play, we were each a cog among many others, and that's what made the whole machine work. From my vantage point, with my fame and my career, I was in a position to do something valuable to enable these nurses to do what they were doing here in the stinking, seething, refugee camps. The other great lesson I took away with me from Bangladesh was that the front line of aid and relief work, horrific as it is, has a kind of spiritual glamour. So we need to be sure that we're doing what God wants of us and not what might be merely self-fulfilling.

When I first became a Christian, I had seriously thought about giving up show business. When I lay on my bed that night, all those years ago, I knew I had to make some changes. I made a conscious decision to be less dominated by my career. Looking back, I realize there was a period between 1965 or '66 and when I recorded 'Devil Woman', in 1976, when I had lost interest. I liked having my career, but I had disengaged from it. If I was recording, the producers would pre-record all the music, and I would go in and add my voice. I didn't even bother asking who'd played it. I would just think, Well that's a good song, that might be a hit. I felt lacklustre, I had no enthusiasm for it any more – until around 1974, when I met up with a producer called Dave McKay, and he's the one who got me interested in my music again. He said, 'I loved the way you played "Travellin' Light" on stage last night, you must record it.' I'd already had a number one with 'Travellin' Light', back in 1959, but he said, 'I'd like to do your live version of it.' So I played guitar on the track and it was a slightly different, musically darker version of the song. He reawakened my interest, so by the time 1976 came along and Bruce Welch was producing *I'm Nearly Famous*, the album with 'Devil Woman' and 'Miss You Nights' on it, I was back in the running. During that down time I guess I'd worked out where I was spiritually. I wasn't a novice at it, I'd been through the period of wondering whether I should and could be a rock star. It was great to be back.

I had struggled and been through some terrible times, convinced I was in the wrong business. All my friends – people like Bill Latham, Graham Disbrey, John Harvey, David Winter – were all immersed in their jobs: Bill had even given up his teaching job to work full time for Tearfund. Graham taught art but was a teacher in his church. David Winter edited *Crusade*, a Christian magazine. They were all involved in what they believed in; I called myself a Christian yet what was I doing? I was simply a pop singer. Such was my self-disgust that I called the press together and said, 'I'm going to give up. I don't know when, I have commitments that I have to fulfil, and it may be two, maybe three years, but then I'm going to give up.' As you can imagine, they had a field day.

During that period, I met the Billy Graham Association again. They wanted a Christian actor and asked me to make a movie. I thought, That's fantastic, I'll make the movie as a Christian and that can be my finale. While I was in the process of making the movie, Norrie Paramor, my then producer, said, 'You say you believe this, so let's do a gospel album.' I thought, Great, that'll be my legacy: I'll do a gospel album, I'll make my movie and I'll go. Then I was invited to do a TV series of six shows based on the parables in the New Testament. Then it clicked. I thought, Wait a minute. I can be a pop singer *and* I can be a Christian. People can see me doing it. I don't have to force it on them, they can turn me off if they want, but I will be there. I can actively be a Christian in show business, I can talk to the press and if they ask me the questions, I can even be a mouthpiece.

The toughest bit of this realization was calling the press together again and telling them I had changed my mind. They revelled in it, of course, saying, 'Oh we thought this was coming and now he's just playing games with us.' It was a big mistake I'd made. Since then I've talked with other Christian singers, and found they'd had the same feelings. My advice now is, 'Look, I don't think you have to make up your mind yet. Just do what you're doing. Make your money, be famous. In your heart you know what you believe, you know what's right and what's wrong, just keep doing it. When the right time comes, you'll also know exactly what to do with your money and with your time.'

The last person I said this to was Daniel Bedingfield. He's enormously talented and a staunch Christian and really wants to use his gifts. I said, 'Just enjoy everything. Live it and love it.' I covered his song 'If I'm Not The One' on 2007's *The Love Album*, and just loved singing it. What a song! He's a very impressive guy, he has fantastic enthusiasm, and he was so open about his faith with me, we even prayed together. I had such a good time with him and he's called me a couple of times since we met, wanting to talk to me, Christian to Christian. I've really appreciated it; I never thought that someone almost forty years younger than I am would think of calling someone who's way into his sixties, to talk and maybe seek advice.

I know I have been able to do far more as a singer to spread the word of Christ than I ever could have done as a religious education teacher – or even an aid worker in the Third World. I've recorded so many gospel songs and been on gospel tours and talked about my faith to audiences all over the world. I never pretended they were anything but 'rock-spell' concerts – a word I coined for them: a cross between rock and gospel. I never misled anyone, although there were probably a few people who expected 'Living Doll' and found me belting out 'What A Friend We Have In Jesus' or 'When I Survey The Wondrous Cross'. I loved doing those shows because the venues were so small I could talk to the audience in a much more intimate way than I ever could at my rock concerts.

They were not always quite so professionally organized, however. One Sunday long ago David Bryce, my tour manager, and I arrived in Würzburg, a small town in Germany, and discovered that we had no lights and no sound. We didn't travel with our own kit in those days and our host was a priest, obviously unused to the needs of musicians. David Bryce was with me for years and years, almost from the very beginning – he was like a brother to me – but he didn't share my Christian zeal. While I said a quiet prayer, David, through clenched teeth, asked for a copy of the Yellow Pages or its equivalent. We both knew that if we had no sound or lights we were going to be standing at the box office in a few hours' time giving people their money back. Because it was a Sunday, everything was shut, but David refused to give up: he scoured the town, leaving no stone unturned, and eventually he found a cleaner in a shop who had a friend with a grubby van – and, miraculously, just in time for the show, all the equipment we wanted arrived.

Over dinner afterwards, our hosts and I said a prayer of thanks to God. This was too much for David, whose own not inconsiderable part in the miracle had been overlooked. 'Look,' he said, '*I* got the lights and the sound.'

'God works in mysterious ways,' we told him, and we all laughed.

One of my early Tearfund trips was even more nail-biting. I'd been doing a series of gospel concerts in South Africa and was due to fly to Sudan to visit the victims of famine and civil war. I woke up in Cape Town, where I was staying with friends, leapt out of bed – and put my back out. I could barely walk. The flight to Sudan was not comfortable, but the Jeep that Bill and I climbed into at the airport was even worse. For hours I had to hold myself in the most curious position, sort of hanging on the backrest so that my backside wasn't touching the seat as we bounced across the most rugged terrain, somehow managing to protect my back from the jolts. Suddenly the driver stopped in the middle of nowhere and got out, explaining we had a leak in the petrol tank. Within seconds, the empty landscape was full of people with cigarette lighters, trying to fill them with the dripping fuel. I wondered if we would ever see civilization again. Then our driver reappeared with some Blu-Tack or something similar – it may have been chewing gum – which he stuck over the hole, and eventually we made it to Juba.

Bill had had a message from the missionary we were meeting to say that he hoped I would give a small concert he had organized. I thought, Ouch, it won't be easy with my back in this state – but that turned out to be the least of my worries. The venue was an open-air arena that held fifteen hundred people, with a stage but no microphones, and just one overhead light. All I had was my guitar. I said to Bill, 'I can't do this.' I have never been so frightened – going into disease-riddled refugee camps was as nothing compared to singing that night in front of fifteen hundred people in the open air without a mic. I walked down the aisles singing like a troubadour, and when it was all over I said, 'Never again – at least, not without amplification!'

In those early days of my Christian commitment I was very serious about it and far more rigid in my interpretation of the Church's teachings than I am today; even, I have to admit, judgemental. I used to read the Bible every night, no matter how late it was or how tired I felt. I set aside time for prayer; I went to church every Sunday without fail. I ran around thinking, The people I meet might be going to go to hell unless I can help them. I felt certain that what was good for me would be good for everyone, and was all but hitting people over the head with the Bible in my zeal to make them see what I had seen. Slowly it dawned on me that it was not my decision. I have no part to play in the judgement of humankind, thank goodness; I am going to be judged just like everyone else.

These days I am much more relaxed. My belief is entirely unaltered, but I don't feel the need to be quite so black and white in my attitudes. I stopped going to church regularly a long time ago because it became too difficult. I would tend to be surrounded by people who wanted autographs. Nothing wrong with that, I suppose, but that wasn't why I was there. I spoke about this to a preacher that I knew. 'You know, people don't understand,' I said. 'I come to church because I need to be spiritually fed. It's all very well being presented as today's showbiz Christian, but it means that I am giving all the time. I need to sit down and receive and have someone else teach me something.' So I persevered, sitting at the preacher's feet week after week, and he was extremely helpful; but the problem didn't go away, and slowly I found myself staying away from church. It had nothing to do with my faith: my faith was still intact.

Then I thought that maybe who I am and what I do and the attention I attract is all part of a grand scheme. I had been seeing it as a problem – but I was looking at it from the wrong perspective. God finds people in a variety of situations. Whenever I go to far-flung places like Sudan, Cambodia or Haiti, I invariably find somebody working there who's given up a comfortable life in some affluent town like, say, Guildford, and perhaps has even brought his family with him, and he is the right person to be in that place at that time. It never ceases to amaze me – and God found me in show business.

I still read the Bible, though not necessarily every day. I dip into it a lot and find it a great book. When I came to it as an adult, having firmly rejected it at the age of fourteen, I was amazed. All that 'gentle Jesus, meek and mild' that I remembered from childhood didn't fit the picture of this man I was now reading about who strode around, possibly barefoot, across terrain that I have tried to walk on in Israel and found difficult enough in boots. This was a strong man with a personality to match, with a brain, wisdom and love – everything good that you could imagine manifested in this one human being. Once I realized that, I was hooked and had to find out more. I tried to read every night, but I would fall asleep halfway through and wake up and be unable to remember what I'd read. So now I pick up the Bible when I want to. I no longer have the fear, instilled in me inadvertently by missionaries I once met, that somehow I am a lesser mortal because I can't wake up at 5 a.m. to go down to the river and read or pray. Looking back, I think it was because I so admired their chosen lifestyle that I felt guilty and therefore less worthwhile.

We Christians must be careful about how we present our faith, particularly to newcomers such as I was when those missionaries made such an impact on me. We have to be sure that we aren't too rigid and maybe say, 'This may not be right for you, you can do it differently. Have Jesus in your life, but how you live with Him or present Him is up to you.' Roman Catholics, Baptists, Anglicans, whoever, we all tie ourselves up with traditions and rituals that are manmade. I just say to people now, 'Look, if you're going to read the Bible once a week, that's OK. If it's once a month, that's OK too. Just be sure it's always around. Trust it and pick it up and use it when you feel the need. Waking at five to read your Bible is fine if you like that, but it's not a requirement for entering God's Kingdom. Jesus is the way you enter into it.'

I have started going to a Catholic church occasionally in Barbados. Catholics don't expect me to be there, so I slip in after the service has begun and sit at the back and most of the time no one knows I'm there until they turn around at the end. I really enjoy it and I like taking communion – I feel it brings me close to Jesus. I was sitting next to a Catholic nun in a church in the U.S. once, and when it came to communion, I said, 'I'm not a Catholic but I would like to go up.' And she said, 'No, my dear, I don't think you should.' So I didn't. I mentioned it later to a priest there and he said, 'You should have gone up and you shouldn't have to apologize. That's precisely what's wrong with the Church.'

And of course it's true; we're so hidebound we don't allow our spirituality to grow and to keep up with changes in our society. I don't think we should throw too much overboard, but there are many areas where compromise is not only desirable but necessary. In the Bible, St Paul wrote about how people should look after their slaves. We don't have slaves any more. We could almost scratch that out of the Bible – except that it is a valuable message, and that particular passage taught me a lot. We outlawed slavery in Britain nearly two hundred years ago, but at one time it was acceptable to be a Christian and to have a slave. Things change all the time, and what we have to do is watch what's happening and keep Christianity relevant.

Same-sex marriages are perhaps a modern example of how things have changed. No one's quite sure what to do any more, but I think the Church must come round and see people as they are now. Gone are the days when we assumed loving relationships would be solely between men and women. In the end, I believe, people are going to be judged for what they are as people. What they are sexually is something else that only they can deal with; no one else can. I know of a couple of same-sex relationships that have gone on for more than fifty years; and yet two of my sisters and some of my friends have been married twice. I don't say that to put them down: we all make mistakes, particularly in relationships; but I think the point is valid nonetheless. The couples I'm thinking of committed themselves to each other and they've remained committed. So what's the difference? The Church is going to have to decide, and it will have to be really sensitive and wise. It seems to me that commitment is the issue, and as far as I'm concerned, if anybody comes to me and says, 'This is my partner – we are committed to each other,' then I don't care what their sexuality is. I am not going to judge – I'll leave that to God.

There was a great line in a movie called *Two A Penny* I made for Billy Graham in the sixties. A guy, who was a non-believer, wanted to sleep with his partner. He said, 'I'm not asking for much,' and his girlfriend replied, 'You're not asking for enough.' And there's another great line at the end, where she goes to a church meeting and says, 'I can see where Jesus fits in my life, I just can't see where the Church fits in.' I would throw that line over and over again at the Church authorities. Whatever they decide to do, they must ask themselves, 'How come so many people can find space for Jesus in their lives, and yet find all sorts of excuses for why they can't go to church?' The Church has got to face that; and I guess that same-sex relationships are just one of the dilemmas of humanity. I have no difficulty saying that I find same-sex relationships acceptable if they follow the pattern that I admired in my own mum and dad. The key is love and, in the final analysis, the best love we have comes from God.

Christianity is incredibly demanding. It demands my thoughts, my time and my actions – and trying to live a Christian life has not been easy. I'm never going to get it completely right and I'm sure I will have my wrists slapped resoundingly by God when I finally meet Him. I know there are many things that I have done wrong and probably done wrong over and over again. But at least, in front of Him I've said, 'I try to be what I should be. You'll have to forgive the bits that I'm not.'

I've been a Christian now for over forty years and I'm still asking myself, What do I really think about this or that? How did I come to that conclusion? The answers don't come overnight. That's what I love about it. It's like life: you're born and you know nothing, and after five years you still know pretty well nothing, but as the years go by you realize that some of the major decisions you've made have been based on about twenty different changes of mind. When I read that a politician was a communist twenty years ago, my question is, 'Is he communist now?' And if the answer is 'No,' then who cares what he was? It's what he is now that counts. It's as simple as that for me. I'm still in the process of changing my mind on all sorts of things, but one thing I've recognized about myself is that I am a solid but non-judgemental Christian – and even that has been a long time coming. Sometimes I feel I'm almost perfect fodder for Humanism, but, of course, the worst thing about Humanism is humans – so I think I'll stay as I am.

In those early days when there were so many questions to ask and so much to debate, most of my friends were fellow Christians because it was easier for me to mix with them than with people from show business, whose lifestyles tended to be wild, excessive and extreme – everything that Christianity warns against. Bill Latham, who became a good friend and confidant, introduced me to his friends – mostly teachers, accountants, bankers, and all involved in their churches – and they welcomed me into their circle and became my friends too. This was not because they were impressed by who I was – many of them didn't listen to my sort of music – but they embraced me as a fellow believer. It was a safe, comfortable and unchallenging environment, and although in our careers we were worlds apart, in other ways we had huge amounts in common. I was accepted as part of the gang for myself, and it felt good. I felt I belonged.

CHAPTER EIGHT

Living Arrangements

At the time when I was searching for some deeper meaning to life, my mother was falling in love. It took us all by surprise. By 1963, my father had been dead for two years and Mum was still in mourning for him, but we probably didn't appreciate just how lonely and miserable she was without him. After Dad's death she started spending time with me. She loved coming to concerts, theatres, restaurants and everything else I did; she would have been with me every day if I had let her. I did take her whenever I could and we did more together than most mothers and grown-up sons, but there were limits. I was twenty-three years old, I had to have a life of my own, and I was busy. I was also preoccupied with my spiritual quest. Looking back, I realize that the combination of all these factors took my attention away from home and family at a time when my mother, in particular, needed me most.

She was only forty-three, slim, attractive and full of life. It is not surprising she wanted a new man to share the future with, and not surprising that she found one – although I would have sworn, as my sisters would have done, that she still loved Dad. I guess that's a not uncommon phenomenon. The surprise was that she fell for my twenty-three-year-old driver, Derek Bodkin. I have no idea why she fell for Derek; maybe she felt excluded from my new life, or maybe she simply needed the sort of love that her children couldn't give her. Whatever it was, soon after I became a Christian she announced that she was going to marry him. My sisters were as horrified as I was, but accepted Mum's decision, though now we all look back upon the marriage as a sad chapter in our mother's life. Having said that, Derek did look after her well and, until the marriage disintegrated some years later when he fell in love with someone else, inevitably breaking her heart, she was undoubtedly happy with him.

When all of this happened we were living at Rookswood, a rather grand house that I'd bought in Nazeing, Essex. It was the obligatory rock star's house – Tudor-style with six bedrooms and eleven acres, swimming pool and tennis court – and a cottage at the end of the drive to house the chauffeur. Fans had made life difficult for us and our neighbours at the previous house in Winchmore Hill and that was part of the reason for the move. The new home gave us much more privacy but it still seemed to attract fans, who would often march down the drive and invade us.

My father didn't live to see Rookswood and the splendour that my earnings could buy, which was such a shame, and Donna never lived there either, because she had married by the time we moved. So the four of us did rather rattle around – although friends and relatives were always passing through, and latterly Mum invited her sister Olive and her two sons, my cousins, to live at the house too. I was away from home a lot – filming, recording, touring – and I spent increasing amounts of my spare time with Bill and his friends. After a long session of theological argument and discussion I would often stay the night with him and his mother in Finchley rather than driving home to Essex. Mamie Latham was a marvellous woman. She became a second mother to me, and it made perfect sense to stay there if I was filming in London or had some recording to do the following day. She was always very tolerant of the unusual hours I kept. Mamie was a lovely person and we grew close.

Derek had spent a lot of time with Mum – he would drive her to the hairdresser and take her on shopping trips or to visit relatives – but her announcement that she planned to marry him came like a bolt from the blue. Within days of it, shortly after my appearance at Earl's Court with Billy Graham, the knot was tied. It was a bizarre situation, but of course I wished them well. We had a party for her at home, showered them with rose petals, then waved them off on their honeymoon. My emotions, like those of my sisters, were very mixed. I didn't know if she was doing the right thing, but I was in no position to prevent her. What I did know was that I didn't think they should be living as a married couple at Rookswood, so I bought my mother a smaller house in Broxbourne in Hertfordshire, and they moved into that.

I soon realized that the time had come to

sell Rookswood. We had only been there for three years, not long enough for me to feel any special attachment to it, and it was ridiculous to keep a house that size with so much land for just me and my two little sisters. It was also impractical. There was no public transport within miles, so they had to be chauffeur-driven everywhere. If I were to organize a personal driver for them today I'm sure they would leap at it, but in their teens they wanted their independence. So I bought a couple of semi-detached cottages, also at Broxbourne: one of them for Aunt Olive and my cousins, the other for Jacqui and Joan, which they shared with a friend. Both girls were virtually grown up now. Jacqui was seventeen or eighteen and working as a shorthand typist. Joan was only fifteen but she had just left school and found herself a job as a receptionist. Neither of them wanted to live with Mum and Derek, but did want to be near them, so this seemed the perfect solution. They weren't stuck out in the country with no transport, they had their independence and, if anything went wrong, Aunt Olive was next door. I could relax.

However, that left me with no house, apart from a holiday home in Portugal; so Bill and his mother suggested that I move in with them on a more permanent basis. This seemed like a very good idea for a number of reasons. It solved the problem of my having to go home to an empty house, which I really didn't want to do; it was practical, because my life and Bill's started to overlap, not just socially but professionally, as I did more and more Christian charity work with which Bill helped me; and last but not least, Mamie was a good cook!

Bill and I gave talks together. We went to church groups, groups of students, anyone who would have us really, and would begin with a question-and-answer session with Bill firing the questions at me; then we'd open this out to the audience. It was all unscripted, the settings were small-scale and intimate, and we had some great discussions about faith, Christianity, spirituality and anything they threw at me. We were doing two or three of these a week at venues all over the country – organized by Bill in his spare time. I have always been hopeless at paperwork, personal and professional, and always had someone else to take care of it. But my management team were employed to manage my showbiz life and had neither the time nor the inclination to get involved with my Christian activities, so Bill offered to take care of those. Eventually there was so much going on in that area that it became clear I needed someone to run it for me full-time and in a paid capacity, so in 1979 I invited Bill to come and join the Cliff Richard Organization, and bring with him his secretary, Gill Snow, who is still working with us today.

I am sure there are countless sayings about the dangers of mixing work and friends, but almost thirty years on Bill is still running all my charitable activity, as well as dealing with all my press and media commitments. He knows me probably better than anyone – he's like family, although now that I spend so much of my time abroad, we don't see as much of each other as we once did. Miraculously, we were never in each other's pockets. We have many common interests but we also have widely differing ones – music for a start – and although we shared a number of houses for thirty-odd years, we did live very independently. People have always made snide remarks about the nature of our relationship. I don't honestly care what it looked like from the outside. I used to, but nowadays I just ignore all those sorts of comments. Let them speculate, because in the end that's all it is: speculation. I'm an enigma – and loving it.

We were two unmarried people, good friends who chose to share a house rather than each go home to an empty one on our own. I have never lived alone and never want to. I'm a gregarious person: I love filling the house with friends and family, and almost always have people staying. My ideal for old age would be to get together with a whole group of friends, buy a huge house and divvy it up so we'd have company whenever we wanted it but, by the same token, could be separate when we wanted to be alone. Nothing wrong with pipe-dreams.

I don't mind being alone occasionally, and sometimes I've chosen to spend a few days entirely by myself, but never for too long. I used to go to North Wales alone, where I've had a cottage since the early seventies that I am currently in the process of selling. It's in a little village called Doiwyddelan near Betws-y-coed and has fifty-seven acres. The cottage itself is quite remote, with just a farm nearby, and I could spend five days there and not see another soul, other than the farmer occasionally driving by in his tractor. Nobody even walks in the area. I used to find it quite therapeutic to get away like that every now and again. I'd go with my dogs, two West Highland terriers, one of which was a present from fans, and I'd build a big log fire – the weather was always terrible – and listen to music and read, or play my guitar, then get the galoshes on, pull the hood up and take the dogs for a long, wet walk. It was wonderful, a great place to unwind, and I would go back home rejuvenated. I also cooked. When I'm on my own I tend to eat pasta or put a leg of lamb in the oven, but give me a recipe book and I can cook anything.

I am, surprisingly maybe, quite domesticated and I enjoy it. When we were kids my mother needed help around the house because there was no way we could ever have afforded to pay someone. So chores were just part and parcel of life, and we all did our bit; my task with Donna, we two being the eldest, was the washing up after meals. When Mum started going out to work, we were latch-key kids. I had the responsibility of looking after my sisters and making sure everyone arrived home safely. Joan used to go to kindergarten at that time and I had to pick her up on my bike and wheel her back to the house. I met the others back home, opened the door, took them all in and looked after them. Every day we took it in turns to sweep the floors, cook, tidy and dust. It's still second nature to me, and many are the times I come downstairs in the morning at my house in Barbados thinking, I'll just... no, Jasmine (my house-keeper) will be here in a minute. There'll be nothing for her to do if I don't leave this washing up alone.

When I was finally able to talk my mum into letting me get her a cleaner, my sister phoned and said, 'I couldn't believe it. I went into the house and there was Mum busy cleaning it. I told her the cleaner was coming and she said, "I know, but I don't want her to see it dirty."' Hers was an amazing generation with a very different outlook, and she couldn't bear to leave things untidy.

The only way I could stop her was by saying, 'Mum, I had to work really hard to earn that money and if I'm giving it to you for the cleaner to clean the house, you've got to let her clean it. I want you to be able to go out, visit a friend maybe and not have to worry about the house being a mess.' In the end she did succumb and enjoyed having help, although she kept stopping the cleaner working because she wanted a natter.

I rented an apartment in Florida recently and before I left I couldn't resist going through it with the vacuum cleaner. I'm sure the guy I rented it from didn't know who I was, but, like Mum, I couldn't leave it dirty. I found some disinfectant and mopped down all the kitchen work surfaces and the toilets and bathroom, I even vacuumed all the floors. I guess that's just what I do – obsessively, some might say. My band used to joke about it. When the newspapers were full of stories about rock stars who went into hotels and vandalized them, my band used to say, 'You're probably one of these people that goes in and cleans it up.' And I'd say, 'You're right. I *would* clean it up.'

Shopping is something else I enjoy. I love going into the supermarket – but I'm a slow shopper. I like to have a good look at everything as I wander round the aisles, just to make sure I don't miss some new product, and I read all the labels very carefully because on my new dietary regime – eating what is right for my blood group – there are certain foods I'm not permitted. I have dieted ever since I was twenty-one because I didn't like the look of myself in *The Young Ones*, and for years I kept my weight down by eating just one meal a day. I would eat at night after the show, at about midnight – not the best time to be eating a big meal, but after years of it, my body adjusted. It had to be after the show because if I eat at lunchtime on a day when I'm singing at night, there is something about the combination of food, and the way one breathes and uses one's diaphragm on stage, that produces burps. Eat a curry at lunchtime and I'm in big trouble.

One meal a day worked very well as a means of keeping the weight down, but when I was on tour in 2006–2007 I met a masseuse, who was recommended to me in Dubai. She didn't draw breath the whole time she massaged; she said, 'Please stop me if I'm talking too much,' but it was so interesting, I didn't. 'I'm working on this section here,' she said, pinching the bit of flesh just above the hip bone. 'Now you're not a fat person, but men collect their fat here. If you believe me then believe this: stop eating dairy, stop eating wheat, and this is where the weight will go.' She explained the theory behind the blood type diet, which was developed by an American naturopath called

Dr Peter D'Adamo, and gave me a big chart showing all the foods that, with blood type A, I should and, more importantly, shouldn't eat. I looked through it and, horror of horrors, there were ten definite foods to avoid – although, tossing little crumbs of comfort, it did say, 'If you can keep the "avoids" down to less than twenty per cent of what you eat then it's OK.' So I thought to myself, every couple of weeks I can have something I shouldn't have. That's what I do and it's not a hardship. My 'avoids' – the things I am not allowed – are red meat, shellfish, potatoes, tomatoes, aubergine, mangos, papaya, cashew nuts, dairy and wheat – all of which I love and sometimes miss; but I'm eating more now than I've ever eaten and not putting on weight. And I think it's making me feel better in my head. I've never been a depressive, so I've usually woken up feeling good, but I've been on this regime for more than a year and a half now and I don't think I've ever felt more positive.

Shopping is the one time when I really begrudge being stopped by fans. I've tried to say to people, smiling through gritted teeth as I sign scraps of paper from their handbags, 'You know, I'm just trying to do what you're doing. I don't think I'm going to get this done if I have to sign everybody's autograph.' Subtlety doesn't work. No one seems to understand that it's impossible to find what I want if I have to stop every two minutes. Weybridge wasn't too bad. People were used to seeing me there, so I could do the supermarket in under an hour – but if I had a record in the charts or if I'd just been on television, then it all started again, even in Weybridge. One person would come up and ask for my autograph and then they'd all come. It's much easier in Barbados and New York. But you know what? I wouldn't change a thing.

Obviously it's difficult for me to do the normal things that most people take for granted. I rarely, if ever, take public transport. I haven't been on a bus probably since we were making *Summer Holiday*. I have taken trains occasionally, but never by myself. I don't think I could cope alone, and I have to pick my times so the trains are not crowded. I was going home from Waterloo once when some youngsters kept looking over at me. After a while one of them said, 'You're Cliff Richard aren't you?'

I said, 'Yeah.'

He turned to his mates. 'Told you so! We couldn't believe you'd be on a train.'

I said, 'Well, it's going to Weybridge and that's where I live.'

'We know,' he said, 'but it's great to see you on a train.'

I enjoyed the encounter – but one of the kids still wanted an autograph for his mother.

I did once take the subway in New York and that was an amazing experience. I was staying with Frank Dunlop, who directed *Heathcliff* for me. Frank divided his time between Dublin and New York, and one day, working on the script, Frank said, 'Do you fancy a trip to Staten Island? But it means taking a trip on the subway.' It was just like it is in the movies. There are people, weird, eccentric people, who travel on the subway and whom you see nowhere else. There was a guy sitting opposite us with a paper bag, and as the train set off he put his book down, and out of the bag came one little tray that he put on his knee, then another, then he undid a box and out came a whole lot of food, a complete meal that he divided between the trays, and then he tucked a napkin into his collar and started to eat. Thank you, Frank, for showing me a bit of real life. I took the Métro in Paris once too because it was much quicker than trying to get a cab to pick us up, but again, I did it with friends, and would never have done it on my own. I just have to accept there are some things I can't do as easily as everyone else. And in the end, do I need to? No. I do them for the experience so that I can say, 'Been there, done that.'

I've never paid a bill in my life. I know how to write cheques and it's my money that's used to pay for things, but if a bill arrives at the house, I send it to the office and they pay it. I do have a chequebook and a credit card but I like having cash, so every week when I'm in the UK I get pocket money from the office; it used to be £50 a week, I think it's now about £120. It's a bit of a joke but they've always done it. Bill drops it round to my house and says, 'Here's your week's money.' I could go to a hole in the wall, I suppose, and when I'm abroad I sometimes have to do that. Once when I got back home I said, 'You owe me three months' money,' and they said, 'Oh no. You don't get it when you're not here.'

I have no idea how much I'm worth, or how much I earned on my last tour; I have never taken a big interest in money. I just need to be told I'm all right – or to be told, 'Pull your belt in, Cliff,' as Joan Hudson, my first accountant, used to do. As long as I know I have money, I feel comfortable. And it's been a great pleasure to have had enough to give some to my family and to have been able to buy my mother the very best care when she needed to go into a home.

I've also enjoyed being able to buy good clothes – although the only time I spend serious money on them is when I'm touring. About nine years ago, I think, I went a little mad. I went into Versace in London and saw the most fabulous shirt – black, covered in turquoise beads: three and a half thousand pounds. I said, 'I can't do this.' And they said, 'Well, we've got a special deal today, we'll give you two for the price of one.' The shirt next to it was red, black and orange, and it also had beading and sequins, and I said, 'OK'. So I got seven thousand pounds' worth of shirts for three and a half. Whether they were worth that I have no idea; but I did feel good in them on stage. I can only spend like that when I'm going on a tour – I keep thinking, 'It's not just for me. It's for the show.' Am I kidding myself...? Hmmmm.

I wish there was tax relief on the clothes I buy for personal use too. When you have this thing called celebrity the public has an expectation of how you should appear, even though you're only shopping or posting a letter. I remember, for instance, someone once saying to me, 'What are you doing driving this crap car?'

I said, 'Well, my Rolls is being done up, I've been lent this one.' It was actually a very nice MG, but his perception was I should have been in something grander.

Clothes are part and parcel of who I am. When I changed my name to Cliff Richard, I had to change my whole outlook on how I presented myself in public. At home I sometimes wear shapeless clothes because they're so comfortable, and I will wear them in the garden, but there is no way I would run out to the shops in them. I don't mind going out in a fairly good looking pair of denim jeans or shorts and a nice shirt, but usually I would get changed. The public doesn't expect to see me looking slovenly and I wouldn't want them to. That's just how it is.

I tend to keep clothes until they fall apart – probably another of the many traits I have inherited from my father. If you buy clothes that are really good, they don't date. I have some trousers that are at least twenty-five years old and one day I'll be able to wear them again and nobody will notice. I'll have to let them down a bit because before I think we all wore our trousers too short. Also, I wear at least a one-inch heel now. I am 5ft 10½in – Mr Normal, average height – but these heels are fantastic. They make me feel and look 6ft tall and when I'm on stage, they stop the girl dancers looming over me; I hate it when we do a sequence and I have to look up to them. I actually wish my legs were an inch and a half longer, then I wouldn't have to worry about the length of jacket I wear. If a jacket comes down too low I think I look like a pygmy; everything is foreshortened. I guess you can see from all this that image has always been very important for me.

Much as I enjoy shopping for clothes, I have to be in the mood, otherwise it's hopeless and I give up. To do it seriously you must try things on, and there are times when I can't face taking my trousers off again, so I guess the size, buy something and regret it later. It usually happens abroad. I say, 'I'm a medium, I'll take the medium,' then get back to the hotel planning to wear it that night and discover it doesn't fit. There are other times when I can spend the whole day trying things on and really enjoy it. The secret, I've discovered, is to use a personal shopper. Selfridges do a fantastic service. Cilla Black recommended it, and gave me the name of the guy there who looks after her. I phoned him and when I arrived, there was a glass of champagne waiting. 'Cilla loves champagne,' he said. 'Since you're a friend of hers, I thought you might like some too.'

As I sipped, I told him the sort of things I was looking for – 'Jeans that are a bit different,' I said, 'and jackets, fitted and preferably in solid colours but not grey or black' – and he and his assistant went away and came back wheeling one of those hanging rails on castors, filled with jackets and jeans, from which I picked out all the things I wanted to try. If I needed to try a different size, if there was anything else I wanted, they went off and found it for me. It must have taken three or four hours but I was completely undisturbed and left at the end of it with some terrific clothes, feeling pampered rather than shattered and not having had to sign a single autograph.

On the whole I think I spend my money wisely. The main thing I have invested in is property – my homes – and they are probably the best investments I have ever made. I could liquidate and be quite well off, and that's what I intend to do when – if– I retire. I'll never be a billionaire but I'll never be poor, I guess. I do watch what I spend, but the danger time is when I come off a tour. That's the moment when I think, Why am I worried? I've just earned quite a bit of money. I could buy ten shirts and no one would blink. It's good to get past that moment because it is very easy to spend and there are too many stories of showbiz people who end up in old folk's homes because they didn't look after their money. This business is great while it's all happening, but in the end everything stops. I'm very conscious of my age and I am trying to make sure that when it all stops for me, I'll be OK and not a liability for anyone.

I'm reaching that stage where I would like to be able to telephone my business manager and say, 'I'd like to build an extension in Barbados and it's going to cost me x amount. How long do I need to tour to pay for that?' I could work, doing what I love, and have my extension at the end of it. I can't think of a nicer way to live – artistically fulfilled and financially flexible.

CHAPTER NINE

The Shadows

I am at a very interesting point in my life right now. Something has changed, and I'm not entirely sure what – but as I embark on this milestone year, I feel happier and less fearful than I can ever remember. I have a great sense of optimism about the future.

Some of it is to do with confidence but, for all my success, I still sit up at night sometimes and think, How did it ever happen to me? I so much wanted what I have, but how did I get it? How did I ever hang on to it? I am not a great musician and really great musicians still intimidate me. I don't understand it; but whatever the reason, I'm here and I'm having a good life. Age has only gilded the lily as far as I'm concerned. There is still all this ambition that burns inside me that makes me want radio stations to play my recordings. But even when they don't, it doesn't depress me any more. I've moved on in my life, and those people who want to put me down can stay in theirs.

Funnily enough, my fans seem to recognize the change. The internet is interesting. I don't like it on the whole because I think it's too intrusive, but every now and then Bill will print out things for me to read, which will say, 'Have never seen him look so confident,' or 'Have you noticed how happy he sounds?' I look at the videos and I can't see any difference in myself, but I can't deny that in general I feel better about my life and better about the people around me in 2008 than I ever have. I'm surrounded by great people who've supported me for years. I have never worked with anybody who has let me down in any way, right from the beginning, from Norrie Paramor on. I have made some changes in the last seven or eight years that have improved my lifestyle, I've made some new friends and I feel I am in a good place at the moment. I know I'm fortunate because I don't think there is any artist alive in Britain who has lasted this long, and had the level of success I have enjoyed.

It is certainly very different from the way I felt forty years ago. I was a very worried man when the Shadows broke up in December 1968; in fact, I panicked. They were so much more than a backing group; they wrote most of my songs. And they had never stood in the shadows by any means. I brought them forward on stage and we had a great rapport, which was very much part of our show. There had been other bands that were good, like the Ventures, who were an American instrumental rock group that also began in 1958, and had big hits with records like 'Walk Don't Run' and 'Perfidia', but the Shadows were somehow different; they were the first of their kind on the planet. It was their personality, I think, that made them so special, and that developed as we played together. None of the other bands had that. Hank and Bruce were huge personalities.

After Licorice Locking left in 1963, the line-up for the final five years had been Hank Marvin, Bruce Welch, Brian Bennett and John Rostill, who replaced Licorice – and they were a fantastic combination. We had done so much together. They had done the films with me – *The Young Ones*, *Summer Holiday*, *Wonderful Life*, *Finders Keepers* – and they had written most of the songs for them. The soundtrack of *Finders Keepers* was entirely theirs. We'd all been marionettes in *Thunderbirds Are Go*. They had written the music and lyrics for two pantomimes we'd played in at the London Palladium: *Aladdin and his Wonderful Lamp*, in which I was Aladdin and they were my friends, Wishee, Washee, Noshee and Poshee; and *Cinderella*, with me as Buttons and them as the Broker's Men. In each of them we'd played twice nightly for four months. And that's not to mention the tours and the hours of recording and rehearsing we had done together. The last album we made, *Established 58* was in

1968, to celebrate ten years of collaboration. And after those ten years it was all over.

I didn't know what I would do without them. They were undoubtedly one of the best bands of that time – not excluding the Beatles: in fact, it was the Shadows who gave the four-piece band an image that the Beatles inherited. The Shadows had a number one hit with their first record, 'Apache'. I like to think I played some small part in that. To ensure they were given the best possible promotion, Peter Gormley asked me to play a drum on the recording and, if you listen to 'Apache', at the very beginning there is a little drum intro – I think two bars. Well, that was me: that was it, my contribution; but they were able to go to the press and say, 'Cliff Richard plays the drums in the opening of the record,' and it had the desired effect. After that, of course, they had many other hits, and they would play them in my shows. We were really so strong on stage because in the end the guys were coming to see Hank and the girls were coming to see me. We had full houses everywhere we went.

Actually, I don't think the Beatles were that great when they started. The Shadows and I had heard a record they had made in Hamburg in 1961, the year of 'Apache', called 'Dizzy Miss Lizzy', and it was not good. The vocals were very indifferent and the playing left a lot to be desired. But whatever happened to them in Hamburg was the making of them. By the time they came back from Germany they had changed; they suddenly had this great songwriting talent and their ability to play their instruments had improved dramatically. When they began recording at Abbey Road – well, they were the Beatles.

It must have been Peter Gormley who told me that the Shadows had decided to break up. I knew things were a bit difficult between them; they were all wanting to do different things, as people with separate talents often do – the Beatles didn't even survive for ten years, remember – and the chemistry between them was on the wane. Bruce could be a real terror. He was such a perfectionist, really finicky; and tuning was his big thing. He and Hank would be tuning their guitars before a show and I would hear a shout and the next thing a door would slam – it happened once in Blackpool – and Hank would come running in, saying, 'Bruce has gone – he can't tune his guitar and he's thrown it on the floor and is going back to London. We have to do the show without him.' Bruce would arrive back home and Peter Gormley would say, 'What are you doing here? Don't be so bloody stupid – get in the car and go back.' So Bruce would turn round and drive all the way back to Blackpool or whichever town it was, and we used to think, 'What an idiot.'

But a fixation like that is hard to deal with, and it was only when Bruce went on to produce my albums that I realized why he had behaved the way he did when he was with the Shadows. He can't bear anything to be out of tune, it's a real problem for him, and if you listen to any of the albums that he produced for me, you will not hear me sing a single bum note. If I did, he'd make me do it again – he would never let it pass. He once made me repair a sound. The word was something like 'things' and he thought it sounded as though I had sung 'thing', omitting the 's'. I did the word 'things' again and he repaired the 's' sound. Perfectionist? Just a bit!

He eventually found the solution to his guitar problems. When John Rostill joined the Shadows as bass player, Bruce would pay him to tune his guitar. John was brilliant and tuned the guitar perfectly, but even then Bruce would always come in and check it. In spite of his tuning fetish, Bruce was the funniest man – the king of the one-liners; he had a line for everything and we were constantly in fits of laughter.

It was he who produced *I'm Nearly Famous* in 1976. That was my first big album since my movie days, and suddenly my records had street cred. Up to that point I had mainly recorded singles – sometimes four or five a year – and the albums that were released, apart from the movie sound-tracks, hadn't been big sellers. This was a new departure – it had songs like 'Devil Woman' and 'Miss You Nights', plus a whole lot more material which was new for me, slightly more edgy than normal, very exciting. It was a huge success and I have Bruce to thank for that. At the studio, he used to get a bit depressed sometimes; I would walk in and there would be this black cloud hanging over the engineers. 'He's heard something out of tune,' they'd say, and we'd have to find what it was and repair it. I worked with great singers like Tony Rivers, John Perry and Stu Calver on that album. We were doing multiple harmonies and having a fantastic time. Sometimes we worked until three in the morning, and we often went out to dinner together. It is one of the happiest memories I have of making an album. Thanks, Brucie.

But while it was great to be able to work with Bruce as a producer, I missed working with him on stage – I missed them all, and I still do. Playing with the Shadows was such good fun. It's not that I don't have the pleasure of a fabulous band today, because I certainly do. My band is second to none – it could actually be one of the best in the world. They have to play 'Living Doll' the way the Shadows did originally, then 'Devil

Woman', then 'Miss You Nights' – songs so diverse in their style, approach and feel that they have to be great musicians to do it so brilliantly night after night. What I miss is the on-stage camaraderie. It's not really their fault. Off stage, my band and I will sometimes eat out together, and we often stay in the same hotels, but on stage they have a specific role, and it's different from mine. I feel nowadays that this is strictly my show – I am the one who does all the talking, and the guys play; but in those days, in the fifties and sixties, I shared the spotlight with the Shadows. I was still the front man, but we had an on-stage relationship that worked fantastically well, and that was what I missed so desperately when I took off on my own. Having said that, within a very short space of time I had a whole deluge of good material and a whole new approach to presenting rock songs on stage – and I know I couldn't find a better band than the one I have now.

This is where Norrie Paramor had been so clever. Long before the break-up, as early as '63 or '64, when the Shadows and I were a really strong force, he was saying to me, 'I think you should use your voice differently. I know you love rock 'n' roll but I think you should do songs like "Long Ago And Far Away" and other classics' – and he would do the arrangements and I would go to the studios without the Shadows and sing with his orchestra. I would do eight tracks with the Shadows and eight with the orchestra. I don't know whether he was planning ahead, but when the Shadows made their devastating decision – which had nothing to do with me, but nevertheless left me rudderless – Norrie came to the rescue. He said, 'I've got a session fixed with the guys who played on those classic tracks you did.' The transition was gentle and I started making records without the Shadows and, you know what? It was OK.

I hope that one day the Shadows and I will have an opportunity to get together again – although sadly it will never be the original Shadows. Tony Meehan died three or four years ago, in the most terrible circumstances. I had been in touch with him a few times in latter years; when he left the music business he wanted to go to college to study psychiatry and needed financial help, which I was happy to provide until he established himself. Meeting him afresh, I thought he was much nicer than I remembered! He was very talented and intelligent – an intellectual – and was living with his second wife, a very nice woman, in London. One day when the family were all out he fell downstairs and hit his head on the floor. He lay there unconscious until his wife came home and found him – by which time he had been unconscious for too long; he died in hospital. I find it horrific that someone could be killed by something as simple as tripping or slipping on a bit of carpet. Fall down the stairs and you might break an arm, yes; but not die. John Rostill also died in awful circumstances – years ago, in 1973. He was electrocuted in his home recording studio. I have great memories of Tony and John – both are sorely missed.

Brian Bennett now writes scores for television programmes and is very successful. He has a house in Portugal near mine and we see each other from time to time. His son, Jonathan, a tennis pro, comes across and coaches me when I'm there. I see Bruce from time to time, too, and there are always big hugs when we meet. We are all friends and we all have a staunch respect for one another – but we are not buddy buddies. Hank, who is a Jehovah's Witness, now lives in Perth, Australia, with his wife, Carole. When I go to Perth I always phone him and say, 'Do you want to come on stage?' One year I thought, I can't ask him again, and I had a message from Gill in the office saying, 'Hank's a bit worried. Has he done anything to upset you?' I said, 'Of course not,' and she said, 'Well he hasn't heard from you, and yes, he wants to come on stage.'

Every time we've done it it's been amazing. I introduce Hank and ten thousand people go so crazy we can hardly start the song. People love Hank, but it's not just him; what they love are the old images: the two of us together bring back memories in people's lives. We all do it: I can remember exactly where I was when I heard P.J. Proby for the first time – driving down the old A10. He was singing 'Somewhere', and I thought it was amazing. We associate songs with memories, which is why I called my anniversary show *The Time Machine*. If people have been listening to my music for most of the fifty years I have been recording, I have metaphorically been alongside them through a whole range of life experiences. That's why my shows get longer and longer, because I have to sing all the old numbers as well as the new ones! It is important to sing things like 'Living Doll' because someone will have had a baby or become engaged at a time when they used to listen to that song. The Shadows and I are part of people's memories.

The galling thing is that I will soon be earning nothing from those songs that so many people want to hear me singing. It was in South Africa that I first became aware of the copyright issue that has exercised me so much in recent years. I walked into a restaurant and they put on a CD called *The Hits of Cliff Richard* with my name emblazoned across it. I was thrilled – until I realized it was nothing to do with me at all. I looked more closely at the cover and, in very small type, it said, 'The Pan Pipes Play – The Hits of Cliff Richard'. People said, 'Oh, we've always loved your music,' and I said, 'But this is not me,' and they said, 'No, but they're your songs, it's your music.' This group was using my name to sell their music, but not a half-penny of royalties would come my way; nor should it, because I hadn't written the songs. My gripe is that they sold the CD on the strength of my name. The royalties would, quite rightly, go to the writers and the publishers. There is a massive imbalance in UK copyright law which seems grossly unfair. The writer's copyright continues for seventy years after his or her death; the singer's for only fifty years from the date of their recording. (In America it's ninety years.) My fifty years are up, and so I am about to lose control of the songs that I made famous. Soon someone will be able to release an album called *The Best of Cliff Richard* with all my songs, *sung by me*, without having to pay me a penny or even ask permission to do so – but they would have to pay the writers.

We singers have given life to songs that might otherwise never have been known. When people think of 'We Don't Talk Any More' they say, 'It's Cliff Richard's song.' Some of my fans may know that Alan Tarney wrote it, but few others do. Songwriters could possibly forget writing their songs, yet

I go on singing them again and again because people still want to hear songs from the past, and every time I sing them, sales go up. Neil Diamond once told me he'd forgotten about a couple of songs he'd written until a royalty cheque came in on the strength of my recording them.

The copyright position doesn't affect me as much is it does some other singers who were my contemporaries. I am still singing, so I will continue to have royalties coming in for the more recent songs I've recorded; but things are very different for those singers who had only a few hits and stopped in the fifties: people like Billy Fury, sadly no longer alive, and Marty Wilde, who's actually still singing but no longer recording. They or their families might be totally dependent on royalties.

So I've been battling for a change in the law, and it's been an uphill struggle; but at last it looks as though justice might eventually come from Europe. Cherie Blair was helpful. I discussed it with her and she said, 'It sounds discriminatory to me.' So, without mentioning her name, I used that phrase when I met the committee in Brussels that is looking into the protection of copyright, and it may just have had something to do with the latest change of heart. There was an announcement in February 2008 that they were planning to alter the rules and bring

Europe into line with the United States. Three cheers!

What I love most of all, though, about having been singing for as long as I have is the fact that my fans seem to have become friends with one another. Wherever there is a curtain at a concert venue to hide behind, I sneak a look at the audience between getting ready and warming up my voice. The hall will be filling up with people and, sure enough, there will always be a group here and a group there, waving at each other. I'm beginning to believe they come to the concerts to meet each other as much as they do to see me! Some of them have best friends they met at a concert years ago; some meet, start writing to each other and get together from time to time; and some only ever meet at my concerts. That makes for a fantastic atmosphere – I love it – and towards the end of the show, just one of them has to start stomping down an aisle and suddenly they are all at the stage and the whole arena is shaking. It's a wonderful sensation and takes me back to being in the audience at my first rock concerts. I can still remember that feeling; and what keeps me going is the knowledge that *I* am giving *them* what Elvis, Bill Haley and the others gave *me*. The day I feel it isn't happening any more will be the day I need to stop.

The question is whether to stop while I am

still ahead. I thought about it a good twenty years ago and talked it over with Peter Gormley. My record company was insisting, 'We've got to get to the kids,' and I was saying, 'No. I'm an adult. I am over forty years old, I make music for adults, not for children. The kids can like it as well, of course, but you've got to aim for a different group, you must find a way of selling me to a mature audience.' But they wouldn't listen, and I was thinking maybe it was time to quit. Then the week I moved into Charters, my house in St George's Hill, which was 1987, I saw a copy of the *Tatler*, with a headline 'Mouldy Old Dough'. The article was all about 'grey power', pointing out that there were more people on the planet now over the age of forty than under, and it was the forty- to sixty-year-olds now, a huge market, that had the money and the power. It was the first time I had seen this point of view expressed. Still nobody in the record company listened; but I realized I had everything going for me. It would have been lunacy to retire.

CHAPTER TEN

The Fans

Bob Monkhouse became a good friend of mine in the last few years before he died in 2003. We got to know each other in Barbados, where he also had a house. He had had such tragedy in his life, with the death of two sons, and then cancer, but you would never have known it. Right up to the end he was such good company, so funny, and he had a lovely wife, Jackie, who also died recently. I was talking to her stepdaughter, Abigail, in Barbados in April 2008 and she reminded me of the story her father told about coming to one of my concerts years ago. I can't begin to remember where it was, or when, but backstage, between shows – we used to do two a night in those days – there was the sound of shattering glass as a brick was hurled through a window. It missed my head by millimetres. Attached to the brick was a note which said, 'I love you, Cliff'. Bob said, 'Can you imagine; you could have been killed by someone who loves you.'

My fans are a loyal bunch, and not many of them have come that close to killing me.

There have been some surprises, though. One girl sent herself to me in a cardboard box. I was in Edinburgh, I think, and when this box arrived I thought it was a TV set. I opened it up and out jumped a girl who wanted an autograph. Some have been coming to my shows and buying my records since the very beginning – one or two even saw me playing at Butlins when I was still an amateur – and inevitably I know quite a number of them by name and many more by sight. They are a wonderful bunch. When Chris Evans announced he wasn't going to play Cliff Richard on his radio show any more, a whole group of them went and set up camp outside the studio to protest. I am very touched by that kind of thing and I have a great deal of respect for people who are prepared to stick their necks out on my behalf, not to mention the discomfort they put up with.

Sometimes, before a new show, I used to be so nervous I couldn't sleep for several nights. Then it sank in that when I am performing there are twelve thousand people out there in the audience who could easily, on a winter's night, have chosen to stay at home with a nice mug of tea and watch a really good movie on television. Instead they have opted to come out to see me; and I thought, So why should I be scared? They want to be there, I want to be there – all I have to do is present the goods. And that's why I rehearse longer than most people in the business. I rehearse for up to six weeks before a show. Many bands apparently get together a couple of times and then go on stage. They can't believe what I do – and I can't believe what they do – but I have to get it right, and that takes rehearsal time. Those people there on the very first night have paid just as much money as the people who are there on the last night, and that first show should not be filled with mistakes.

Many are the times I come off at the intermission on that first night and say, 'That song doesn't work there. It's too early in the programme, we have to change it.' We will swap it with another and, believe it or not, just changing the position of a song will make all the difference. Sometimes you have to build up to a new song. You woo the audience with as many songs as you can that they already know, then you hit them with a brand new one – and by that time they are so happy that they accept the new one. That process of worrying and rearranging things goes on for three or four days but after the fifth day, it's pure excitement. I can't wait to do it again. It is hard work, and I have to deal with my days being upside down and eating at odd times and never being in bed before 2.00 or 2.30 a.m. I have to eat wisely to stay slim and practise so I can sing properly, and I have to exercise to keep fit enough to do the routines.

The disciplines in my life are enormous; but who cares? I do love what I do.

Yet the nerves haven't diminished. I didn't sleep for about a week before the start of the 2006–2007 world tour. It was the usual pattern. I suddenly realize that the songs aren't under my skin yet, the show still isn't one hundred per cent in my head, and I just can't sleep. I sit up, I put the light on, I get my pen out; a good way of learning songs is to memorize them and write them down. So I write out the lyric, and if I forget a line I don't worry; after a couple of days I've filled in the gaps. Quite often when I'm on stage and I'm losing a lyric, I can visualize my writing on the page. I think, It's the third line down and the last word was 'heart'. OK, so the first one was 'start'. It does work; but it means I have really disturbed sleep, and probably explains why when I finish a tour I am so whacked. After the last tour I spent nearly a week doing hardly anything except sleeping. It was the most wonderful tour: I had more days free than I have ever had, I went out and saw things, did things, relaxed, played tennis, skipped about in sea and sand, I loved it. My band loved it too. But I was still worn out by the end of it.

Sometimes I go to concerts given by other people in my profession and the artist will come on stage and say, 'Hello,' and that's it. I can't understand that. I find it's such a natural thing to talk to an audience. It doesn't take much; you could talk about what you've had for breakfast and the audience would love it. What they want is some little insight into your personality and your life, and just by talking I can give them a flavour of what it's like to be Cliff Richard. I think it's very important to make them feel they know me and to let them know that I love them – and I do love them. It is not the same love that I feel for my close friends or family, of course it's not, and it's not really a one-to-one relationship; but it is a relationship: an artist–audience relationship, and I feel I can be free with them and honest with them. I'll always believe what we have is special.

During a gospel tour once I remember talking about love. Love is such a strange word. You know, in the Bible they have different words for love. If you loved your mother it was one word; if you loved your wife it was another word; if you loved a friend it was another word. We are stuck with *one* word. For instance, I love God and I love the skin of custard – same word, yet God and custard are miles apart; I shouldn't have to use the same word for my taste in food that I use to describe my feelings for God. I thought I was being quite profound. Blow me down, another night, as I started the custard story, I saw two girls walking towards the stage carrying a large shallow tray. The previous night I had embellished the story, saying, 'If it's true that skin forms when the custard cools, then if you made it in a flat dish a quarter of an inch deep it would all be skin.' And I was proved right: in the tray was custard and it was all skin. It was funny and I was delighted by their experiment – but people only do things like that because they're comfortable with me and want to participate in my story.

It doesn't take much, but without that openness a lot of artists miss out on the joy of reading a letter or an email from someone who's been in the audience, saying, 'I didn't know you thought like that.' I enjoy hearing people laugh at some experience I've recounted. I told them about the night I went to a party when the Shadows were on television. I went up to my hostess, whom I didn't know very well, and said, 'I hate doing this, but do you mind if I put the TV on? My band, the Shadows, is on at eight o'clock.'

She said, 'Your band, the Shadows? You're Cliff Richard? You're *the* Cliff Richard?'

I said, 'Yes.'

She said, 'I can't believe it, you look too young to be the original.'

Maybe I was lucky starting when I did. A lot of people in the business will say, 'My music's enough.' I don't think the music *is* enough. Everyone's out there making good music; you have to give your audience something extra. That's probably what that early training with the stars of vaudeville taught me. Every night I go on stage, smile and say, 'Hi, good evening, it's really nice to have you here,' even if I'm not feeling too good and inside I'm thinking Oh please let it be the end, I want to have a steak and go to bed. Suddenly, whoops, I find the enthusiasm and warmth of the audience has revived *my* enthusiasm, and within three songs I am right back up where I should be. Their response gives me a fantastic high and everything else vanishes.

I also think we have a responsibility towards our fans, all those people out there who, for better or worse, admire us; and, as an industry, the pop world doesn't always set a particularly good example. It's not for me to say what people should and shouldn't do with their lives, but when I think of the sixties, the drugs and how desperate it all was, I feel very angry. That was the part of the sixties that I find hard to forgive. Who knows how many people died of drug overdoses and how many lives were totally destroyed because of the example set by some of my contemporaries? As artists, we have to take the blame. Yes, it was an exciting time; we were breaking down barriers; but the freedom we achieved has to be tempered with responsibility or it becomes dangerous and people get damaged.

I never took drugs. I guess I was just lucky not to have liked smoking – hence no pot, which could have led to something worse; and once I became a Christian, I had my faith and so had no need for artificial props. It is interesting to conjecture what would have happened to me if I hadn't found Christianity when I did. I might have had the same success in my career, but I would have been a different type of artist. And who knows where I might have ended up? I might have got into drugs, I might have done all sorts of things. I might have been dead by now. It is all speculative. All I do know is that I live my life as best I can according to my faith; and perfection is something we can only ever chase, never achieve. There is a quote I love: 'In Jesus we are accepted as though we were perfect.' It means that I don't have to fear the fact that I am never going to be perfect, but by giving myself to Him, I'm accepted as though I *am* – and that motivates me to try and try again!

I considered myself a radical because I didn't want to do what everyone else was doing. I didn't want to throw television sets out of hotel windows, I didn't want to kick journalists or punch people on the nose – well, maybe I did sometimes – but I didn't do it! I remember, on some show to celebrate my thirtieth year of performing, a whole bunch of people were interviewed and Adam Faith said of me – and I paraphrase – 'He's an enigma. Everything he seemed to do was wrong. You can't be too nice in our business, you can't be a Christian, you can't stand up and say the sort of things he's said about drugs. He seemed to be out of step with what everyone else was doing and then it turns out that he wasn't wrong after all.' I really appreciated what he said; he acknowledged that I had swum against the stream, and that I was outspoken about all the things of which I disapproved – because I felt I had to: I said what I thought of the apparent adults who behaved like drunken yobs and poured marmalade over the first class seats of a British Airways jumbo jet. I always steered clear of that sort of behaviour.

I used to have someone working for me – Ron King, he was such a funny man; sadly he died, and we still miss him. Anyway, one day we were coming out of the stage door at the back of a theatre, rushing to get to a book signing, and I said to a woman waiting with a group of people outside, 'Sorry, we're in a rush. Nice to see you, thanks for coming, we'll see you later,' and she turned very nasty and said, 'Huh! We *made* you.'

Quick as a flash, Ron turned to her and said, 'Darling, you couldn't make a rice pudding. We'll see you later,' and we left. And

I thought to myself: my fans and I, we do owe each other a lot of things in life, but in the end if I make a record you don't like, you won't buy it; of course not. You are not giving me my career out of the goodness of your heart. We need to have reciprocal respect, so I do my best for you and if I can't stop to sign an autograph, I hope you'll forgive me.

I don't quite know my fans by name, but I recognize some of them easily. As soon as tickets for my shows go on sale, there are a few hundred of them who go to the venue and queue. They set up tents and camp by the side of the road, some of them for as long as three weeks. They camped outside Wembley in 2005 and 2003, and two years before that they camped outside the Albert Hall. I sometimes visit them and have pictures taken with them, and once I arranged for people to go and cook them breakfast. I hope they know just how fantastic I think it is that they do this for me – a sixty-seven-year-old rock 'n' roll singer. I mean, I don't think Westlife's fans do it. The publicity value is incalculable – the press are astounded. Of course, the husbands are the ones that I have real respect for – they take over in the queue while the wives go back home and shower and wash their hair and change clothes. What a crowd!

Here's something interesting I noticed on my last world tour: the age of my audience seemed to have dropped by twenty years or more. There were a lot of people in their forties among the crowd. The women in their sixties are still there, but they've been joined by these younger people, and also by men. I guess that's because couples are coming together now, which they very rarely did before. I've had letters saying, 'You know, I wasn't really a fan but my wife insisted that I come to the concert and you know, I quite liked it.' I said to Bill and the others, 'This is fantastic. This is the invisible audience I have never been able to get to because they've been told, "Oh, Cliff's a goody two shoes, he's the Christian."' What difference should that make? Plenty of singers are Buddhists, but no one stays away from their concerts because of their faith.

Anyway, I can't help it. Christianity demands a commitment, and I've made that commitment – but it doesn't make me 'holier than thou'. It's the 'holier than thou' effect that is so negative, and that comes from the way Christianity is presented by the media, and sometimes even by the Church. People are put off by it, understandably; so when they do come along to one of my concerts, I hope they realize that I do a perfectly good rock 'n' roll show. I rock with the best of them. I've had people come from other bands and say, 'Ooh, you're loud!' I don't know what they expected; that I was going to play afternoon Palm Court music?

My band is a rock 'n' roll band, and they play what the music demands: so when we do 'Devil Woman', it's insidious; when I sing 'We Don't Talk Anymore', it's upright and brash. If it takes loud – then I'm loud.

It has been a great thrill to see those couples at my concerts. It's right across Europe that the change has been so noticeable. Far Eastern audiences have always been different, with a far greater mixture of age and gender. They love their music and will go and see anybody who sings. They love karaoke too, so when I sing some of those oldies they're up on their feet, all singing the lyrics with me, even if they don't speak English that well. I get a great buzz playing in Japan, Hong Kong, Singapore and all those far-flung places.

There is no official Cliff Richard fan club and hasn't been for many years. The original one, started by Jan Vane, the girl who saw us play at the 2i's when we were just starting out, grew to be the biggest fan club in Britain at that time. It was good while she ran it with her family and some other girls; but then they married and had children, other people took over and it ran into trouble. They were selling photographs and a few other bits and pieces, and when money starts to change hands there are all sorts of tax implications of which they had no concept. I suddenly found myself with a huge bill and having to bail them out. So my manager stepped in and we wound it up in about 1966. He said that if people wanted to run fan clubs at a local level on their own, that was fine, but we shouldn't be involved. Otherwise I was likely to be bailing people out for the rest of my career.

So now there are dozens of local fan clubs and what are known as Cliff Richard Meeting Houses. These started with people getting together not just to play music and do all the things that fans normally do, but to raise money for charity as well. In the early days the money they raised was for Tearfund, because that is what I was most involved with, but now they tend to raise it for my Charitable Trust. There are dozens of Meeting Houses around the world, and I'm shocked sometimes on tour when I am handed a cheque for something like twelve hundred pounds. I'll ask how they raised the money and they'll say, 'Well, every time I take a picture of you I sell it to the fans, and here's the money for it.' I'm always bowled over by their ingenuity and generosity.

So I feel very good about my fans. They have followed me not just through my music but through my lifestyle. They enjoy the gospel concerts, even though they are not all Christians – many of them may have chosen some other way; but in the end I feel good because they have respected my choice, and they seem to enjoy participating in the many different things in which I'm involved. They have been incredible over the years – they once bought an incubator for premature babies in hospital. All I had to do was sign a photograph; they raffled it with a few other things, raising thousands of pounds, and we now have The Cliff Richard Meeting House incubator in Birmingham Childrens' Hospital. It's really thrilling for me that they've done so many things like that.

Probably my biggest fan club now is the one run from the Netherlands by a couple of guys called Anton Husmann and Harry de Louw, who somehow know more about me than ever I will. They publish a bi-monthly news-sheet called *Dynamite International*. Occasionally I say to my office, 'Am I going to be in so and so?'

And they say, 'Oh yeah, but that's not for another year.'

'Well, I've just read all about it,' I say. I am amazed that these Dutchmen know things that haven't been announced yet, and every scrap of news goes whizzing all over the world to anywhere that I am known. It's the internet, I presume, which makes everything so accessible. I don't look at it but I believe there are thousands and thousands of pages about me out there.

As a recording artist you need a nucleus of fans as your bedrock, who will always support you; but important as those fans are, they don't give you the million-seller, and they don't necessarily let you have the number one hit. To achieve that you have to go beyond the borders of your fan club into the wide open market. There are people there who may not want to join a fan club but have enjoyed the shows, maybe, or have liked a record every now and then. If you can make a record that appeals to *them* as well, that's when it becomes a really big hit. I did that with 'We Don't Talk Anymore', 'Millennium Prayer' and the other million-sellers. I went beyond the loyal core, to all those other people who are just waiting to hear something they will spend their money on; but it's a constant problem trying to cater for those people – and, without the help of radio, just gets harder and harder.

'Millennium Prayer' in the year 2000 (the Lord's Prayer set to the tune of 'Auld Lang Syne') was huge, and brought me a lot of free press coverage. EMI had turned it down, saying, 'We don't hear this as a single.' After all the years I had been with them and all the hit records I'd given them, I couldn't believe that they didn't recognize the potential. So I gave it to Papillon Records – and because it was a charity record, the press had something to get their teeth into: 'EMI has turned down Sir Cliff's charity record.' When the radio stations then said they wouldn't play it, the press said, 'How dare they ban Sir Cliff's charity record?' There were stories day after day after day, so everybody became aware that I had a record out. What capped it for me, was that, because it was for charity, my record cost twice as much as any other single – and still it sold. I think we charged £3 for it, and although it wasn't being heard on the radio, people bought it. It went to number one within a fortnight of its release, and stayed there for three weeks. It sold 1.4 million copies and raised £1 million for Children's Promise. Satisfying as that was, 'Millennium Prayer' was probably the most painful hit record I have ever had because I constantly felt as though I was fighting a battle.

It was baffling. I wasn't at war with anybody. Forget the merits of it; I'd made a record which was unique. It was a prayer. The Lord's Prayer can be spoken by Muslims or Jews. It doesn't mention God or Jesus. Its message was simple: 'Please feed us, forgive us, make us forgiving' – all the things you might think would be beneficial for humankind at the start of a new millennium: making resolutions to improve ourselves, and improve our relationships. I thought it was perfect; and yet, somehow or another, it turned out to be one of the most controversial things I've ever done – and to this day I don't entirely understand why. A

Christian said to me, 'Well, they crucified Jesus for even speaking those words, so you can't expect much better yourself, can you?' So I thought, OK, maybe there was a spiritual message hidden in there that people didn't like. Ironically, George Harrison's 'My Sweet Lord' was a wonderful hit, played everywhere, all over the world, and nobody batted an eyelid at its Hindu overtones. Yet my singing the Lord's Prayer was unacceptable. One high-profile and popular singer referred to it as 'this vile record'! Bizarre.

CHAPTER ELEVEN

Tall Poppy Syndrome

Years ago, my mother sent me a letter. She had read some story about me in the press and she wrote, saying, 'I'm really worried about you. I don't like what your management are doing. They seem to take control of everything you do, you are completely in their hands.' I didn't phone her: I thought, she's written to me, I'm going to write back; and sometimes it's easier to express oneself on paper. So I wrote to her saying, 'Do you really think that I've survived thirty-five years in the music business by being weak, by not knowing what I want to do?' I said, 'Mum, I only do what *I* want to do. If they advise me, or come up with an idea that I haven't thought of and I think it's a good idea, then I do it; otherwise I don't.'

I'm generalizing, I know, but I do feel that the press has spent too much time in the last forty years attempting to put me down and portray me as some sort of wishy-washy weakling. They seem to confuse meekness with weakness, and the two do not necessarily go hand in hand. The truth is quite the opposite. Nobody could survive for as long as I have in this business if they were weak.

I am not worried about the reviewers any more because I stopped inviting them to my concerts – and if you don't give them free tickets, they don't come. I said to Bill one day, 'Why are we paying for these guys to come to the show and sneer?' So that solved that problem. We take out national advertisements announcing that tickets are on sale, but otherwise there is very little, if any, newspaper publicity and reviews are few and far between.

I reached the same conclusion about interviews. Bill used to set them up and I would come out of the session saying, 'I really enjoyed that, we had such a good conversation, we've talked about so many different things, really nice guy.' Then I would read the resulting article and somehow I'd been made to look like an idiot. Finally I said, 'Look, I can't do this any more. No more one-to-ones in future. I don't see why I should put myself through this.' It's not just reading the thing that upset me. Having read it, I sometimes wouldn't sleep for three whole nights. I wouldn't go out to the shops because I knew people would have seen the article and would be looking at me sideways, thinking who knows what about me, and I just didn't like it.

But even that's changed. Over the last six or seven years I have reached the conclusion that I don't give a darn anymore. The internet has helped. The minute a journalist writes something unpleasant there will be fans saying, 'Why have they written this? We know Cliff could never have behaved like that!' The support is so unwavering, so constant. Of course, I don't want anyone to think ill of me so in terms of dealing with adverse publicity, I say to myself I don't value their opinions anyway so they can write what they like.

I remember one particular article. It was in the mid-eighties when I was nearing the end of my run in the West End musical *Time*. I spotted a headline which said, 'God Speaks to Pop Star Backstage'. I thought, that's got to be about me – and sure enough, it was. I had signed a year's contract, and my year was almost up. This article said I claimed that God had spoken to me backstage the previous day –'telling me that I should leave the show'. I wish! The only person I had spoken to about leaving *Time* was my manager – who was arguably almost as important as God in my career! Oh no, God himself has never spoken to me – not with a voice anyway. And more to the point, *I* had never spoken to this journalist. I rang the office to see if someone there had spoken to him and no one had. The entire thing was fabricated. I just couldn't understand why a newspaper would want to do that. The article made me sound like a religious nut, and I've spent all my life trying *not* to be a religious nut. I like to think I am rational about my faith. I do not go around saying, 'God spoke to me last night and told me not to have porridge for breakfast.' He speaks through what I see people do or say; he speaks through the words I read in the Bible. I haven't, as yet, heard an audible voice.

I once had a stalker who followed me for several years – she clearly had problems. My dog used to go crazy when I let her out at night, running off barking into the bushes, and I was convinced someone was there. I called in the police and they found a girl. She said, 'God told me to come and look at the house because Cliff has the answer. I have to see him to find the answer too.'

I was far less afraid of her than I am of the media. I have lived in fear of journalists for most of my career. It's not the interviews themselves – as I've said, I usually quite enjoy those. It's how the journalists interpret or manipulate what I've said. The *Time* piece was laughable – not only had God not said anything to me, I hadn't said anything to anyone either – but there are other instances when what they've written about me is just painful. And some of the time it's dishonest. They use half of a sentence and leave out the bit which qualified what I said in the first half. Or they make it sound as though I have issued a major statement when all I have been doing is answering a question. Thank goodness, there are some excellent journalists who are genuine and do their job properly, but there are many others who have their own agenda, and that frightens me because the written word is very powerful.

I once spent the whole day with a journalist from the *Times* magazine while I was preparing for a charity gospel concert. We had lunch together, then we carried on talking while I got ready for the stage. I don't use liquid make-up any more because I find that when I sweat it runs into my eyes and then my eyes fill with water, so I use powder and shadow. It's a very personal thing and quite egotistical, but I try to get the lights in the dressing room to replicate the effect the stage lights will have on my face; so there's a lot of posing in the mirror, wondering how I look. As a mature journalist, this interviewer should have known what I was doing. I liked him: we talked about my charity work and I thought we'd had a good conversation, but when the article came out, the opening sentence was, 'Cliff Richard: his face is like an iced-bun with a cherry on the top.' The whole thing was a terrible put-down.

You don't have to like someone's singing to appreciate what they are trying to do. I go and see people I don't like at all. I'm not a great fan of Meat Loaf but I look and I think, Yeah, this guy knows exactly what he's doing; so I can applaud that. The fact that it's not the music I would play for myself doesn't negate the talent. Of all the music I do love, I think Michael Jackson's *Thriller* is probably the best album ever made. I listen to it now and the sounds still excite me. I don't necessarily think he's the best singer there's ever been – his voice is a bit too thin and piping for me – but his dancing and his physical approach to his music are second to none, not to mention the fabulous songs. When I watch his videos, I find them compulsive, even if I don't really like the song; but I loved every single song on the *Thriller* album. My taste is very eclectic nowadays. I never used to like Frank Sinatra, but now if I see an album with him on it I buy it; I listen to Ella Fitzgerald, Peggy Lee, Mariah Carey, Bonnie Raitt – who's never really been big in England but she's cross-over blues/pop, has the most fabulous voice and plays slide guitar amazingly – those sorts of people. My little CD player takes five CDs and I put them all in and sometimes one of my own and I set it to random, and I hear Peggy Lee and then mine comes on and I think to myself I'm the luckiest person on the planet. I mean, when did you last hear your record alongside Peggy Lee?

To go back to the press, sometimes it is the headline that causes the damage. The article itself will be fine but the headline's completely misleading. I have occasionally had apologies from journalists when that's happened, which I appreciate, and it's not their fault – it's a sub-editor who writes the headlines – but it's still very annoying. In 2006, when I sold Charters, there was a headline announcing that I had sold my house in England and was planning to move abroad. It was just not true. I already had three properties abroad, I didn't need any more; and the day before I sold Charters I bought a new three-bedroom bungalow at Wentworth, twenty minutes away, in England. I wasn't packing up and leaving the country, as the headline implied; I was simply downsizing. It's true that I do spend more time abroad these days, but I will always have a

Left: Dad (Rodger Webb) in India where we all enjoyed a comfortable lifestyle.

Below: 1941 aged 14 months — check the pose. Dad on left, Mum fourth from left.

Left to Right: My parents and me — quite a family resemblance!

Above: Dad beside our first TV set.

Above right: Mum on a works outing — she is the one with a handbag at her feet.

Right: Was it hopscotch? With Jacqui, Joan and a friend. Whatever it was I needed my sisters to keep my balance.

Below: Always a player! Me in the school football team 1951-52, back row third from right.

Above: Me with my little sister Joan in the garden at Winchmore Hill.

Above, right: What a line up — me, Mum, Donna, Jacqui and Joan in our council house at Cheshunt.

Above: Getting me up in the morning was never easy.

Left: What a fearsome team. No prizes for guessing which one's me.

Above: Jay Norris and the class of '56.

Below, left: but first there was Ratty in 'Toad of Toad Hall' in 1955, when Jay Norris made me sing.

Below, right: And as Bob Cratchit in a school production of 'A Christmas Carol'.

Above, right: Could this have been my first open air concert? Our house in the background.

Right: The King — without whom. . .

EVERETT COLLECTION/REX FEATURES

Above: Getting used to what it's like to be famous —
just having a family breakfast was a photo opportunity. . .

Below: . . . and as for signing autographs, that was
something I had to get used to as well.

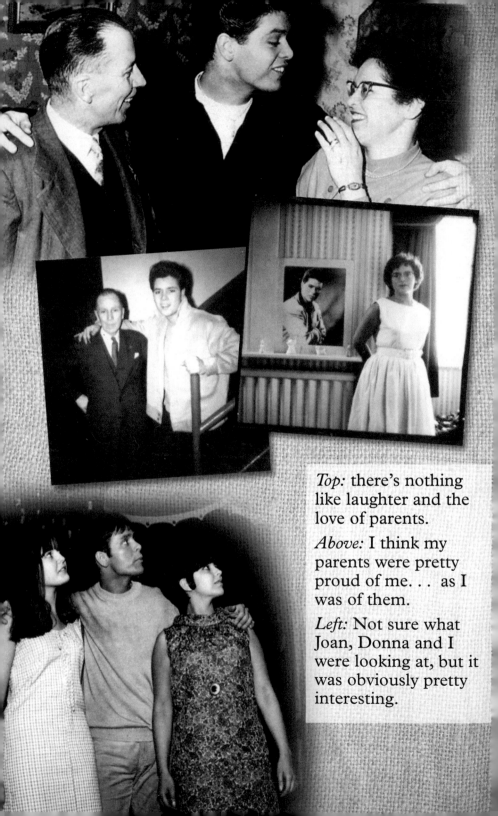

Top: there's nothing like laughter and the love of parents.

Above: I think my parents were pretty proud of me. . . as I was of them.

Left: Not sure what Joan, Donna and I were looking at, but it was obviously pretty interesting.

From top to bottom: Me and the Shads, left to right: Brian 'Licorice' Locking, bassist with the Shadows, me, and Bruce Welch, rhythm guitarist; Taking time out at the London Palladium with Des O'Connor in 1960; Backstage with Ian Samwell, the man who 'moved it'; I was never going to be the world's greatest drummer, but it was fun for a time.

Left: Meeting Her Majesty is always an honour. With (from right) Rosemary Clooney, Harry Secombe and Eartha Kitt.

Below: Doing what we do best. Me and the Shads.

AP/PA PHOTOS

RONALD GRANT ARCHIVE

Right: What a way to spend a premiere. The crowds in Leicester Square for the premiere of 'Summer Holiday' were so huge I couldn't get in to see my own film!

Above: Sunday night at the London Palladium with Bruce Welch and Hank Marvin.

Right: Off to America — the land of promise.

Above: With Una Stubbs in 'Aladdin and his Wonderful Lamp' at the Palladium, 1964.

Below: And again on the set of 'Wonderful Life' with the Shadows — life sure was wonderful!

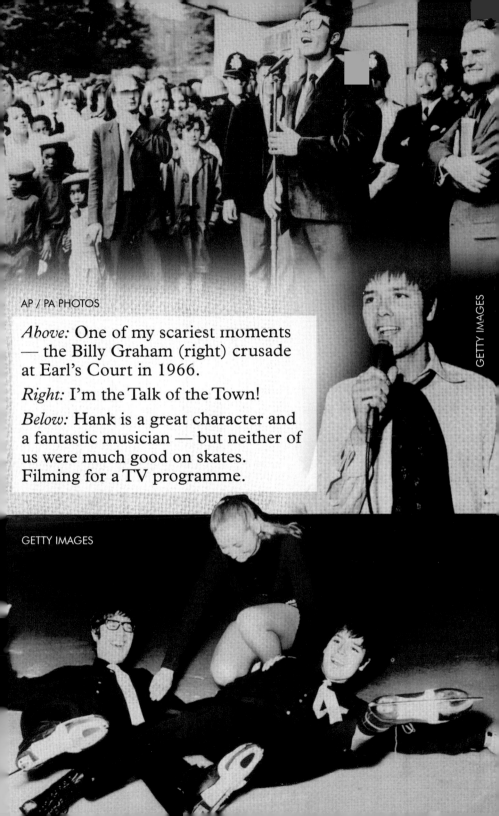

Above: One of my scariest moments — the Billy Graham (right) crusade at Earl's Court in 1966.

Right: I'm the Talk of the Town!

Below: Hank is a great character and a fantastic musician — but neither of us were much good on skates. Filming for a TV programme.

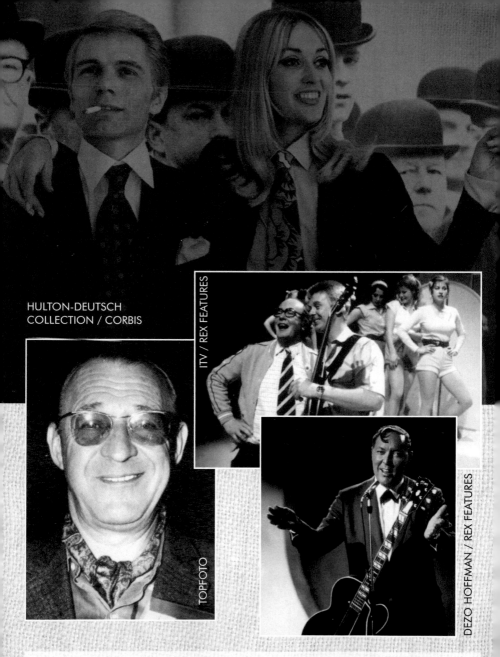

Top: Jackie Irving — Dad thought she was a real cookie.
So did Adam Faith!

Above, left to right: The man who made it all happen —
Norrie Paramor; Jack Good in glasses with Joe Brown
on the set of 'Oh Boy', Jack taught me so much; The man
I lost my prefect's badge for — Bill Haley.

Clockwise from top left: Wish me luck for the Eurovision Song Contest; Pipped at the post by Spain and 'La, La, La'. Here I am with Massiel and the two composers; How young we all were. . . with Cilla Black and Lulu, all of us picking up awards in 1970. I was 'Best Dressed Male'; On stage: though we might not have won, we had a fantastic time.

Top: With George Hoffman (centre) and Bill Latham in Bangladesh. Tearfund trips added a new dimension to my life.

Above left: It never ceases to amaze me how resilient children are.

Above right: That first trip to Bangladesh was the hardest. I felt I should stay and help but the nurses pointed out that I was more use raising money as a singer.

Clockwise from top: With Morecambe and Wise — variety was where I began; It was such a shame that Dad didn't live to see me collect my OBE; Diana was a very special person — a princess who knew about Marigolds; If ever there had been any sign of it all going to my head, my family would have brought me down to earth. Joan, Mum and Donna; I have Sue Barker to thank for my enduring passion for tennis.

Left: I've always had a bit of a weakness for cars.

Right: 'Time' was not the greatest musical ever written but I had such fun and so much friendship during my year in the West End.

Bottom: 'The Event' at Wembley Stadium — June 1969 — it was packed for two nights — I have never played to such a large audience.

PAUL COX

ANDRE CSILLAG / REX FEATURES

DAVID REDFERN / REDFERNS

Above, left to right: In Austria, 1996, at the Viennese Opera Ball with my dear friend Jill Dando; I never lose my sense of excitement when meeting Prime Ministers: here I am in 1991 with John and Norma Major, and, more recently, with Tony Blair.

Right: Being Heathcliff.

Below: In my thirties — if I could, I'd like to go back to that period!

Clockwise from top left:
And here I am actually playing — at my Tennis Classic in Birmingham in 2004; Two of my favourite dames — Dame Vera Lynn and (*below*) my dear friend Olivia Newton-John; Tiring work playing tennis — but always fun; That moment at Wimbledon in 1996 when rain stopped play. One of my most famous performances — with Virginia Wade on back-up.

GETTY IMAGES

REX FEATURES

PAUL COX

REUTERS / ANDREW WONG

SIPA PRESS / REX FEATURES

Top to bottom: With a helping hand even the most hostile terrain can reap rich rewards; It isn't just the rain at Wimbledon that gets me singing!; If this looks like hard work, it was! But what a warm welcome I had in Brazil; The victors — but I fear it was rigged! Football with a team of kids in a children at risk project in Recife.

Clockwise from left: My friends are my support network — and vice versa! With Gill, Bill and Marion (my housekeeper); John McElynn; and (*below*) my oasis: the courtyard at the Quinta in Portugal'

MARY KHAN

ANN CHAPLEO AND MYRTLE HORLOCK

TANYA WHITEHEAD

Main pic: Arriving at Butlins Holiday Camp in 1958.

Above: Nice to be wanted! Mary Khan collected 100,000 signatures to persuade me to stay in showbusiness in 1966.

Below: What a difference a decade makes! I think I've changed my image since those days.

Left: Putting the boot in — backstage posing.

Below: After the publication of my first book for Hodder.

Bottom: Live at 'Her Kurhaus' in Holland 1964. The screaming was so loud who knows if anyone actually heard me.

ELAINE LEE

BRIAN LONG

BAS VAN EIJK

NAOMI YOKOCHI

SYLVIE PLESTED

NAOMI YOKOCHI

HEATHER WOOLHAM

LESLEY CODMAN

Clockwise from top left: Cliff on Cliff; Caught unawares in my seventies hairstyle; I love meeting my fans anywhere in the world — here I am in Japan and in Hamburg; Out in the country — happening on a farm in Guernsey.

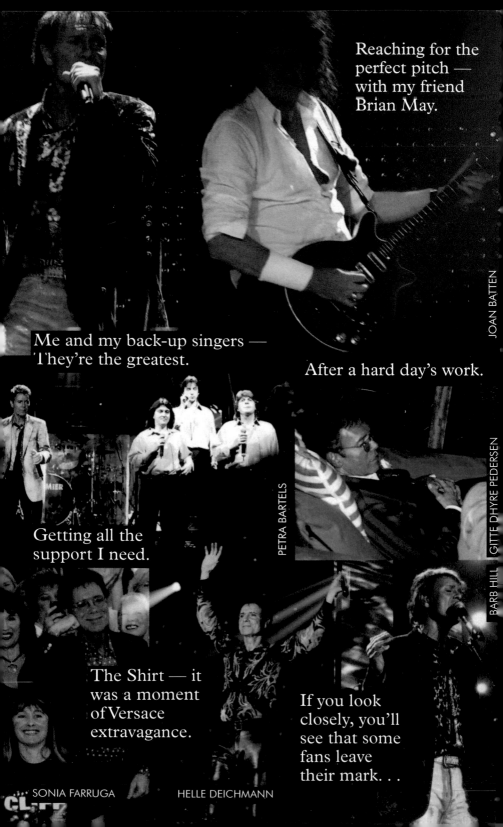

Reaching for the perfect pitch — with my friend Brian May.

JOAN BATTEN

Me and my back-up singers — They're the greatest.

After a hard day's work.

Getting all the support I need.

PETRA BARTELS

GITTE DHYRE PEDERSEN

BARB HILL

The Shirt — it was a moment of Versace extravagance.

If you look closely, you'll see that some fans leave their mark. . .

SONIA FARRUGA

HELLE DEICHMANN

base here, and I will always come here so long as my family is here; but it seemed silly to keep such a big and expensive house going when I wasn't living in it for more than a few months of the year.

Occasionally I wonder whether I may be partly to blame for the things the media say about me because I am so upfront in acknowledging the people who've helped make me what I am. I have always talked about the songwriters, the musicians and producers I have worked with. I have made a running joke out of how I couldn't do what I do without them. I have said how talented they are and how lucky I am that our paths have crossed. I plug and plug them – people like Dave McKay, Norrie Paramor, Bruce Welch, Terry Britten, Alan Tarney. They are all huge talents and they have all helped me build mine. I speak about them with absolute respect and sometimes envy, because they're writers, and I would have liked to have been a writer; I gave it up rather early. What I try to convey is that none of what I do is a one-man show. The backstage crew alone runs to about forty people and there are nine others on the stage with me. OK, I stand up front, I control everything, I decide what I'm going to sing and where I'm going to sing it; but I couldn't do it without them. I see that as being honest and giving credit where credit's due, but maybe the press see it as weakness.

All I can say is if that's weakness, then I'll always be weak.

Or maybe it is just the tall poppy syndrome that we have in Britain. The media help build you up, then when you are at the height of your success they seem to take pleasure in cutting you down. Perhaps they still feel that I need to be put in my place. Well I don't need them because my family and friends do a great job of that.

Americans have a different approach to success: they love it. It's a real regret of mine that I missed the boat there – although it's never too late! About three years ago I was invited as a guest to the Country Music Association Awards at Madison Square Garden, New York. So I phoned Olivia Newton-John and said, 'Look, they want me to walk the red carpet. Are you free? Would you come with me?' and she said 'Sure.' She was on a tour but she had a two-day break. I said, 'They're all going to be waving at you and *I'm* going to be waving back, so when they show clips of it in England no one will know that it's not me the crowds are waving at.' She was so sweet, she came and we did all the waving and the interviews together.

Before I went, the CMA people had said to me, 'We have a night free at a place called Joe's Pub. You can use our name. You can say "CMA presents Cliff Richard" and you can do a showcase and invite the American industry to see you perform.' It was a great venue, a cabaret and supper club, part of the Joseph Papp Theater, very intimate and close, with plush red velvet; it held about eighty-five people. So I brought a band up from Nashville (guys who had played on my *Something's Goin' On* album), put them up for a couple of nights while we rehearsed, and played with them to a packed house. It was fantastic. One of my conversational pieces was about Elvis. 'I've sold a lot of records in England,' I said. 'Elvis sold more after he was dead – but I'm not that ambitious.' People laughed and I assumed it had gone down well. Afterwards someone came up to me and said, 'If you're going to talk to Americans, a piece of advice: don't do that joke. Better you tell them that you outsold Elvis in Britain, they'll love it – you outsold Elvis, you outsold everybody.'

I am the first to admit that I don't know why I've been so successful. If I had appeared on the television programme *The X Factor* when I was starting out, I wouldn't have got past the first round. Now, I think I could compete – but it's taken all this time to become what I consider to be halfway good. *The X Factor* is a great title for a talent show because sometimes no one really knows why a star is born, not even the artist himself.

I have tried really hard to make commercial rock, and to emulate my heroes – Elvis,

Jerry Lee Lewis, Ricky Nelson etc. – who all had fantastic songs and great musicianship, and sang well and in tune. I've really worked at it and I think that's definitely had a part to play; but fifty years on I am no closer to fully understanding why I am still here when others have fallen by the wayside. I don't even know what makes one song so much more successful than another. We all had the feeling that Alan Tarney's song 'We Don't Talk Anymore' was going to be a hit – it turned out to be the biggest-selling hit single I ever had, and sat at number one in the UK charts for four weeks – but it was only after the event that we said 'Told you!'

The last record I'd had at number one before that was 'Congratulations', eleven years earlier, in 1968. It was the British entry in the Eurovision song contest, in which to my disappointment I came second, by one vote, to a Spanish song that came and went in a flash called 'La La La'. I was amused by the idea, suggested recently, that the Spanish dictator General Franco rigged the voting so that the Spanish entry won. Who knows whether it's true? I do remember being surprised at the time that Ireland and Yugoslavia, two countries where I was very popular, both gave me 'nil points'. My youngest sister Joan teases me to this day about the way I danced while I was singing 'Congratulations' – she didn't like what I did with my legs. To be honest, I was so nervous my legs had taken on a life of their own; but it doesn't matter, every time the clip is re-shown she is overcome with embarrassment. Silly I may have looked, but it didn't hurt sales. 'Congratulations' sold over two and a quarter million copies and in my downstairs loo in Barbados I have the original of a Mahood cartoon of me kneeling before the Queen, who, after dubbing me Knight Bachelor, bursts into song with 'Congratulations'.

People still denigrate that song, but people go on singing it everywhere at weddings and anniversaries – it's the equivalent of 'Happy Birthday', and if someone had given me the rights to be the first person to sing that I'd have jumped at the chance.

'We Don't Talk Anymore' also did very well in America, where it sold a million copies. My other big hit there was 'Devil Woman', which reached number four in the charts and sold 1.4 million copies. It had been released in Britain with EMI and went straight into the charts here, but EMI America did nothing with it. Elton John's company, Rocket Records, said they loved it and asked if they could release it. I said, 'Yes, please. Go ahead.' Funny how things work out.

'Devil Woman', which Terry Britten wrote, was a departure for me. He sent me the demo version of it and I had it in my sweaty palm for about six months, thinking, 'Will my fans allow me to sing this?' I was Mr *Summer Holiday*, who sang 'Bachelor Boy' and 'Living Doll', and this was very different. Finally we went into the studio with Bruce Welch producing and he said, 'Just sing it through a couple of times', which I did. He said, 'It's OK, but I don't know that we have done anything that special to it; it sounds like the demo. Try another voice.' This is where he was so good. I thought, Try another voice? What's he talking about? But I did. I sang the verses as though I was singing a ballad, and Bruce said, 'Stop, stop, stop. That's the way to do it. You sing it with that breath and I'll put an old fashioned rock 'n' roll echo on it, like Elvis used.' So he did: this echo follows the breath, which you can hear if you listen carefully. It has powerful drama about it that was never there on the demo, and I think it's one of the best records I've ever made.

'Devil Woman' was anti-occult – although Bruce Welch will tell you otherwise. He always makes a joke about it, but you know, it's absolutely there. It's about an occult experience, and I insisted on changing some of the lyrics before we recorded, so that it became a warning: 'You'd better get out of there fast, beware, she's just a devil woman.' I received a letter from a girl in Australia who said the record had changed her life. She had been planning to dabble, exactly as I once had, in a desire to get in touch with the dead, but a Christian friend of hers had said, 'Hold on a moment. I know you like Cliff'; play this.' She wrote to me, saying, 'I just wanted to tell you that I have heeded the warning in the lyrics. I did not go where I was going to go, I've now become a member of a church in Melbourne and I am running the children's Sunday school.' That was quite something. That record may have sold a few million copies, but as far as I'm concerned, it was made for that one girl.

'We Don't Talk Anymore' is no more a gospel record than 'Devil Woman', but I had a strange and similar experience with that song too. At the time when Bill Latham and I were going around talking to groups about Christianity, a black girl stood up and said, "We Don't Talk Anymore" will always be a wonderful gospel song for me.'

I said, 'What do you mean? It's not a gospel song, it's about the breakdown of a relationship. People don't talk enough, you know?'

And she said, 'Oh, well, it worked for me. I woke up one morning and I heard you singing, "It's so funny how we don't talk anymore," and I realized I'd been through a patch in my life where I had stopped praying.'

Those words had reawakened in her a spiritual life that, for whatever reason, she had given up. God does move in mysterious ways.

Twenty years ago I wrote a book with Bill, called *Single Minded*, in which I spoke about my faith, and after it was published I had a letter from a woman who said that, because of what she had read, she felt the urge to start going to church. Then her husband joined her and then the whole family, and they became Christians; and previously there had been no religious interest. I thought, That was fantastic, that one little thing that we said in that book clicked with them – and I don't even know what it was. I am not suggesting I converted them; that would have happened somewhere else, probably after they found a church and got into discussion, arguing and asking questions; but the book had obviously kicked off the process, and I was uplifted to know I had been some small part of their journey.

Another strange thing: when I was living at the first house I had in St George's Hill, Weybridge (before I bought Charters), a fan once said to me that she had come down the driveway and had taken a whole lot of photographs of the house, also from the house looking back up the drive. She sent me a copy of one, saying, 'I can't believe it, but look, Jesus is obviously up in the trees guarding you.' I thought she was talking nonsense. I couldn't see anything – but then I turned the photograph round and held it up to the sunlight and looked at it from the back, and, sure enough, in the middle of the trees there was this image, the typical long hair, sunken eyes, jaw, face – the picture we all have in our heads of Jesus. So whenever I meditate now, I think of that. I know it's not real, and on any other day of the year, in a different light or with the leaves at a different stage, it would be gone. But it gives me a shape that helps me focus. Otherwise it's Jeff Hunter, Max von Sydow, Robert Powell, James Caviezel – the actors who've played Jesus – that flood into my mind when I try to visualize Jesus, which is not helpful because it all becomes human. *That* image was in a tree, part of nature, and so it was perfect.

I never cease to be amazed by the number of ways in which God can manifest himself without ever uttering a word to me. I wish He'd shake the table sometimes. I've longed for it and I have met people who have had that kind of experience, but I never have. I'm not worried about it. There's a story in the Bible of doubting Thomas, who needed the earth to shake. He said, 'I want to feel your wounds before I believe.' So Jesus appeared before him and said, 'OK, feel them. Here are my hands, here is my side.' He said, 'Blessed are you that believe because you've seen me; more blessed are those who believe and have never seen.' When I read that I thought, That's about me. I've never seen Him, never felt the wounds, never heard a voice say, 'Well done.' It hasn't happened and I don't think it will. I don't need it; my faith is still intact. But I've often said to God, 'If you want to talk to me, you're very welcome!'

CHAPTER TWELVE

Dreams Fulfilled

Ever since I was at school I had dreamt of appearing in a play on the West End stage. Jay Norris, my English and drama teacher at Cheshunt Secondary Modern, was responsible for that: she had instilled a love of language in me and given me the opportunity to play out my fantasies. She used to make me read poetry at school. 'I love your speaking voice. You go ahead and make your music,' she used to say, 'and then we'll find the right poems to accompany it.' Today they call it rap. Jay was always way ahead of her time! I had to wait almost thirty years to find the right poems.

In 1986 Dave Clark, formerly of the Dave Clark Five, approached me with a proposal for a sci-fi musical he had written called *Time*. Sci-fi is my weakness. I have to confess to being a fully signed-up Trekkie. I wasn't extreme, I didn't go to the Star Trek conventions, but there was a time when I had about sixty of the original sixty-something shows on video. I used to watch them every now and again, but I don't have a video player any more so I gave them to my gardener, who still does. He said his children would love them, and of course the great thing about *Star Trek* is that it's perfectly safe for kids to watch. The original series was brilliant for its time, but it hasn't bridged the years well and the stage set looks so obvious now. It doesn't begin to compare with the *Star Trek* movies made with modern technology. They are something else...

Dave Clark's script was not actually poetry in any sense of the word, but the music was tremendous and *Time* gave me one of the most enjoyable years of my professional life. It was partly the music, which I never grew tired of singing, partly the thrill of being on the stage at the Dominion Theatre in the West End of London, partly the opportunity to act and mostly, if I am honest, the camaraderie with the rest of the show's cast. We were bonded by a multitude of things: by the hostility of the critics, by the fatigue of performing eight shows a week, and by the sheer exuberance of belting it all out to packed houses night after night. Because, although the critics sneered, the audiences kept coming. We broke box-office records. Nearly three-quarters of a million people came to see the show in the year I was in it: more, I have been told, than had ever been to a West End theatre in the same period before. The Dominion is bigger than most theatres in London – it seats two thousand people – and we were never less than 85 per cent full.

It was a morality play, about the fight between good and evil in a world on the verge of extinction. In a nutshell, the human race is on trial in the High Court of the Universe for exploiting and destroying the planet; it is the case of the Time Lord v. the People of Planet Earth. The celestial judges plan to call a politician to plead the earth's cause, but there's a cool character called Captain Ebony who thinks a politician would fail humanity. Instead he takes a rock star he knows about, someone he feels has integrity, who would have a better chance of putting up a good defence. The rock star, my character, is transported into space, where he successfully pleads for mercy. Throughout, a figure called Akash, represented by a fifteen-foot-tall hologram of Laurence Olivier's head, hung suspended over the stage. Dave Clark called him a 'Time Lord who went to Nazareth two thousand years ago' but I insisted, because of the obvious suggestion that this character was Jesus, that he be called something else. I think he was referred to as 'a guiding light' or something.

It was like no theatre I had ever seen before, and I am sure that was true for most of the audience. However scornful the critics might have been about me or the script or the lyrics, I was amazed that they were so ungenerous about the sets. They were designed by John Napier, who designed shows such as *Cats, Starlight Express* and *Les Misérables.* They were incredibly high-tech and drew gasps and applause night after night; but sadly, the theatrical establishment seemed to look down their noses at the whole venture.

As a result, perhaps, the cast developed an unusually close bond. After the show, we would often go out to dinner together. I remember smuggling pizzas into a late-night movie, and sometimes we would go down to the David Lloyd Centre and play tennis at midnight. We became good friends, and when the year came to an end I am not sure what I missed most in saying goodbye – the exhilaration of being on stage each night or the friendship of all those people I worked with.

What I didn't realize until about three months into the run was how frustrated they all felt because I never spoke to them about my faith. I went right through rehearsals thinking, If they want to know about my beliefs they're going to have to ask me, because no one's going to be able to come to me afterwards and say, 'You shoved it down our throats.' Finally they elected somebody to speak to me.

'How come you don't want to talk about your Christian faith?'

'Oh I do,' I said. 'And if you want to listen to it, I can arrange it.'

So one evening we went to the Christian Arts Centre in Waterloo, which was run by some of my friends: we had a good meal, then we all sat around with a few bottles of wine and talked. They asked us questions, we plied them with questions, and we all talked long into the night.

I like to think I have never let fame go to my head. I can't pretend I don't have people to do things for me, or that I don't get tables in restaurants or the red carpet treatment on aeroplanes and all of that sort of thing, but when any of this happens my thoughts always go back to my father saying, 'Why can't you be more like Jerry Lee Lewis or Marty Wilde?' With that attitude thrown at me by the people who mattered most in my life – my mum and dad and my sisters – from the very beginning, there was no way I could have been an egomaniac!

It is always a danger, though. Fame can give you so much, so quickly, that you can very soon start believing things you read about yourself. When I first went to South East Asia they used to call me the Golden Boy, and so there was a temptation to say to people if I got frustrated or cross, 'Don't you realize I'm a star – the Golden Boy?' I have actually only said something like that once, and it was Dave Clark who drove me to it. I know he won't mind my saying so.

Dave was a very tough taskmaster during the production of *Time*, and he was adamant that there should be no changes to the script. We were happy with most of it, but one of the actors said, 'Look, dear boy, I have said this twice before in the first two scenes; do you mind if I cut it?' Dave wouldn't let him touch it; he behaved as though we were dealing with the Bible. There was one very dramatic scene where I was on earth, in the middle of a rock 'n' roll concert with my backing group. This was the moment, at the beginning, when Captain Ebony transported us all into space, and as a ray came down on to the stage there was a massive roar, the stage shook, a wall came apart and revolved, lights flashed and we were miraculously beamed up to the High Court. The effects were extraordinary and the noise thunderous (we had to have signs outside the theatre, warning people with epilepsy). As we arrived in space, the orchestra continued playing, and this annoyed me from day one. Finally I said to Dave, 'It annoys me night after night because after that cacophony it should be absolutely quiet for maybe thirty seconds with a gentle echo on my voice so we can give the impression of space and its silence.' Time and again he said 'No,' and after a week or so the issue came to a head in front of the whole company. I said, 'OK, Dave, I am the star of this show and either that goes or I go.' Next night it was gone.

Maybe I should say it more often.

For the next nine months, the remainder of my time in the show, we did it my way and the effect was fantastic. Suddenly you really were in space – and then slowly the orchestra crept in. I did notice, however, when I went to see David Cassidy, who took over the part from me, that the intrusive under-score was back in. Peter Gormley said to me, 'You would have gone on if he had refused to back down, wouldn't you?'

I said, 'Of course I would – I had the whole cast to think of, but Dave has probably dealt with people who *wouldn't* have gone on and I had to let him know that I was really serious about this. I wasn't asking for much – just thirty seconds of silence.'

My year in *Time* was a very happy period in my life. On stage I felt magnificent every night. We used to have fun with it, it was a frolic. Jeff Shankley played opposite me as the great Time Lord, while I was the innocent human trying to persuade the celestial judges to let the earth survive. He said to me, 'We don't have a world-shattering script, even though the songs are good, but it's interesting and if you and I can believe it when we're up there on stage, we'll be all right, it will work.' I found that so helpful – and I did believe it while I was up there. I was never bored, as everyone predicted I would be, and I never lost my enthusiasm for the show; it wasn't until it was all over that I realized just how exhausted I was.

I came away from *Time* with a strong desire to sleep – and a new recruit to my management team. Roger Bruce was Dave Clark's company manager; he had stood in as my dresser a few times and generally looked after me. We had a good rapport. He had been in the theatre all his life, had been company manager for Cameron Mackintosh for many years and worked on a number of his big musicals, but he was becoming disillusioned and had plans to disappear to Wales. When those plans fell through, Roger became my tour assistant, driver and security man – and a good friend. He's still a good friend.

Another one in the team with a theatre background was David Bryce, my tour manager, who was with me for nearly forty years until his retirement in 2002. He was Dickie Valentine's brother, and had been working for Leslie Grade when I was one of Leslie's clients; he looked after me when I

241

was at the Palladium. It was David Bryce whom I have to thank for introducing me to Weybridge, which is where I lived for most of those forty years. He and his wife, Jean, lived there, and many were the times we would go back to their place in preference to some glitzy showbiz party in London, and I'd lie on the floor watching films – he had underfloor heating. It was a home from home; I loved them both and I loved the area, so one day I asked Jean to find me a house. This was when I was living with Bill and Mamie, his mother, in Finchley. One Saturday morning Jean rang and said she had found me one – Feather Green, in St George's Hill. I drove down the next day and bought it; Bill and Mamie moved in with me. That was in 1973 – when 'Power To All My Friends' was in the charts – and it cost me £74,000. I sold it fourteen years later when I bought Charters.

When David Bryce retired he left a gap that was hard to fill. I have been incredibly lucky with the people who have worked for me. There are fewer of them these days, partly because I am less busy than I was at the height of my career and partly, sadly, because a number of people have died – it was as if we were hit by a plague of cancer – and that has been very painful. Nevertheless, we still have a very happy office at Claygate in Surrey and I regard all of the people who work for the Cliff Richard Organization as friends. There's Bill Latham, who still looks after my charity work, as well as all my media and promotional schedules; Gill Snow, my secretary, who's been with me for as long as Bill; Margaret Webb, my book-keeper; Tania Hogan, secretary to Malcolm Smith; and Malcolm himself, who after twenty-odd years is almost the newest recruit! He used to look after my account at Touche Ross, the big City accountancy firm, and left there to became director of the CRO in 1987. He is the money man, and whenever I want a new car or a new house, he's the one I have to get it past. When Peter Gormley was retiring in the early eighties, I said, 'Please don't attempt to replace yourself because I don't think I could cope with that.' I didn't want to have to build a new relationship again, or have to learn to trust all over again; so the others have been doing the job he did between them ever since. And when David Bryce retired, Bill and Malcolm were happy to take over his role between them.

Roger joined us in 1988, after *Time* closed, and with his theatrical pedigree introduced me to a lot of people from that world: people like Chris Ellison, who played DI Burnside in *The Bill* – they had worked together on *Oliver!* in the West End – and Gareth Armstrong, who played Sean Myerson in *The Archers*. I listen to *The Archers* avidly – I've even been known to cry over it – but I didn't realize who Gareth was until I heard him speak. Roger was the joker in our pack and great at laying on little surprises. Every year we used to have a big party at Charters, usually with a theme – we had a Viennese ball one year, and rock 'n' roll on my fiftieth birthday. We had quite a gang of friends in those days: there were neighbours from St George's Hill, my tennis friends – by this time my passion for tennis had already taken root – a few more from showbiz and a lot from the Church. One year, unbeknown to me, Roger had hidden an entire choir in the woods, and at the end of the evening we were all gathered round the pool when a rocket shot into the sky and fifty choristers – all in choirboy outfits – emerged from the woods singing the most beautiful hymns, before suddenly launching into an Elvis number. Roger had excelled himself.

Whenever we were touring Roger would find interesting people for us to meet after the show. He arranged a blind date for me once in Manchester with Liz Dawn, who played Vera Duckworth in *Coronation Street*. I am a big fan of *Corrie*, and once Roger even got me on to the show, which was a real triumph – they had a shot of me in the Rover's Return with my back to the camera. Without telling me, Roger sneaked Vera into the theatre so we could all go to dinner together, and told her to wait by the side of the stage while I did a bit of meeting and greeting after the show. Suddenly this brassy blonde came waltzing on to the stage singing 'The Hills Are Alive with the Sound of Music'. It was hilarious! Then we went off to a smart French restaurant with soft lights, packed with people, where she continued to be outrageous. Everyone stopped eating as we walked in and in ringing tones she said, 'Oooh, Cliff, I love a bit of breast of Duck, don't you?'

There are always people to meet and greet after shows – sometimes fans who are unwell or have some special request that they have sent to the office. Either Gill or Roger decides which of them I should meet, and Roger used to have some great ideas. There was a woman once who had lost her husband and children – I can't remember the circumstances – but she had won some prize in a magazine and was coming to see the show in Brighton. Roger's plan was that she should get into the lift and I would be hiding behind a huge bunch of flowers. When we all got out of the lift she said, 'Who's the gentleman with the flowers?' and I pulled them away from my face and presented them to her. She was so thrilled. On another occasion we were in Scotland and went to the home of a little girl who was in an iron lung. Roger knocked on the door and on entering said he was delivering some things that Cliff had asked him to give her. She was very pleased; then, just as Roger was shutting the door, I popped up in person and she was overjoyed. We went inside and chatted for half an hour or so. It was very touching; I am always surprised and rather humbled by the effect that something so simple – a word or a couple of moments of my time – seems to have on people.

Time was one dream come true, but nearly ten years later I realized an even greater ambition in *Heathcliff*. There is a press clipping in existence from the beginning of my career when a journalist asked me whether I would like to play a straight role as an actor and, if so, what it would be. Apparently I said, 'I'd like to play Heathcliff.' I don't remember that any more than I remember wanting to sing at the age of twelve and a half; but I was shown a letter that I wrote to a pen friend in Australia which said, 'Dear Gladys [I've changed the name to protect the innocent], my name is Harry Webb, I go to school at so and so, I am twelve and a half years old and my ambition is to be a famous singer.' So there it is; I obviously had articulated both ambitions – and I achieved both. Heathcliff was out of the question for many years, and unless I had made the opportunity myself it would have remained out of the question. No one would have taken a chance on giving me a part like that, particularly in my fifties. Even I had serious doubts at one point.

When the project became public, the press were vicious. They said, 'He can't do it, he shouldn't do it, he's too old, he's too pure, he's not passionate enough.' I woke up one night in Portugal and thought, What am I doing? Why don't I just phone everybody and say, 'It's not going to work'? But during the course of the day I started to get angry and think, How dare they? I haven't tried to do it yet, we don't even have a script, or any music – and I became utterly determined to go ahead. The press had a go at Tim Rice too. He wrote a fabulous rebuttal to *The Times* saying, 'How can I be criticised? How can you knock me like this when I haven't written a single word yet? I have merely agreed to do it.'

I had read *Wuthering Heights* at school. Jay Norris was responsible for that. I found the first couple of chapters of the novel tough going and was very tempted to skip bits, but I became immersed in the story. It was complicated, but I was drawn in to the various relationships, most of which ended up being destroyed by this one man. When I read the book again as an adult I found it even more compelling and began to fantasize about playing the part of Heathcliff in the stage version of the novel. I asked

247

Frank Dunlop to direct, and he said, 'We can't do the whole book; it's spread over two generations and the show would be too long; but you could do a musical study of Heathcliff on his own if you like.' I did like.

So that's what we did. We took him and the characters that touched his life and made a show. I think it worked, and what's more, although other people might argue, I think it is the best thing I've ever done. It was a combination of everything I love most. It was my sort of music and an opportunity to act – an area in which I always felt I had been slighted by the critics. My films were arguably not the best vehicle for me as an actor. They used to say I was a 'natural actor', by which they meant I was comfortable as myself, but real acting is more than that, as I discovered when I played James Callifer in *The Potting Shed by* Graham Greene at the Sadler's Wells Theatre in north London in the early seventies. What I discovered in that play and again with *Heathcliff* was that I was able to draw myself out of Cliff Richard and be someone else. The moment I went out on to that stage I stopped being Cliff – and it was the most exhilarating experience.

Some people say it's putting on the wig and the make-up. Sure, I enjoyed the wig and the make-up – and in fact I specially requested the wig, so I didn't have to worry, as I constantly do in my concerts, of my hair falling out of place. But for me the moment when I began to be the character was the moment the music began. I would go on stage and stand behind a door that used to open up, and the mist – dry ice – would start to swirl at my feet. Suddenly a solo guitar would bleed its first notes and that was it. I took on the persona. Every worry, every other thought went out of my head. I stormed out to the centre of the stage, and I *was* Heathcliff. And when I see myself on the DVD of the show, I still think to myself, I really can do it. I really did do it. It gives me enormous satisfaction – particularly since the critics had said I wouldn't, couldn't and shouldn't.

Out of the whole fifty years of my career, that show was the one achievement of which I am most proud and which I enjoyed most. I know it wasn't perfect, but there again, what is? I just loved it. It gave me a chance to be with other actors on stage and to be things that I could never be in my life. I would never smack my pregnant wife to the ground, I would never desire to find my brother and beat him to a pulp. But I enjoyed doing these things as Heathcliff. I enjoyed expending the emotional energy that goes into hating someone as much as he did. Heathcliff was a vile creature: he was in love with Cathy but couldn't have her, so he married her sister-in-law so that their child, when he grew up, could be destroyed by him in just the way he felt the world had destroyed him. Cathy herself, of course, died in childbirth but even that didn't change him. He wanted to destroy everything and everyone, but in the end he was thwarted by the children, his son and Cathy's daughter, falling in love with each other. The daughter finally turns to him and says, something like, 'I couldn't be you, it must be terrible to be you. Nobody loves you.' I used to love scrabbling over the side of the grave where Cathy was buried. Heathcliff had bribed the sexton of the church so that he, rather than her husband, would be buried next to her. 'Our bodies will mould and we'll be one,' he says. 'If anyone ever found us we'd be clenched together and no one would know which is which.' He was so obsessive – evilly obsessive – and that was what I found so interesting.

I remember coming off stage after the first night and saying to Roger Bruce, 'I feel as though I've had amnesia – I haven't thought Cliff Richard for one second in the last two hours.' I couldn't; I couldn't afford to let anything drop. *Time* had been different from anything I'd done before, but *Heathcliff* was different again: it was so overpowering, totally dominating in every way. Even when I turned my back to the audience, while singing 'I Do Not Love You Isabella', I couldn't drop the role for a second. I was completely immersed in the whole process. Originally I thought *Wuthering Heights* was a romantic novel – the romance of Heathcliff and Cathy running across the moor – and movies had only reinforced that; but when I reread it as an adult, I realized that, as Frank Dunlop pointed out, it was a very ugly story. There was not one redeeming character in it, with the exception of Cathy and Heathcliff's children. The interesting thing is, you can play the part of someone who is extraordinarily nasty and people believe it; but play the part of someone unbelievably good and people have difficulty accepting it's real.

My concentration was absolute while I was on stage, but the minute I came off I was out of it. My sister Jacqui used to come and see me with the kids and I had no problem with that. They came to my dressing room before the show too. The children would creep in and say, 'Uncle Cliff, give us the Heathcliff face,' and I would scowl at them and they would run out of the room, shrieking excitedly. But everyone had to go before I put on my wig; the wig was the cut-off point. Lord Olivier, whom I met once when he came to a performance of *Time*, said, 'Give me the costume and wig and I can be anything,' and he was right. Concerts are different. These days I do a whole series of voice exercises to warm up before I go on stage and I ask for half an hour alone beforehand so I can go through all the strange sounds I need to make. I don't even like my family being there. I find it difficult to go through the routine in front of people.

The press were as unkind to me after we opened *Heathcliff* as they had been before, but for once I didn't really care. I almost felt that I didn't need them any more. What I did need was an audience to come and appreciate what I'd done – and they did. No fewer than sixty of my fans camped out in freezing temperatures to buy tickets for the premiere, and when we finally opened at the Birmingham NIA Academy in October 1996, after quite a delay, we played to a full house. From then on, for six and a half months, we had full houses wherever we went – and we didn't play in small theatres, mainly in big arenas. The show had cost me £4.5 million to put on – I financed the project myself, I had no backers – and we broke even in four months. There have been plenty of musicals that have played for two years in the West End and still not broken even. So the last two and a half months were all profit; but I had such a fantastic time doing it, I would have been happy if I had done nothing more than get my money back. Nearly half a million people came to see the show and we had advance bookings of £8.5 million – more than there ever were for *Phantom of the Opera* or *Cats*. I even think it was a British theatre record.

So I feel I can hold my head up, and although I found what the critics said hurtful and puzzling, the audience didn't seem to pay much attention to them. Tim Rice, who wrote the lyrics, was comforting. 'It's just unfortunate that your career has been in pop music,' he said, 'because what you're doing here deserves to be recognized for what it is. You're an actor.' The rest of the cast said much the same: 'When we're on stage with you we regard you as one of us,' they said. But Tim was right, because repeatedly the critics had said, 'Oh, this is the guy that sings "Living Doll". He can't possibly be a credible Heathcliff.' But I was – so there!

I love breaking records. I love the fact that I've had a number one record in every decade and that no one has come near me in the number of sell-out concerts I've given at the Albert Hall. It's not often you get the opportunity to be first at something. Peter Gormley once said, 'Look, there's no money in this, but I tell you what, this is going to be great publicity and it would just do you good to do it. It'll be great for your career.' My trip to Russia in 1976, shortly after 'Devil Woman' was released in America, was one of those instances. I spent six weeks preparing for that tour and hardly made more than a brass farthing. When we arrived, I said to the band, 'We're all millionaires,' and they said, 'What do you mean?' I said, 'We've all got at least a million roubles each.' But you had to spend them there and there was precious little to spend them on, so we ate caviar daily. However, I was the first internationally known artist ever to go to Russia. Elton was the second and that was ten years later. We had a great concert tour and I was able to go home knowing that it would be in the history books. Peter encouraged me to do that, and had my father still been alive, I just know he would have been behind it too. He would have been saying, 'Yeah, don't worry about the money. Be the first one to go, it will be fantastic.'

That's the reason I play the Royal Albert Hall so much. I certainly don't go there for the money. The Albert Hall can never be a big money-spinner because debenture holders have so many of the seats; there are only two days of the week on which you can sell the whole house. So I can do little better than break even. But it's a great venue, a prestigious place, audiences love it – and I love being the record-holder for the number of concerts I've played there: thirty-two shows, all sell-outs. I would like to have finished off my fiftieth anniversary tour at the Albert Hall, doing a couple of shows there for charity maybe, but the set will be too big for the stage. Shame; maybe after the next fiftieth!

My shows are not cheap to put on. They

never have been, because when the fans come in I want them to be knocked out and to be curious about what's going to happen that night. They should be able to see instantly that it's going to be different and exciting. I want the lighting to be knock-out and I want to be wearing fabulous clothes; I want the sound to be mind-blowing. And all of that costs. It was in the mid-seventies when we really started splashing out. We'd spend a quarter of a million pounds before we'd even started rehearsing – and those shows were out of this world. We used lasers in a way they had not been used before – a way we discovered quite by accident. It's called a flat scan; they create a solid green slab. If you then pump smoke into it, it becomes even more solid. I started doing songs like 'Ocean Deep' standing in this slab of light, and then we discovered, again by accident, a way of producing a jagged effect, so it looked like waves. On one of our last nights one of the crew held a board up into the laser and it looked as though I was about to be attacked by a shark. Usually 'Ocean Deep' makes people cry; well, not that night!

I spend weeks with my team working on the stage effects before each tour – and we've come up with some interesting ideas for my fiftieth anniversary concerts, which I think will be very exciting. The problem is that if I leave out something that people have liked,

I'm in trouble. I always used to use mirror balls hanging above me for 'Miss You Nights'; then I went one further and hit the ball with laser lights; then, just for a change, I dropped the whole thing – and had furiously indignant letters from people wanting them back. I spend weeks and weeks deciding what songs to sing; that's almost the hardest part, and another bone of contention because everyone wants their favourites. Getting the right balance between old and new is not easy. Let's face it, I don't carry the words to all the songs I have recorded over fifty years in my head. Sometimes people mention the title of a song which I could swear I have never heard before and, lo and behold, I discover I have recorded it!

This is an exciting time for me and I find I am still looking ahead. I thought when I hit the age of forty my career would be coming to an end or at least slowing down. I thought that again at fifty and again at sixty, and now I am wondering whether seventy might be the moment to stop – to do one big, final concert, say, 'Thank you so much' to all the wonderful people who have supported me all these years, and bow out gracefully.

And yet... There's something about singing and having people want to listen that gives me such a buzz. Maybe when I'm eighty...

CHAPTER THIRTEEN

Tennis

Tennis is one of my greatest passions. I play everywhere I go, no matter what the temperature, and if I have one burning ambition left it is to have a game of tennis on my hundredth birthday. Well, two: and to die smiling.

But I was a late starter. At school, tennis was regarded as a girls' game, a sissy game, so I didn't grow up with it. I was in the rugby team and the football team. I didn't play cricket in those days either, for some reason, but the only people that I ever saw on the school tennis courts were girls. So it was never in my psyche. It wasn't until the early eighties, when I started dating Sue Barker – who had been ranked number three in the world: she had won the women's singles in the German and French Opens and reached the semi-finals at Wimbledon and the Australian Open – that I picked up a tennis racquet in earnest. She said, 'Come on, let's play some tennis.' I said, 'I can't play,' and after we'd played for a while, she said, 'You're right, you can't,

257

but keep going and you can only get better.'

We first met at the Brighton Conference Centre. The Shadows were playing in concert in Brighton at the same time as Sue was taking part in a tennis tournament there. Hank was very keen on tennis, so he made a point of meeting her and invited her to come to the show. He then rang me and said, if I was planning to come to the concert, I should come that night so that I could meet Sue Barker. So I went, we met, then all of us had dinner together after the show and we all thought she was great. Back in London I rang her and planned to meet up at David Lloyd's original tennis club, at Heston by Heathrow Airport. David became a good friend and I'm a life member of all his clubs; we quite often play together in Barbados, where I also play with Virginia Wade. Am I a name-dropper or what?

My tennis improved a little over the years but never enough to give Sue a run for her money. The funny thing was that, after having a hit with Sue, I would be in the men's room, showering, and the guys would ask, 'Did you beat her?'

I would say, 'Are you seriously asking me if I beat Sue Barker? The only time I even hit the ball is when I serve it.'

Sometimes on court she would say to me, 'Do you mind if we play flat out for a minute?' So I would run like mad, and not even touch the ball. She was a very hard-hitting player. Martina Navratilova and Chris Evert both said the one player they feared was Sue Barker. And yet Sue didn't beat them. David Lloyd told me that he couldn't beat Sue unless he played flat out. So Sue could give a man a run for his money, and yet she could never beat Chris or Martina.

Sue introduced me to Charles Haswell, who co-owned the club with David and is another fantastic tennis player. 'Look,' she said, 'I'm going away on tour but it you phone Charles he'll play with you any time you want to play.' So I did, and we are still playing together – it's been more than twenty-five years now – and in all these years I have only ever taken one set from him. One set! But I grew to love tennis and Sue said, 'The trick is to learn how to do it properly, or as well as you can'; so a lot of the time, particularly when I'm on tour, I choose to play with professionals. I will play for hours on end, often in the blazing heat of the day, and I am pleased to say it is quite often the pro who wants to pack up first. The reason I like playing with a professional is because he knows exactly what he's doing; so if you mis-hit the ball and it flies to the wrong side of the court, he'll be there, he'll get it back; and if you say you want to practise your backhand, every ball he hits will come back to you to within eight inches of the perfect spot for a backhand. Having started at over forty, I've obviously got no chance of getting the technique perfect, but Sue was adamant that I should try. She would ask who I liked to watch, and when I said Ivan Lendl she said, 'OK then: when you're doing a backhand, think what Lendl looks like when he's playing one.' I found that very helpful. I'm never going to be really great at tennis, but I get huge pleasure from it – and Sue was right, the more you practise the better you become.

To be a natural player you have to start when you're young. You watch one of the top players, his opponent strikes the ball and almost a millionth of a second after it's been struck, the receiver has his racquet in either the backhand or forehand position, because he's already seen where the ball is going to go and is running with the racket ready to strike the ball. The rest of us tend to watch the ball coming and at the last minute decide, 'Oooh, it's my backhand,' and then whip the racquet back and push it forward, but always late. My responses are never going to be that quick, but playing as much as I have over the years has helped. I'd say I was a good average player: better than some, worse than most.

I started thinking about this level of skill that really only comes from starting young and fostering natural ability from the beginning, and I asked Sue whether there were any pro-am or pro-celebrity tournaments in England. She said, "They do them a lot in America and occasionally here, but there's no reason why we couldn't start one.' I became rather excited and said, 'Why don't we try and raise money for potential stars? Everybody grumbles about the Lawn Tennis Association, saying, "Why have they never found a champion? They're doing it all wrong."' I was as guilty as the next man of this, so now I said, 'It's silly; let's put our money where our mouths are. Let's try and do something ourselves to raise the interest in tennis.'

We called the project the Cliff Richard Search For A Star; nine years later it morphed into the Cliff Richard Tennis Development Trust and came under the umbrella of the Cliff Richard Tennis Foundation. The idea was to send a team of experts around schools looking for talent, giving coaching and taking sports lessons; if they found a child who was outstanding, we would support that child – paying for their clothing, their coaching, their court fees and transportation to tournaments. We held our first pro-celebrity fund-raising event at the Brighton Centre in 1983. The first year we sold about half of the arena, so we had perhaps two thousand people; the very next year it was sold out. Audiences loved seeing

Virginia Wade and Sue Barker; they loved it when Elton John played or Jason Donovan, Bruce Forsyth, Brian Connelly or Des O'Connor. A whole load of stars came and supported me. Personally, I played some of the worst tennis I have ever played in my life at those tournaments because I'm not good enough to cope with having a comic on the other side of the net who has the audience in stitches of laughter while I'm trying to get my second serve in. It could take eight minutes from the first serve going into the net, and of course I double faulted. So I didn't enjoy that aspect of these evenings very much, but as fund-raisers they were very successful. In later years, when we had moved the tournament to a much larger arena – the NIA in Birmingham – we raised between £135,000 and £150,000 on one night alone and the audience had a wonderful time. And ironically, more people came to our tournament than to any of the other indoor tournaments in England.

After twenty years of this, I had had enough. It was the most tiring day of my year. I had to be at the venue from midday and was never home before 2 a.m. And in between I never, ever sat down until it was time to have a meal at the end: tennis apart, I was giving interviews, meeting people, meeting groups and winners of raffles: I ran myself ragged every year. So I wasn't sorry to call a halt: but in those twenty years we did introduce tennis to about half a million young people in Britain. That is a huge number; but we need to get through to even more. What we need is a bedrock of people playing tennis because, the minute you've got the whole nation playing, it is far easier to find the one person who will rise to the top of the pyramid. We've had Under-Ten champions but we've never been able to get them past that age. Once a kid gets to eleven or twelve, girlfriends and boyfriends come into the picture, or football or shopping. That's when you find the true champs: they are the ones that stick with it all the way through, like the Beckers and the Samprases, the Federers and the Nadals.

The LTA has now taken over the Cliff Richard Tennis Foundation and we have become part of their charitable wing. It is a great weight off my mind as we had lost our sponsors – something Sue reassured me was nothing to do with us, but was happening all over in the world of sport – which put a huge pressure on me. There were five people working for the Foundation, all dependent on me, and I knew I couldn't keep it going for longer than another three years without further funding; and then, like the cavalry, the LTA came along. It saved my bacon because those people working for the Foundation had been with me for years and had been wonderful; they had pulled out of everything else for the sake of the Foundation, and they were brilliant with the kids. They had such a wealth of experience, including working with disabled children. The only time I've ever been booed in my life was when I was serving to a girl in a wheelchair and accidentally aced her. These kids in their wheelchairs are incredible to watch. The only concession they get is they are allowed two bounces, which is a little disconcerting to say the least, but absolutely fair. The LTA is keen to encourage disabled children into tennis, so we know this work will continue.

If we are to get this bedrock of players from which future stars will emerge, the LTA must target eight-year-olds in schools. They are a captive audience and we need to grab their interest really early. The LTA already has coaches networked all over the country. The question is, are those coaches tough enough, strong enough and experienced enough? The kids who go to the Nick Bollettieri Tennis Academy in Florida, for instance, are coached by people who have been in finals themselves, who know what it's like to be match point down and still win the match. That is not the kind of thing you can pretend to have done. Our coaches are certainly good enough to teach eight-year-olds the technicalities of tennis, but it seems to me that only winners can teach children how to win.

Having said that, I have heard that Nadal is coached by someone who was never a professional player. There is always the exception!

Finding champions was what we originally set out to do, but it became very clear early on that we could do far more. We came to realize that going into schools and putting tennis racquets into children's hands can be helpful in all sorts of other ways. Sue Mappin, who runs the Foundation, started playing tennis at the age of six, played for England, played in all the Grand Slam events and at the end of her playing career moved to work for the LTA. She knows about tennis and the psychology of the game. She's a tough Yorkshirewoman, but once when I met her she was almost in tears. She said, 'I can't believe what we're experiencing. We are meeting kids whose only decent meal of the day is the one they have at school, and the only relationship they have is the one they have with the teacher. Some of them come from single parent situations, and, in some cases, the parents simply don't care.' She was so concerned for the children – and it was obvious to her that tennis could be used to change a child's outlook on life.

Years after we began, I was doing a publicity stunt for the Foundation at a tennis club in north-west London. I was playing with a young Asian who was aged about twenty-five, and I said, 'Make me look good, please, they're taking photographs; hit me balls that I can volley back.' Well, he gave me some great shots that I was able to whack back as though I really knew what I was doing, and afterwards he said, 'Before you go, I have to tell you, your Foundation saved my life.'

I said, 'Hold on, you're surely being slightly over-dramatic here.'

He said, 'No, I'm not. Some years ago I knew that people were selling drugs at the front gate to my school and my friends and I were getting closer to these people. Your Foundation came to the school and I suddenly discovered tennis and got hooked. Looking back, I dread to think where I would have ended up had that not happened. I'm married, I'm having my second child and I have a job as a tennis coach. Yes, your Foundation saved my life.'

I thought to myself, This is wonderful! I told Sue and she said, 'Well, remember it, and tell that story whenever you feel you can.' There have been other stories about people with asthma who have benefited – one girl in Scotland had it so acutely she could barely breathe but, for some strange reason, probably because she was using her lungs more in playing tennis, her asthma pretty well disappeared. She's not going to be a champion but it changed her life.

And so the Foundation has grown and grown. We came to the conclusion that our brief should be to endeavour to bring health, both mental and physical, to young people everywhere. Because tennis stays with you for ever.

When I was going out with Sue Barker we would play tennis at Wimbledon, and on the court next to us one day was a woman called Kitty Godfree. Sadly, she's no longer alive; at that time she was eighty-three years old and she had won Wimbledon twice, in 1924 and 1926. She was playing with three other people, two of them wearing splints, all of them strapped up to the knees, and I have never heard such laughter in my life. Sue and I had to stop. Sue said, 'Just take a look at this. That's Kitty Godfree. They can hardly move. They are drop-shotting the ball and making their opponents attempt to run, and the laughter is unbelievable.' I thought, That's exactly what tennis is: you can play it at your standard, until you drop. It doesn't matter if you are a mediocre player, so long as you have friends who are a similar standard; one of you will pop up as being the strongest in that group, but you'll always be able to have fun among yourselves.

That's what happened to me. I found friends who liked tennis and throughout the summer they used to come round to my home on a Saturday and we'd play doubles for about four hours. Then one day I said, 'Don't go, why don't we get a takeaway?' We all showered at my house, got a Chinese takeaway and went on playing tennis right through to the evening, and that became a habit. It's a very social thing, and our hope and prayer is that these kids we introduce to tennis will take it with them throughout their lives – and now that David Lloyd has built so many tennis courts around our country, that will be easier. When we first started the Foundation Sue Mappin said, 'There's no point taking tennis into a school if the nearest courts are ten miles away.' There were so few, but that has changed in the sixteen years we've been going. Here's to more clubs.

I don't think David Lloyd was too happy when the Foundation decided to link up with the LTA – he has had many disagreements with them and has always told them exactly what he thinks. Several of our group were against it, too, but there is new blood there, most importantly a new chief executive, Roger Draper, who is young and tough. He saw that we were doing what the LTA should have been doing long ago, so I am confident that our Foundation is in good hands. Besides, until the LTA came to the rescue, everything we had done was in danger of being lost, and now it isn't! Anyway, I hear that it's all going well and the team are happy in their new surroundings, so I'm very happy. They used to be crammed into my office in Claygate, but now they have plenty of space at the LTA premises. And I am still involved. We have an annual charity dinner at Hampton Court every year, which we will continue to organize. It doesn't raise as much as the tennis tournaments used to, but we still get over £100,000 and it's always a great evening. I have told the LTA that they can carry on using my name if it helps, and that if they give me a call any time they come up with a fund-raising idea, if I am able, I will join them. You bet I will.

I love playing tennis, and I also love watching tennis – as several million people know, thanks to rain famously stopping play at Wimbledon one year! It was not my idea to have a sing-along, and I have to say it was one of the more daring things I have ever done. I was talked into it by Jenny Gorringe, the wife of the Club Secretary. I agreed to be interviewed and, just before the interview was over, she asked me to sing something. I have a feeling that one day some people won't remember me for my fifty years in show business but simply as the bloke who foolhardily sang on Centre Court. Thank goodness I hit the right notes, because with no accompaniment, nothing is guaranteed. Singing aside, one of my greatest pleasures in recent years has been watching top-class tennis. There's something very theatrical and gladiatorial about the sport, and it's much easier to watch than twenty-two people running about on a football pitch. And, of course, I can honestly say that I played Centre Court!

I really enjoyed my time with Sue Barker. She is a wonderful girl with a good sense of humour and she's definitely no blonde bimbo. On the contrary, she is a really bright woman. A lot of sporting careers don't last; you begin professionally at eighteen and by thirty-something you're retired. She was among the top ten players in the world for eleven years – she started late in life, at eleven (most kids start at eight) – so she must have been playing for nearly twenty years. When she finally decided she'd had enough, she was offered a job in television. It was winter sports. I said, 'Sue, what are you doing? You don't know anything about winter sports.' She said, 'I've got books.' The next time I saw her she was using all the various technical terms for what they do on skis and ice skates. She'd read it up and knew exactly what she was supposed to look for and was able to make knowledgeable comments about the competitors' prowess on snow or ice. I thought, Sue, you are fantastic.

But while my love of tennis endured, my relationship with Sue shifted gear. I've given up being regretful, and the truth is I am just so happy with where I am right now, there's nothing to regret. There are things I might like to have done differently in the past – all sorts of things over the years – but if I had, I wouldn't have what I have now. We've all seen those movies about what happens if you change the past: it totally changes the future, and therefore the present, and I kind of believe in that. Things that at the time seem to be negative are really not because in the end, with hindsight, everything becomes clear and you realize you needed to live through those things. At the time you may have been hurt, upset or disappointed, but then you have to think, Look what's happened since. And on the whole, most people get over loss and even allow love to happen again, because love isn't strictly a one-off thing. It *can* be, and in fact, if you work at it, it can last you a lifetime; but if it has broken down, it doesn't mean that you've lost the capacity to love somebody else. Most of us just get on with living, get over the past, have a little moan and start smiling again. Sue and I have done that.

Not long afterwards when I heard that she'd met somebody, I felt happy for her. Lance is a really nice man, utterly charming. Now she and Lance are happily married and I'm so pleased to still be able to call her a friend.

I don't think marriage was for me. There

was a time, when I was really young and with the Shadows, when girls were throwing themselves at us. The Shads all got married and I thought, help, I'm the only one left. To be married was all I wanted. Then they were all having babies – my sisters too – and I just felt left out. Now I look back and think, Thank goodness I didn't chase it further. Feeling left out is not a good reason for marriage: remember, you're committing yourself to someone else for the rest of your life – giving them the right to know where you're going, what you're thinking, what you're feeling. So I know it wouldn't have been right for me. And though I hate to say it (and I know it happens for a lot of different reasons), so many of my friends who did marry in earlier days – Hank, Bruce, Jet, Peter Gormley, Olivia among them – have since been divorced. No one wants love to end; sometimes it just does.

I think I would have made a pretty good dad, though; but, having said that, I don't sit around worrying that there's no one to carry on my genes. I'm not the only one who had my parents' genes. I have sisters who have done the job for me – and in any case, there's no guarantee that any child of mine would have been a singer. If Jacqui's grandson Josh, who is so far the only one of my relations to show signs of being musical, turns out to be half as good as his grandma says he is, I can at least be beneficial to him in some way. I wouldn't tell everybody he's my great-nephew, but I could certainly encourage and give him some help. After all, I do have a few connections!

Show-business marriages are not easy, but I don't know that they are any more difficult than married life is for businessmen who are always travelling, or doctors, or over-stretched teachers who have to mark home-work every evening. I think all couples who work have to figure out how to find precious time together. The difficulty with show business is that it's not as simple as going to work in the morning and coming back in the evening. Sometimes you go on tour for three months and don't get back at all during that time. Had marriage come my way, I would have had to change my life completely. I would have had to ask my partner, 'Are you going to tour with me?' And what about children? Would they have gone too? That couldn't have happened. I would never have traipsed a kid around with me on tour. It wouldn't have been fair on anyone – especially the child. And so we would need to have set up some kind of complicated arrangement. As a single person, I have never had to worry about any of this.

As it is, I'm not answerable to anyone. I couldn't live the way I do if I were married – and if I were I'm sure I wouldn't want to; but

I love being a free agent. Hank Marvin thinks it's selfish, and I know what he means, but I disagree. It would only be selfish if I *had* a partner and only thought about myself. I'm not hurting anyone or leaving anyone behind. I have a life that suits a single man: I can be loving with people, I can have lots of friends, I can care for my family and I can go wherever I want, whenever I want. It's the lifestyle I have chosen and I love it.

CHAPTER FOURTEEN

The Year 2000

January 3, 2000 was a day I shall never forget. I woke up in my bed at Charters and I thought, 'I have nothing to do today;' and what's more, 'I have nothing to do for the rest of the year!' For the first time since the age of seventeen I didn't have to worry about my voice, my health, my weight, my wardrobe or whether my hair was sticking out at odd angles. Stretching out ahead of me was a year of total liberation, in which I could travel, explore, make new friends and be like everyone else. In some ways it was life-changing.

That year off taught me a lot about myself. I'd always told people that there was huge pressure in my business, but it wasn't until it was missing that I appreciated quite how great that pressure was. I had spent my whole life terrified that something was going to happen to my voice that would stop me singing; I would dread waking up with that terrible sensation of swallowing razor blades, and knowing that I'd picked up an infection. When it didn't happen I would thank God for that; but then wonder if it might happen tomorrow night? Even the slightest tickle and I would pray that I could get through the performance before it developed into anything more. It was the constant fear of making a fool of myself or, worse, of having to cancel a show. One hundred per cent of my working life I was worrying about whether my throat would stand up to the demands I placed on it. Our vocal cords are two little bits of gristle; they're not even muscles. You can make them work better but I don't think you can make them stronger and you cannot stop them getting infections, or becoming swollen. That was the main pressure. It was nothing to do with the business; it was, How do I keep singing – sometimes for six months at a time?

For the first time in all these years I was so relaxed I didn't care if I caught an infection. The fact is that when we tour in Britain, and Europe in general, it is usually winter, when people tend to have coughs and colds. If I am singing nightly to twelve thousand people, and two hundred of them have flu or coughs and colds, there's a very good chance that somebody in our forty-strong backstage touring group is going to pick it up. It's inevitable, because we're all trapped in the same building. If one of us gets a cough, two or three other members of the crew get coughs or bad colds too, and that's where I become so vulnerable.

I warned everyone in the office about two years in advance that I was planning to take a sabbatical and so they made no bookings for me until the year 2001. I had promised myself I would go to Australia and get a Winnebago and travel right across the country – but many times I woke up thinking, Shall I go to Australia? Nah, it's a long way, isn't it? So I never went. Instead I went to America. I went to California, L.A. and San Francisco, where I had never spent much time, and then to New York and Barbados, and I travelled alone. It was quite a scary prospect. Always before I had relied upon having someone with me to take care of things, to steer me in the right direction and to keep the fans at bay. But the dollar was still pretty strong against the pound at that time so there weren't many Brits travelling to America, and so I had the joy of being able to walk about the streets un-recognized. I was waved at in San Francisco by some Australians, but in Los Angeles I was completely anonymous.

Only once before had I taken off on my own – a couple of years earlier. I'd bought my own tickets, made my own hotel book-ngs, and told the office I'd let them know where I was travelling to next after I'd arrived there. Bill was the only one who knew what I was planning and he said, 'You know everybody in the office thinks you're going through the male menopause?' And I thought, Maybe I am. To this day I don't know; but what I do know is that I needed to prove to myself that I could do it. Gill said, 'Can we get you a car from the airport?' and I said, 'No, there will be taxis there. I've seen them, they all queue up, I just get in line and get in one and go to my hotel.'

In New York, I went to the tennis. In the mornings I wandered the streets looking for somewhere nice to have dinner that night; I'd book a table in the window, then when I went back later I'd take my newspaper or my book and sit and eat and watch the world go by and enjoyed the fact that nobody knew who I was. That's not to say I don't enjoy being recognized – in fact, if I walk into a restaurant in London and nobody recog-nizes me, I feel disappointed – but it does wear you down, and it was nice for a while to be incognito.

Anyway, back to the year 2000. I went to

stay with friends. I visited Olivia Newton-John, and John Farrar, who wrote the music for *Heathcliff*, and his wife Pat. I often stay with John and Pat. Before I took off, Pamela Devis, sadly now dead, who was a choreographer in some of the early Palladium shows I did, heard that I was going to New York and knew no one there and asked if I was taking my tennis racquets with me. I said, I take them everywhere, whereupon she and some of her friends gave me the name of a friend of theirs in New York who was also a keen tennis player. He was called John McElynn; they thought I would like him and told me I must look him up.

The first thing I did was phone a friend of mine who works for British Airways and say, 'Do me a favour – I have got to ring this guy. I don't know who he is and I don't know how this is going to go – could you book me a room in a hotel in New York so that I have an escape route?' He booked me into a little Irish hotel called the Fitzpatrick that my dear friend Gloria Hunniford had recommended, and, knowing I had somewhere to go if things didn't work out, I breathed a little more easily when I met John and his family. We played tennis together – John, his sister Janet and her husband Jack; they were very friendly and, as Americans do, immediately invited me to the family home for dinner. I needn't have worried. The evening turned out really well and we've all become very firm friends. I cancelled the hotel.

The joy about being with this family was that not one of them had the first idea who I was. Like my nephews and nieces, they seemed genuinely to like me, and not because I was famous. And that makes them very special to me. Of course I realise it's so much easier to like someone if you know when you meet them that they do something people admire, whether it's singing, dancing, acting or running the country. It has been so rare for me to find friends who I know like me for myself. I am not always the best judge of character; I am often too quick to think the best of people, only to realize later, sometimes painfully, that they were not as genuine as I thought. As a result, perhaps, I have been quite reticent about making new friends. The ones I made when I became a Christian, most of them Bill's friends originally, have been the ones with whom I have chosen to spend time, both at home and on holiday. I don't see them so much these days because I spend so much of my time abroad, but for decades they were the people with whom I felt happiest.

The McElynn family had never heard my name, and it wasn't until we met some friends of theirs at dinner at their club that they had any idea I was a singer. It was Memorial Day weekend in early summer, and there was a special dinner at the club for which they invited me to join them. Janet belonged to a book club and had been reading *The Mammy,* a novel by Brendan O'Carroll set in Dublin, in which the heroine, a widow living from hand to mouth with seven children, has a dream that one day she will dance with Cliff Richard – and her children arrange it. Janet had been convinced that 'Cliff Richard' was a fictitious character and was amazed to find herself sitting at dinner with the real thing. The ladies from the book club said they'd never met a real fantasy before!

I became friends with the whole family – and I was very touched the next year, when I was working again, that several of them came and saw me on stage at the Albert Hall. It was so flattering that they had come all that way to see me. Last year I spent Christmas with the family, and before that they gave me my first experience of Thanksgiving. As soon as I arrived, Janet said, 'What do you want to do? Brussels sprouts? Potatoes?'

'Brussels sprouts,' I said, and was handed the recipe for a maple syrup and mustard glaze. It was magic to be thrown into the kitchen like that and be given something to do with a group of people who treated me as though I were one of them.

John and I have over time struck up a close friendship. He was about forty-six when we met, and at that time he was a Roman Catholic priest, so we immediately had a lot to talk about. He belonged to a religious order that worked with the poor and had been a missionary in Panama, but was currently working among Hispanic immigrants on Long Island. I hadn't realized that priests in a religious order don't have much choice about where they work; that is decided by the order, which sends them to different parts of the world to take on projects of one sort or another. John had taken his vows at the age of twenty-two and, having worked among a variety of communities for more than twenty years, he had reached a watershed; he felt he was burning out a bit.

It seems that, whether you're a priest or a pop singer, you reach a certain point in your life when you need to step back and reflect and wonder about the future. John had reached that point. Soon after we met he took a sabbatical and travelled the world for a few months, visiting me on the way. He hadn't had any thought at the beginning about giving up the priesthood; but when it became clear he was thinking of the possibility, I suggested he might help me with some charitable projects, and he said he would.

That was seven years ago, and our arrangement has worked out really well. John now spends most of his time looking after my properties, which means I don't have to rely on management agencies or local people, and it takes a great weight off my mind. He is very good at it – in fact, I am amazed how good, because you wouldn't necessarily think a priest would be good at dealing with workmen and architects or even a vineyard – but he's very practical: as he points out, he used to run the churches in the various missions he lived in, and if the roof was falling in, he was the one who had to find someone to repair it. He has also become a companion, which is great because I don't particularly like living alone, even now; and, crucially, he knows how to work computers and send and pick up emails and handle all those technological things that seem to be so vital today and that I know so little about. Nearly all my communications with the office now go through him. And after twenty years of simple living, I don't think he's having too much difficulty adjusting to the odd glass of fine wine!

I have no interest in computers or the internet; I do have a mobile phone, but no one calls me on it because they know I rarely have it on. I take it if I'm driving alone in case I break down and need to call for help. I can't send text messages either – all that predictive stuff baffles me. I have an iPod, too, but I don't know how to use it. I can switch it on and off but I can't upload and download – that's all been done by friends' children, so there's some strange music on it and a lot of Christmas songs which through the summer months have been driving me mad. I know I'm being left behind and I'm sure I could find someone to teach me – but not when I'm in Barbados and not when I'm in Portugal. Maybe in England when the weather's horrible ... the truth is I can't summon up the interest. Email is a great invention and if I want to send one I can always phone Bill or Gill, or ask John to send one for me. I refuse to get bogged down by a computer – I'd rather be in the garden or playing tennis.

My days of sharing a house with Bill Latham had come to an end shortly before I took my year off, when he and his girlfriend at the time found a little house in Weybridge and moved out of Charters. We had been housemates, in one house or another, for about thirty years – and his mother, Mamie, had been with us too until she died in 1986. For me, losing Mamie was like losing a second mother. Over the years the arrangement had worked very well, but sharing the house with a couple would be different and was not something I wanted to do. And so I moved on in my life; I took my year off and had a slight re-evaluation.

Finding John was a blessing. I was not enjoying having the house to myself – and it's such a big house at that! I have no idea whether the arrangement between us will work for ever. There are obviously aspects of John's old life that he enjoyed and that he misses but for the moment he is un-encumbered and happy doing what he does. I trust him; he's a staunch friend and I think I could probably open my heart to him as I knew I could to Bill – although I am not sure I'm ready to have him hear my confession just yet!

I remember years ago, fans would write saying, 'You give us such pleasure, we'd love to see you happy, married and settled.'

And I would reply, 'I'm happy, I'm settled, I'm just not married. Two out of three isn't bad!'

People very often make the mistake of thinking that only marriage equals happiness. Now, of course, I may suddenly meet someone and feel differently; but right now I am not sure that marriage would enhance my happiness.

I proved in the year 2000 that I could manage on my own. I have done it, and I am pleased that I was able to do it, but I don't particularly want to do it again. I do prefer having someone around: if not John, then Bill or Roger, because I do feel a need to be sheltered – even travelling to America. It's not the same as it was a few years ago; the pound is strong against the dollar and I get recognized on every street corner and stopped by people all the time – not Americans, but Germans, Swedes, Japanese and Brits – in fact people from almost any other part of the world – and when that happens, I like someone with me to say 'We have to move on, Cliff.' I quite enjoy being recognized when I'm travelling, but I like being led through it. I feel vulnerable. In airports I try not to look at anybody – I know that if I make eye contact I will be stopped. That's fine once, but if I stop for one person then everyone seems to get in on the act. Airports are the most stressful places anyway; all I want to do is get through the darn thing and on to the plane as quickly as possible. Travelling by ship is far easier.

I always gave very good parties at Charters but for my sixtieth birthday I thought it would be fun to do something different; so chartered a ship called the *Seabourn Goddess 1* and cruised round the Mediterranean from Nice to Malaga with my family and friends aboard. They were a real mixture – showbiz, church and tennis. I didn't invite my sister Jacqui and her family because Jehovah's Witnesses don't celebrate either birthdays or Christmas. I didn't invite Hank Marvin for the same reason, but Bruce Welch and Brian Bennett came, and Olivia Newton-John, Gloria Hunniford, Tim Rice, Shirley Bassey, Bobby Davro, Mike Read,

John and Pat Farrar – almost everyone I cared about was there, although it was very hard to whittle the numbers down to eighty-odd from the list of about five hundred possibles. On the night of my birthday, 14 October, we had a big party in Monte Carlo.

The difference in faith within my family has made Christmas and other celebrations very difficult. Jacqui and Peter have been, I think, very wise. They take the attitude that they may not believe in Christmas or birthdays but they do believe in the sanctity of marriage, and so each year the whole family celebrates their wedding anniversary and they exchange gifts on that day as the rest of us do in December. I am sorry we don't have Thanksgiving in Britain. It is a wonderful celebration, because there is no pressure about presents and people of every persuasion, philosophy and religion get together and are thankful for having each other. I'd much rather have Thanksgiving than Halloween.

Years ago, when my sisters' children were all young, the entire family spent some time in Portugal. I booked three houses: one for my mother and me, so we had some escape from the ten kids, and a cottage each for my sisters. The nephews and nieces came running up to ours every morning but I said firmly, 'Not before ten,' and between eight and ten my mum and I had the most fantastic discussions over breakfast. We talked and talked – a lot of the time, many times, about religion. It was just fantastic. It was the closest I ever felt to her. At home it was rare to get her to sit down long enough to talk; she always seemed to be working, cooking for someone, phoning someone, busy and active. I think it was during that holiday that I said to her and to Jacqui and Peter, 'You must do what you feel is right about birthdays and Christmas, and I'll respect that. But I am going to do what I want to do too and I hope you will respect that too. When I celebrate Christmas I am celebrating the greatest gift that mankind has ever received. The gift I buy for the people I love is just a symbol of that gift that God gave us.' So I carry on buying them gifts, I just don't send them at Christmas or wrap them in Christmas paper. It has worked well over the years.

As for birthdays, I know it doesn't say anywhere in the Bible that Jesus celebrated his birthday; but the Bible is a book about spirituality, so why would they write about that? It doesn't say what Jesus ate for his breakfast either, but we can safely assume he ate something. There are loads of things it doesn't say because, in the overall picture, they're unimportant. Being born is important; why not celebrate the birth of somebody that you love? I may never win that argument with Jacqui and Peter, but again we've come to an understanding. We don't talk about it, but we accept each other's standpoint and nothing will stop us loving each other.

It was on my fiftieth birthday, which I celebrated with a big party at Charters, that I realized I didn't fear ageing. It was a 'Come As You Were' party, meaning dress the way you did in those early days – in the fifties – but everyone cheated and lied about their ages – and not just the ladies! The party began on the eve of my birthday; there was a band, we all sang and it was great; then, just before 12.00, the radio was put on, and at the stroke of midnight I switched it off and said, 'Look, nothing has changed!' Everyone had been saying what a milestone fifty was, as though it was something to fear. 'I fear nothing any more,' I declared, 'I don't even fear ageing.' But, of course, I am one of the lucky ones because I continue to enjoy good health, so it's easier for me to say I have no fear.

That year I treated myself to a Mercedes, and gave each of my sisters £50,000. Every now and again my accountant says I can give away money without being taxed on it, and that was one of those moments. I can't describe how wonderful it is to be able to do that – even though I've always felt I shouldn't give my family so much that they become reliant on me. I've never wanted to turn them into poor little rich girls who don't face life for themselves, and I'm glad to say that hasn't happened: throughout the family, those who can work all have jobs and therefore they have their independence. They haven't been spoilt; they are all normal, natural, fun-loving people and can actually manage without me.

And it's such a thrill for me when I do give them something. I remember the first time I ever did anything for the kids – all ten of my immediate nephews and nieces. I called them all together, they came to see me at the Wembley Arena, and after the show I said, 'OK, I've got a big surprise tonight. I'm going to give you all a gift.' They all looked round expectantly. I said, 'It's not wrapped. I am going to give you each ten thousand pounds – but here's the catch. Call me old-fashioned,' I said, 'but you can't have it until you're twenty-one.' Some of them were only ten or eleven at the time, so by the time they came into that money it was worth a lot more. There is just one still waiting to turn twenty-one, and his pot should be worth about £22,000 by now. I've been so tempted sometimes just to say, 'Go on, take it.' But I remember when the others received theirs they said, 'But this is more than £10,000.'

'Yep,' I said, 'but that's why I made you wait – to show you that if you look after your money it can grow.'

Jacqui has three girls and two boys and I

was a bit disappointed that Rachael, her youngest girl, was not interested in going to university. She is bright as well as good-looking and vivacious: she got eleven GCSEs, and she is the first one of us who could have been university fodder, but it wasn't to be. Instead she took herself off to Brazil, saying she'd be back when the money ran out. She will be all right, and, like my other nephews and nieces, she's personable, so she'll never be out of a job; but I've told Jacqui that if ever she changes her mind and wants to go to university, I will deal with the finances. And that goes for all the kids.

I have had the most miraculous life and I wouldn't change a thing, but I know I am undereducated. There are a lot of things I feel that I can't articulate as I'd like to, and I think that better and further education would have helped that. I was talking to someone in my office once and I actually made her cry. Lord knows I never meant to, but I was talking about my faith and couldn't find the words I needed. I said, 'What's wrong with me? I can't seem to speak English properly,' meaning I knew what I wanted to say but couldn't express it. She took it to mean, 'Why can't you under-stand me?' I guess that is always going to be a problem for me. My education stopped when I was sixteen and a half – in fact, if I'm honest, it actually stopped the moment I was keen to sing. I started missing out on home-work and school life, and from then on I was really just killing time until I could leave.

Since my fiftieth birthday my health has been monitored regularly. Since I reached that magic age my insurance company insists on having everything tested annually and it drives me crazy. Every time I go on tour I have to have my blood tested, my heart, my liver, my kidneys and my lungs – and so far they all seem to be in perfect condition, so I must have done something right. Of course I've been very lucky, too, but I know it's possible for cancer or something else to be lurking, and no one's immune to sickness. Every time I go to places with Tearfund where people are sick, paranoia kicks in and I get back to the hotel and think, Please don't let me die of anything horrible.

I was in Portugal once and I thought I was having a heart attack. It was actually kidney stones and I was hyperventilating. Bill was staying and I got out of bed and knocked on his door and asked him to call a doctor. My lips and fingers were all tingly and I was con-vinced I was going to die. Then I thought that if I did, at least the album I had coming out would be a smash hit. That was when I realized I wasn't afraid of dying. I don't fear death, I fear pain. I would like to die as my mother did, falling asleep and just not waking up. Birth and death are so natural,

I'm not quite sure why as humans we accept birth but remain so fearful of death. Is it because we believe there's nothing after life, or that there's something horrible awaiting us? I'm lucky, I guess. I know there's going to be something good after life – that's a great part of the Christian faith. Once you lose your fear of something, you feel liberated. The Bible says, 'Eye has not seen and ear has not heard of the glories that await mankind,' so I can only assume it's going to be beyond my imagination, this paradise, and there's the added comfort that I will see my parents again.

Donna had a far more serious health scare than I have ever had. About fifteen years ago – at much the same time as my mother was beginning to go downhill – Donna had a massive brain haemorrhage. She was found on the kitchen floor at her house in Hertfordshire having collapsed. Her husband, Terry, rushed her to hospital in Hampstead for emergency surgery; Jacqui, Joan and I all met him there, having raced across from various parts of the country. We were there for three days and were told she might not survive. We didn't know what to say to each other. When she opened her eyes for the first time after the operation, Donna looked up and said, 'Oh my goodness, it must be serious for you all to be here.' The relief was short-lived. Two weeks later she had a second massive bleed into the brain. It was Jacqui who spotted that something was seriously wrong; she had experienced so many crises with her son, Phil, during the first two years of his life. So she was the one who called for help. Donna went straight back into hospital and more surgery. It was a miracle she lived. The doctor treating her told us that she was the only person he knew who had come through two brain haemorrhages, and he warned us there was a strong possibility she might be left completely paralysed and possibly unable to speak again.

Thank heaven, this didn't happen, though she did have trouble with her speech initially. It was all jumbled up. She would say, 'Can I have one of those windmills?' when she meant 'chocolates', or use the word 'tap' when she meant 'hair'. She knew what she was saying was wrong but couldn't stop it. We laughed a lot – an antidote, I'm sure, to all the days of stress and uncertainty – and her speech eventually came right.

As far as my own health is concerned I don't feel any different today from how I did when I was eighteen – and I have more energy now than I had at that age. I always feel I must be a disappointment to Elizabeth, my doctor, because if I was ill I think she would enjoy curing me. She's always saying to me, 'Anything goes wrong, you've got to let me know. Are you eating the right things? Give me some blood. I'm going to check that you've got everything that your blood needs.' She loves it. 'You haven't got enough folic acid. I knew there was something!' So I get myself a pill, which is a multivitamin, and it says it includes 'folic acid'. It has thirty or so different vitamins but it is only providing, say, 25 per cent of the magnesium you need, so you take another pill that supplements that. And the next time I go for a test she says, 'Very good, your folic acid is perfect.'

She's concerned about me. She said, 'Look, you told me your father died of a heart condition. This is genetic. You could easily die of a heart condition. And your mother. She has dementia, it could easily run in the family.'

And I said, 'Stop a minute. Look. Test my cholesterol.'

She said, 'It's up a little, just a little bit.'

Three months later a specialist who had scanned my heart said, 'What were you concerned about?'

And I said, 'My cholesterol.'

He said, 'Here's the chart,' and pointed to a patch of white the size of a pin prick.

I said, 'I don't understand what it means.'

He said, 'It means that you are part of the three per cent of the nation that have as little cholesterol at your age as this. What I should do if I were you is think of something else that might kill you and work on that.'

The one thing I am still afraid of is spiders, which as a man I find a terrible thing to admit. I feel embarrassed about it sometimes, but I have this stupid phobia. If I go into my bathroom to have a bath, and look down to put the plug in and see a spider, the shock is such that I feel an electric jolt shoot through my body. I can't describe it any other way. My mother was even worse and so is Joan. She can't even see a money spider without screaming the place down. Those tiny little things don't bother me, but I can't handle anything bigger, and if I can't get it out of the window I have to kill it.

I had a couple of friends staying in the house in Barbados once, and the wife came out one morning and said, 'Darling, I'm not complaining, of course I'm not complaining, but there's a spider in my room, it's on the ceiling and it's quite large.' And so I came in and I looked and I thought, Blimey. It spanned about three inches; the body was bigger than a thumbnail. It was really big, and not hairy but coarse. I said, 'OK,' and I got the husband and I said, 'OK, this is the deal. I don't like spiders,' and he said, 'Well, I'm not crazy about them myself.' So I said, 'Well, I'm going to get the Hoover and I'm going to take the brush off so I've just got the nozzle. We'll get it plugged in and we'll switch it on. You're going to knock the thing off the ceiling with the broom and when it drops on to the bed I'm going to hoover it up.' Well, does it go according to plan? No. Having dropped off the ceiling, the spider shoots under the sheet, and I'm standing by with the nozzle, and the other guy's lifting up the sheet and the hoover is going for all it's worth but even when I get it over the spider it doesn't suck it up, the thing is clinging on to the sheet, but finally it disappears up the tube and it's gone. By this time we are both covered in sweat. It was ridiculous. I said to my Bajan housekeeper, 'Jasmin, there's a spider in that Hoover bag and I think you should get it out.' I think she thought I was mad, but she released it outside while I got myself a large gin and tonic!

Acquiring the house in Barbados was another part of the liberation of 2000 and completely unplanned. Charles Haswell, my tennis partner, asked me if I had ever thought of living in Barbados. I hadn't. A few years before I had gone there for a short holiday on my way back home after watching tennis in New York. I rented a little house called Bachelor Hall, which was managed by a woman some friends of mine knew. It was owned by the man who built some of the first hotels on the island, and it came with a butler, a laundress, a maid and a cook. After a couple of days I had to put the brakes on the cook. For breakfast, I said,

'I'll have a couple of poached eggs.' They were fantastic At eleven o'clock, I was lying in a deckchair reading, and the butler said, 'Cup of coffee, Sir?'

I said, 'Yes, I'd love a cup of coffee – and do you have a biscuit or something?'

'Yes,' he said, and a couple of biscuits arrived. Then he said, 'What would you like for lunch today, Sir? We've got fish…'

I was having six meals a day, and I had to say, 'It's nothing personal but I cannot keep eating like this, so I'm going to have a light breakfast and I'm going to skip lunch and then I'm going to have dinner here. And if I go out to eat, I'll have lunch here but I'll skip dinner.' But we kept the elevenses, the cup of coffee and biscuits. It was a great break, I loved it – I did nothing but read, drive around the island and put on weight; but it wasn't somewhere I thought I might want to live.

So I told Charles I had been there a couple of times and didn't think I was interested. 'I wouldn't want to live on the beach – it's full of tourists,' I said – thinking I'd be signing autographs all day. 'It's not for me.' What I didn't know was that David Lloyd had bought a big piece of land for development in Barbados; and Charles, of course, who had been in partnership with David when he was first building tennis centres, knew of the venture. He should have been working on commission from David, he was so persistent. 'Supposing I could find you something...' The next time I saw him he had photographs of a substantial plot of land hidden in the hills with the most stunning views of the sea. The next time I was passing – on a cruise with friends – I went and had a look. There were seven major plots for sale and the one Charles had shown me was the only one with mature trees already standing. There was instant privacy, and I realized it was just what I wanted. This was where I chose to build my house, Coral Sundown.

So in my year off, I flew to Barbados, booked into a hotel and met with the architect who was drawing up plans for the house. Every day he would come over and lay a huge sheet of paper on the table and we'd spend a creative time drawing pictures and talking through what I wanted. I couldn't be happier with the result. It is the most fabulous house, the most opulent of all my homes, with six bedrooms so there is room for family and friends to come and stay, a swimming pool and a tennis court. I have had such fun with the garden. I planted palm trees and ferns, flamboyants and poinsettias, bougainvillea, hibiscus, orchids, ylang-ylang and frangipani – all sorts of exotic and colourful plants and trees; and I searched for and found wonderful statues. There is a great gully, so rather than fill it in, I built a bridge across it leading to the front door. I have two oversized bronze Great Danes on either side of the driveway and a couple of elephants on one of the lawns. The climate is hot and humid, and everything grows so quickly that it's a constant battle to cut back and prevent the garden becoming a jungle. The first year I planted some dark green, big-leafed plants – the sort you grow in pots indoors in England and when I left they were below the level of the windowsill. When I came back the following year I couldn't see out of the window. But I'm a secateurs man; I enjoy cutting back though my gardener does the cleaning up. I enjoyed planning the garden, and, having spent so long working on stage, I made sure it was well lit!

I've discovered I really like Barbados. I love the heat and the pace of life and the sociability of it; I have made all sorts of new friends there, and got to know some old ones very much better. Cilia Black is one; she has a penthouse apartment right on the beach and is such good fun. Some friends I've made live there all year round, others have holiday houses and tend to be there between January and April. Some are from America, some from the UK and a few from elsewhere, and there are many people there whose wealth makes me look like a pauper. I'm sure you know the phrase 'how the other half lives': well, I thought I was the other half until I went to live in Barbados. I am not even nearly in the same league as some of my neighbours. But who cares? They are great people, everyone is very friendly and generous with their hospitality and we enjoy seeing each other. We play tennis – Virginia Wade, a friend from way back, comes and plays on my court when she's there – we swim, and we drink wine and party in each other's homes. It's very different from my life anywhere else now and from the rather low-key kind of life I've lived in the past, but I've discovered I love it – and I love knowing that I don't have to spend a cold, miserable, drizzly, grey, damp winter in England ever again. Those of you who have been there will know what I mean.

CHAPTER FIFTEEN

Princesses And Prime Ministers

I first met the Princess of Wales at 10 Downing Street when Margaret Thatcher was Prime Minister. It was an evening reception, something to do with African student exchanges, and I presume I was invited, as were other celebrities, to mix with the businessmen and make it a bit more exciting for the students. I was thrilled, because the princess and Mrs Thatcher were two women I had very much wanted to meet and I had never previously had the chance. It was a great coup to meet both in one night – and my perception of them both changed substantially on that one occasion.

Mrs Thatcher was busy with guests at one end of the room when a young waitress came in through the door at the other end carrying a full tray of prawn and mayonnaise canapés. The girl's foot caught on the rug and before she could save herself she was on the floor, mayonnaise and prawns everywhere. I happened to be standing right by her and was beginning to help her up when Mrs Thatcher came flying across the room and took over from me. 'Don't worry about a thing,' she said with a maternal arm around the girl's shoulders. 'Go back into the kitchen, calm yourself down and when you're ready, come back.' The Prime Minister then dropped on to her hands and knees and began retrieving the prawns and mayonnaise and putting them all back on to the tray. I thought, this is the Iron Lady? She was behaving just as my mother might have done.

I voted for Margaret Thatcher. For years I hadn't voted because at election time all the parties seemed to be saying much the same thing and I found myself agreeing with them all. But I liked her, and I thought she was one of the best and strongest leaders we've ever had. That evening at Number Ten I asked her whether she enjoyed Prime Minister's Questions. 'It's my favourite part of the job,' she said. 'I know they can't catch me out. I know the answer to every question they might throw at me. I love it.' I was impressed, and she went up in my estimation. I guess Tony Blair felt differently – he cut the number of times they held PMQs each week; still, I liked Tony too, and would have voted for him if he had been a presidential candidate – but we vote for a party in Britain, not a prime minister. The ballot box is a secret so I don't feel obliged to tell you who I might or might not vote for at the next election!

Originally, I suppose, I didn't vote Labour because my father never did; but as I grew older it was because Labour gave me the impression that they wanted to build a society in which people got something for nothing. Having been imbued with my parents' work ethic, and watched them struggle but succeed in improving their situation, I believe it is better to give people an incentive to work, pay them fairly and encourage them if they become successful – not clobber them with punitive tax when they do. I was paying exorbitant taxes in the sixties when Labour was in power – it was 83 per cent on earned income. If I invested the remaining 17 per cent, they took 98 per cent of the income on that. I don't think Labour are any better at handling taxation today. Some of their current taxes almost certainly damage the poor more than they damage those of us with money, which is strange given that Labour is supposed to be the party that looks after the less fortunate in society. Maybe there's a stratum that shouldn't be taxed at all.

John Major was another political leader I liked. He impressed me from the start, and I thought it so unfair when they dubbed him 'grey'. He was anything but! I met him once at Wimbledon; he sat down at our tea table and none of us spoke again. He told one wonderful story after another, and such funny jokes, we were laughing so much it hurt. I had met Norma Major first – she had contacted my office and said she would like to come to one of my concerts. So I gave her some tickets and we met up afterwards. Cherie did the same thing, which was how I first got to know the Blairs. John himself never made it to a show but Tony sneaked in once during the second half of a concert at the Albert Hall.

When Tony first stayed in my house in Barbados, I really did not know him that well. I'd seen him on television during the Iraq invasion, and I thought, This man is really struggling with his decision. He almost seemed to wither and get older as I watched; so I phoned Cherie, whom I had met a couple of times by then, and simply said, 'I'm not going to be there in August and if you'd like to use my house during that month, you'd be most welcome.' They accepted, and I was horrified when shortly afterwards the *Daily Mail* ran a story about the Blairs' holiday plans. They showed an aerial view of my beautiful house and I thought, Oh my goodness. This is a targeted man – one of the two most targeted men in the world – and the newspaper is saying, 'Hello, you want to bomb the British Prime Minister? This is the place to get him.' Of course I was concerned about Tony – but I was also just a little concerned about my house being dropped on! They have been back most years since. Tony says he has the best holidays ever in my house, he finds he can just switch off and relax. 'My favourite thing,' he said, 'is to sit up on the terrace outside the master bedroom, draw the curtain, switch on the fan and read.'

The same newspaper suggested that I had an ulterior motive: that I had invited him to my house to nobble him over the music copyright issue. I was incensed. I have never asked Tony for a single thing, not once, and I never would have dreamt of doing so. We didn't talk politics, which is a shame – I would like to have probed him further over what happened in Afghanistan and with Saddam Hussein in Iraq. The only hint he's ever given on the latter subject is that he felt he was in a no-win situation. If he *didn't* go into Iraq, and Saddam *did* have those weapons of mass destruction, he'd lose. If he *did* go in and they *didn't* have the weapons, he'd lose. They didn't have them: he lost! He's an interesting man and I like him – and I like Cherie too; they are very family-orientated. We've come to know each other better since they started using the house. I went to dinner at Number Ten and a couple of times to Chequers. My hope is that we don't lose contact and that we might one day become good friends.

I think the word 'friend' is over-used. Unless I am able to pick up the phone and say to somebody, 'Hi, do you want to come over and have a meal and go to a movie afterwards?' how can I regard that person as a friend? Olivia Newton-John is a friend. We have known each other for a long, long time. We worked together: she was in my backing vocal group in the early seventies and worked with me on my television series *It's Cliff Richard*, which is how it all began for her in England. Peter Gormley became her manager too; we recorded some great duets together. These days, whenever I am in Los Angeles, which is where she lives, I'll ring her, and if she's around we'll meet up; and she'll do the same. Unless I have that kind of easy, spontaneous relationship with a person, I am always reluctant to call them anything more than a good acquaintance.

The night I met Margaret Thatcher at Number Ten, Diana was also working the room. She came over to join me and a couple of African students with whom I was in conversation, introduced herself and we all began chatting. After a while one of her minders came across and whispered in her ear, 'You're needed across the room, Ma'am.' She said very quietly to him, 'I'll be over when I've finished talking to these students,' and then made a point, it seemed to me, of carrying on talking to these young Africans for a good five minutes or so before she excused herself and went to see whoever was so important on the other side of the room. She wasn't going to be rushed around; she was in control. I liked that.

The next time I met her was at Lech, in Austria, in 1992. I was on the first of many skiing holidays with Charles Haswell and a small group of chums including Mike Read, DJ extraordinaire. Diana was with Prince Charles and their children. Charles Haswell's wife was a really good skier, far better than him, and he wanted a few other people around him who skied at his level; so he asked me and the others to join him. I hadn't been on skis before, but after a couple of days on the nursery slopes the balance quickly came and for many years after that we had some very good times together. Lech was marvellous: a pretty little town with a river running through it, the surrounding mountains high enough that, even if there wasn't much snow around, you could still find enough to ski on at the top of the higher slopes.

That first year, my meeting with Diana was very brief. Rumours abounded that her marriage to the prince was in trouble, and they were always hiding from the paparazzi, the curtains in their suite permanently drawn. But by the time our holidays overlapped again, she and Prince Charles had separated and she was with the boys and a couple of girlfriends. I was with the usual gang. We only ever stayed for a week, and always on the final Friday night Mike and I would sit with our guitars in the little bar after dinner, as it was getting on for midnight, and strum and sing all the old songs together. We did it every year and it was good fun.

Diana heard about this little tradition and asked whether we would perform for William and Harry, who would then have been aged about ten and eight. We agreed it shouldn't be too late because they had to go to bed, so Diana suggested we do it at about eight o'clock, after the boys had had their meal and before we had ours. So Mike and I joined them in the empty bar and I sang all my hits. One of the boys started to yawn and I thought, Oh dear, poor kids. After one of the songs I stopped for a moment and Harry said, 'Do you know "Great Balls of Fire?"'

I said, 'Of course, but how on earth do you know it?' That song was way before his period, after all.

He said, 'Because Mummy likes it.' Diana must have played them Little Richard and some good old rock 'n' roll. So I sang it, and Harry was beside himself with excitement. He grabbed a Toblerone packet that was lying on the table and, using it as a microphone, gyrated like Michael Jackson while Mike and I did the number. William meanwhile sat back and just moved his arms a little. He was obviously aware, even at that stage, that he was going to be king one day and remained totally cool. If I ever meet him when he's king, I will remind him that my first royal command performance for him was at Lech when his mum asked me to sing for him and his brother. It was fun, and all the more enjoyable for knowing that the paparazzi were massed outside the hotel that night, blissfully unaware of the good time we were having inside.

Diana and I met again over dinner a few times at Charles Haswell's house in London. She astonished me once at the end of the meal by asking Charles whether he had any

Marigolds because she wanted to do the washing up. I was impressed that she even knew what Marigolds were – I didn't know what they were for years because there were no such things when I was doing the washing up at home, as a child. On another occasion she was distraught because she knew some story was about to break, which it did a couple of days later, and she felt so helpless. I knew the feeling well. She recognized she was in an impossible situation: she needed to use the media to promote her work, as we all do, but she was never sure of their agenda. She asked if it was the same for me, but I made it quite clear to her that what I have had to put up with over the years didn't come close to what she went through.

The last time I met her, she'd invited me to Kensington Palace and I had no idea why. Among the other guests were a couple of Indian businessmen and, after the most lovely lunch, one of them said, 'Look, what are we doing here?' – something I would never have dared say. Diana laughed and said, 'I want you to meet this gentleman here.' And sitting further up the table was a man who stood up and started talking about the Leprosy Mission. Funnily enough, I had been supportive of the Leprosy Mission years ago, but had lost touch with them. At the end of this man's long spiel, the Indian guy said, quite correctly, 'Well I guess you want money then?' I said, 'Well I'm not in the same league as these gentlemen,' whereupon the man from the Mission said, 'But maybe you could do a concert.' I said, 'I certainly could,' and then Diana said, '–and I could come.'

In the end I had to do it without her, because Diana was killed in the intervening months before we ever sat down to discuss the detail. But the following year I was booked to do some shows at the Albert Hall and decided to give the profits from one of the nights there to the Leprosy Mission. So we did do the concert and the Mission was very happy with the evening's proceeds. But I was sad to have missed the opportunity of working with Diana. She was a very hands-on type of person and I had been looking forward to planning what we could do together. Who knows, she might have presented something of her own that night; she might have come on stage and danced. We'll never know.

I heard about her death on the radio. I woke up on the Sunday morning and switched on Radio 4, as I always do. They were talking about the demise of somebody who was clearly important, but I lay there for quite a while before they actually mentioned the name Diana. It shook me rigid, because all of us – even celebrities – are struck by other people's celebrity. We're all affected by people who suddenly become so much larger than life, and we expect them to be immortal. It never crossed my mind that Diana would die in a road accident. I felt completely shocked. I was due to leave for America the next day to watch the US Tennis Championships, and it never occurred to me that I would be invited to the funeral, so I asked the office to send my condolences and left for New York as arranged. On the Wednesday Gill, my secretary, rang me and said, 'You have been invited. They found your name on Diana's Christmas card list and thought you should be there.' Yes, I thought, I should.

That was in the days of Concorde, which took less than half the time of normal aeroplanes to cross the Atlantic. I said, 'I need to be in London on Friday night and back here again in New York on Sunday morning,' and it was doable. I took a limousine to the airport and I asked the gentleman driving me whether he would pick me up when I arrived back on Sunday. He said, 'You're coming back on Sunday? Can I ask where you are going?'

I said, 'Well, I have been invited to Princess Diana's funeral.'

And he said, 'My God!' and he started to cry. 'You knew Diana and you're going to her funeral? That is so wonderful. Of course I'll be here to pick you up.'

At the tennis that week I had been a guest

of the United States Tennis Association, and as people were introduced to me they said, 'Cliff Richard? Are you from England? Oh, I'm so very sorry.'

At first I said, 'Why are you sorry?' I panicked; I thought they must know something about my family that I hadn't been told yet.

And they said, 'Well, Diana died.'

Then I understood. People over there were overwhelmed by her death and all week I was being consoled by them. It's no wonder the limo driver fell apart.

That Friday night in London was unforgettable. There were thousands of people all round Parliament Square and Buckingham Palace, the Mall – everywhere Bill drove me – thousands and thousands of people but no noise. All these people, yet absolute silence. It was eerie. I stayed in a hotel very close to Westminster Abbey, and the next morning went there in plenty of time before the start of the service and took my seat with everyone else. I was amazed at how emotional everybody was, myself included. I was sucked into it, at times tearful; and when Elton started singing 'Candle in the Wind'... How he got through it I shall never know. I was standing opposite Brian May and we were both blubbing like children. Everywhere I looked people were crying.

I have good memories of Diana. Gone are

312

the days when I used to think people might be perfect. No one is perfect, and we all have to learn to live within the limits of our imperfections. She impressed me and I liked knowing her, and sometimes she was positively saint-like – but I often catch myself thinking that a real saint died that week in 1997, and in the emotional outpouring over Diana, Mother Teresa's death was almost entirely overlooked.

I met Mother Teresa just once. George Hoffman and Bill and I went to Calcutta in 1976 to interview her for Tearfund about her work with the destitute and the dying. It was a phenomenal experience for us to meet such an icon. I remember we were all very amused when we arrived at the door to her hospice, which was down a tiny alley, to find one of those old-fashioned name boards with a piece of wood which you slide from left to right to indicate whether someone is In or Out. There were a whole lot of names but among them we found 'Mother Teresa'. 'She's in!' we exclaimed with one voice. She was then in her seventies, a frail, hunched little figure, dressed in the familiar white nun's habit with the blue edging that pertained to the Missionaries of Charity. This was the order she founded in the fifties when she gave her life to caring for the poor. She was awe-inspiring but also delightful. She introduced us to some of her fellow nuns – all dressed as she was – and showed us round; she showed us the holy area where they prayed, and the area where the people came in off the streets, many of them on stretchers. She was hugging the patients as we passed them, saying, 'These are sweet people and when they die they will know that we have loved them.' That was her premise, that no one should die alone and unloved; everyone should die with dignity.

After the tour of the hospice, I interviewed her, and then – I had my guitar as usual – we all sang and then we prayed together. In the car on the way back to our hotel at the end of the day, someone said, 'Let's listen to the tape.' So we put the tape into the machine, pressed 'play' – and nothing happened. We turned it over; nothing. We tried every inch of it: there wasn't a single syllable to be heard. As soon as we got back to the hotel I rang Mother Teresa and said, 'I'm so sorry to have to ask you this but would it be possible for us to come back?'

'Why,' she said, 'what happened?'

I said, 'There's nothing on the tape.'

Her reply was simple: 'OK, something you said or I said must have displeased Jesus. He wiped the tape. You'd better come back. We'll do it all again.' Mother Teresa could not have been more gracious and I thought, No matter how much we make people icons, a part of them has to remain real, and she was one hundred per cent real.

I came away thinking, Why do we complicate our faith? Why do we have to intellectualize everything? Sometimes the intellect clouds the issue. For Mother Teresa, it was simple: One of us said something that Jesus didn't like, so come back and we'll put it right. Second time around, the recording was perfect, and it was the same tape. I would have said it was the same interview too, but maybe not.

She was a most humbling and inspirational woman, and it is still a source of amazement to me that her death should have passed with so little ceremony. This was a woman who had set up 610 missions in 123 countries; she had won a host of prizes and awards, including the Nobel Peace Prize, and was posthumously beatified by Pope John Paul II. I suppose the difference is that she had reached the end of her allotted span; Diana was young and beautiful and her life had been brutally cut short.

Another life brutally cut short was Jill Dando's. Like everyone else I found it totally shocking, but I knew Jill much better than I knew Diana – she was a very good friend – so my loss was great. We had met in Vienna in the nineties. She was presenting *The Holiday Programme* and the producer had contacted the office to ask whether I would go and be Jill's surprise partner at the Viennese Ball they were filming. She apparently had had quite a crush on me as a teenager and thought she was awaiting an Austrian prince. As she was talking to camera, saying, 'I am told my prince is on his way,' I appeared in tails, white tie and gloves and swept her on to the dance floor. Her shock and surprise had to be seen to be believed. It was a magical moment of television and a huge thrill for me.

We became good friends after that. She too was a Christian and she got on well with all my friends; everyone adored her. We all loved Alan Farthing too, the gynaecologist who became her fiancé, and were very excited about their forthcoming wedding. My gardener was over the moon because Jill had asked him whether he would drive her to the church. I had said she could use my Bentley.

The day she was murdered I was on tour. Several people had called Roger on his mobile to give him the news, but we were on an aeroplane and it wasn't until we arrived in Copenhagen that he switched his phone back on and picked up the messages. Soon after we checked into our hotel, with a packed show looming over us in the evening, he came into my room and said he had something to tell me. I couldn't believe it any more than he could. Somehow I managed to get through the show on autopilot and afterwards we went out for a meal and I rang Alan Farthing on my mobile phone. The office had arranged with him that we might speak. It was one of the most difficult calls I have ever had to make. We had all talked about the wedding at such length. They were going to be married in the church on the north side of Putney Bridge and had talked of having the reception in a marquee in my garden at Charters. It wasn't to be.

Instead, on the night of what would have been their wedding, I invited Alan to come to Charters for dinner with his choice of friends. He invited a fellow gynaecologist, an anaesthetist and his wife, and some of our joint showbiz friends, and it was a lovely evening. And over coffee after dinner, at Alan's request, Roger played the sonatina that he had written and planned as a wedding present to him and Jill.

Jill's funeral was in Weston-Super-Mare, where she had grown up, and all the people who were to have been invited to the wedding were invited to the funeral. A big group of us travelled together, including Gloria Hunniford and her husband, Stephen Way and some friends from British Airways who also knew Jill well. On the way back we stopped at a restaurant in Hungerford and sat round an enormous table, like King Arthur and his knights, and Gloria suggested we took it in turn to tell stories about

Jill. It was a good way to finish off the day.

One of the stories was about the night that twelve of us – most of whom were sitting round that table in Hungerford – were having dinner at the home of a neighbour in Weybridge called Robin Williams. He was the gang leader of the BA crowd. His house was immaculate, and among his ornaments was a set of fabulous terracotta warriors. While Robin was out of the room Jill was rocking on her chair when she fell back and decapitated six of these men. She and Gloria collapsed with laughter, and then wondered if Robin would freak. When he came back into the room and asked what was going on, we all exploded. He didn't freak at all. What we didn't know was that he had bought the figures for two a penny in Saigon on one of his trips and was completely unconcerned.

Jill had agreed to open a hotel at Heathrow for an Indian businessman called Surinder Arora, and after her death a mutual friend suggested I might be a willing substitute. As soon as I heard I was standing in for Jill, I was only too happy to help and duly officiated. One afternoon not long afterwards, I was playing tennis at Charters when Surinder turned up unannounced. He didn't want anything; he said he was just calling by to say 'Hello'. I liked that, so I gave him some tea and off he went. Then an invitation for dinner arrived, after which I invited him back to dinner with me, and we soon became good friends. He has a sweet family, two girls and a boy, and Sunita, his wife, is wonderful. He has a very interesting life story. For whatever reason, his mother gave him away to her sister soon after he was born and he spent the first years of his life in India believing his aunt and uncle were his parents. His real mother had moved to England and she reclaimed him when he arrived as a twelve year old to live in Hounslow, where she and his real father had been in the intervening years. He began work as an office junior at British Airways, and he is now a very wealthy self-made man. The hotel I opened at Heathrow was his first; now he is chairman of a multi-million-pound business, the biggest family-run independent hotel chain in Britain – Arora International – and owns a chunk of Wentworth too.

As our friendship grew, Surinder kept saying to me, 'Why don't you come in with me? I like sharing my success.' The more he talked about it, the more appealing it sounded. He was thinking of a hotel in Barbados, which sounded perfect, and asked John McElynn to look at some properties for him. John and I went together and saw some lovely places, but John pointed out to him that staffing would be a problem in Barbados. Next thing, Surinder was saying, 'What about Manchester?' I said, 'Manchester, from Barbados? It's a big difference.' and he said, 'Well this hotel has come up and it's a good deal, a good price, I'm convinced I can make it work, and I guarantee I'll double your investment in a couple of years.' He was right, my input has doubled and I didn't have to do any work. I have never made that sort of money without having to work really hard, and I rather enjoyed it. Maybe I'll get the chance to do it again sometime.

CHAPTER SIXTEEN

Bolt Holes In The Sun

My love affair with Portugal began in 1961. I had no thought of buying a property in that part of the world, any more than I had planned to buy in Barbados. I had never been to Portugal and had no interest in going. The man who talked me into it was Peter Gormley – and the person who talked him into it was Muriel Young, the television presenter, who was once a disc jockey on Radio Luxembourg. She had bought a house on the Algarve coast and told Peter he must go and look. So he went for a holiday in 1960 and was so besotted with the place that he bought six houses above what was then a sleepy little fishing village called Albufeira. The first I knew of it was when I had a message telling me that he had bought a house on my behalf. He had bought one for me, one for Bruce Welch, one for Frank Ifield, one for himself and two for Leslie Grade. I said, 'What do you mean you bought me a house?' and he said, 'I just think it's a fantastic investment. You can sell it if you don't like it.'

The houses were three tall semi-detached buildings in a row, all facing the sea. Mine was on one end with Frank Ifield's next door, Bruce's and Peter's were at the far end and Leslie's were between us. Muriel's house was to the east of the village, and ours were to the west. I didn't rush down there straight away – in fact, I didn't go for a year. I didn't think I would like Portugal; but when I finally made the journey, I discovered a little piece of paradise. The journey was a killer, though. There was no airport in the Algarve at that time, so we had to fly to Lisbon and take a taxi down to the south. It was nearly 300 kilometres and with no motorways it was a long, hot drive. Whenever I went there afterwards with my family – in a convoy of taxis – we always knew when we were getting close because in the distance we could see a huge black figure in a hat and cloak – the famous Sandeman Dom port advertisement – silhouetted against the sky. The tiny road ran beneath it, and we always used to get the cars to stop at that point on the brow of the hill and look down on the little village snuggled at the bottom of the hillside, with a light twinkling on the church in its midst.

Today Albufeira is vast. It has a population of over 35,000 and is one of the most popular tourist destinations in Europe; but at that time there was no one there at all. There was a tiny market square with stalls selling fruit and vegetables, beneath the shade of the trees, where you could buy a melon for three old pence. It was nothing. What's more, you could buy Mateus Rose for seven shillings and sixpence –and they gave you four shillings back on the empty bottle. So it was about 20p a bottle. We got into the habit of drinking quite a bit of it while we were there.

At night everyone went to the Boite Sete Maia (Club Seven and Half) the one and only nightclub, where they played *fado* music. There were no discos in those days, but we still danced, and then somebody would come out on to the stage and the locals would sing *fado* songs, their version of the blues. We would stay until about four in the morning, then go down to the beach and wait for the fishermen to start coming in with their night's catch. We'd help them pull their multicoloured boats out of the sea. It was heavenly; but the trouble with paradise is that you can't keep it to yourself. The minute people started reading or hearing about it – and I confess I am partly responsible, because I talked about Portugal all the time – it was over. The tourists began to invade. It was good for the Algarve, but it sent me back into hiding. My name lives on, however. They named the street where I'd lived after me. It's called Rua da Sir Cliff Richard, and in brackets 'Cantor', which means 'singer'. A great honour.

Those days in Albufeira were so special. It was like being in the Third World but with mod cons. Yes, we had electricity and water, but almost daily there would be a water cut. So every morning, after we'd showered, we would fill the bath with water and fill every pan, kettle and jug for cooking purposes, because you knew when you came back from the beach there wasn't going to be any. So if you were going to bath or shower, there was no alternative but to save your water earlier. All that's gone, of course, but the disappointment for me is that the old fish market, next to where we helped pull out the boats, has also gone. The fish is now sold elsewhere, as are the fruit and vegetables. The old market is now a very nice square where they have light entertainment and pretty little lanes are filled with arts and crafts stalls and meandering foreigners.

The problem for me is that a huge number

of these meanderers are British. I have nothing against the British – far from it – but when I go on holiday the one thing I try to do is get away from being recognized. If I am recognized then people want to take photographs, they want autographs, and when I'm with friends or family, trying to relax, I just don't need that. I do so much of it for the rest of the year, and I have done so much of it for so many years, that I really try to withdraw and recharge while on holiday. If anyone barges in while I am deep in conversation and expects me to drop everything and sign a menu or smile for a photograph, I do it – but I grit my teeth.

So, in the early seventies, I sold my house in Albufeira. I was very lucky to sell when I did – Portugal was on the verge of a communist uprising – but a local woman came along with carrier bags full of cash and paid me £24,000 for it. She then proceeded to put a refrigerator, a stove, a bed and a couple of couches in the garage, moved in there and rented out the house. Very enterprising, and I am sure she made a fortune.

With no house, I began to holiday elsewhere. I went to America and Israel and a few other places, but I always gravitated back to Portugal and rented. By this time Peter Gormley and his fiancée, Jean, had parted. Peter fell for a dancer in one of my pantomimes called Audrey Bayley, whom he later married. He gave Jean his house in Portugal, where she lived full-time, and he made sure she never wanted for anything. I think he must have carried great guilt about leaving her because he was always saying to us all, 'Please don't forget to visit Jean,' and he went himself quite regularly. Jean was lovely and had always looked after my house for me when I was away. It must have been in the early eighties when I rang her and asked if she knew of anywhere I might rent for a couple of weeks. Going back made me realize how much I missed having somewhere of my own, and when I mentioned this to Jean she said she knew of a four-bedroom property for sale on the clifftop in Ses Marias a couple of miles along the coast from Albufeira.

It was 200 metres from the sea, across a field, with room for a smallish garden on the seaward side and a tennis court on the other side. I loved it the moment I saw it, and would still be there today had it not been for a Swiss German couple who ran a very good restaurant nearby, where I became a regular. I would often go to Portugal on my own, which I quite enjoyed, and one evening I was sitting in their restaurant when the proprietor, with whom I had become friendly, came across and joined me. He asked if I was selling my house.

I said, 'No.'

He said, 'Well, would you be interested in seeing another house?'

He proceeded to pull out a black and white photocopied picture of an old farm-house. It looked fantastic, so I said, 'Look, I am not selling my house but I'd love to see this one.'

The next day he drove me round to see the Quinta do Moinho and I completely fell in love with it. 'Yes, I'm going to sell my house' I told him. The Quinta was beautiful, very quiet and completely isolated, sitting in thirty acres of farmland. It is said to be 350 years old but I've always been conservative, so it may be merely 250 or 300 years. As the crow flies it's four or five miles from the sea and I can see it from my kitchen terrace. It's a typical Portuguese farmhouse – 'quinta' means 'farm' – whitewashed stone with yellow and blue doors and shutters, and from the terrace it looks rather like a small street of town houses. The ground falls away and steps lead down to another part of the house that's twenty feet below. Architec-turally it's curious but utterly glorious. I phoned Malcolm Smith, my business manager. 'I think I could probably sell the other one, and this one,' I lied, 'just needs a lick of paint and it will be ready to go.'

I paid less than a million pounds for the house, but that 'lick of paint' cost another three-quarters of a million – I had to gut the whole thing to make it habitable. The wiring was completely gone. The plumbing was routed down the back of the chimney stack, so if I had lit any fires, the pipes would have melted and we would have been afloat. Electrical wires ran just beneath the tiles or just over the top of the curtains. It was just ancient and uncared for; but I did it all up and restored it exactly as it had been originally, even down to the tiles on the floor. It's big; there are seven bedrooms, each one with either a double bed or twin beds, so fourteen people can sleep in the main house, and I've built extra accommodation next to the garage – a two-bedroom cottage with fabulous arched windows that look straight down the field to a windmill ('Moinho') in the distance.

I built the cottage so that I could let family and friends holiday there without needing to use the farmhouse itself. I was finding that if I had a sudden whim to go to Portugal, sometimes I couldn't because other people would be in the house. Now I say to some of my friends, 'Please feel free; use the flat, you can have the whole run of the farm, the tennis court, the swimming pool, but I am going to keep the house for myself so I can drop in whenever I want to.'

It's all beautiful, but for me the magic is the fantastic feeling of peace that comes over me when I'm there. Partly it's the design: the different levels, the sunken bit of garden, the pool invisible from everywhere and the neat rows of vines that encircle the house. Sixteen acres are under vines; then there is a field that must be a couple of acres, which Carlos, my gardener, keeps mown, where I have palm trees growing, along with apricots and a couple of avocados. The tennis court is tucked out of sight, surrounded by rockery and trees, with a tiny woodland above it which sweeps down towards another garden, full of beautiful flowers and plants, and a lawn that stretches into three areas, and a kitchen garden too. When I go there in January nowadays, I have oranges from four or five trees, likewise lemons and grapefruit, then later in the year apricots and peaches; and I've now asked the farmer to grow two types of melon for me, as well as tomatoes and onions.

Carlos is a gardener-cum-handyman and general factotum. He used to be married to a Newcastle girl so he speaks English with a Geordie accent, and I would be lost without him. He lives in a little two-bedroom cottage that I built for him and his wife and daughter in the hope that if they were happy he would stay. Finding reliable labour was a huge problem when I first bought the farm in 1992 and having found Carlos I didn't want to lose him. He did stay, though the marriage broke up so now he's in the cottage on his own. There's a lot of garden work for him to do, but he has sorted out a friend to help him, and I think he's happy with the set-up. If something goes wrong with the electrics I say, 'Carlos, what can I do?' And he'll say, 'Let me have a look at it,' and if he thinks it is beyond him, he will have the phone number of someone who can come and do it. Half an hour later somebody's there and the problem's fixed. A situation that would otherwise be so stressful is sorted in no time.

There was a story in the *Mail on Sunday* two or three years ago, saying that my staff in Portugal were in revolt because I had sacked Michael, my estate manager, and that my brother-in-law who had been put in charge was throwing his weight around. Michael was actually a real-estate agent, who looked after the Quinta on my behalf; my contract with him had run out, and he resigned. Relations hadn't been too good between us, it's true – it may have been something I said – but I paid him for an extra six months, so I didn't feel he had any reason to resent me. I don't think we parted with any acrimony; and since Joan and David had bought a house nearby and were moving out to Portugal, I asked David whether he would consider taking over. He was delighted to. As for my staff – that's Carlos and Maria, my housekeeper – they were mortified by the article and were definitely not in revolt. So once more I am left asking, Why do the press do this?

Barbados is incredibly social; Portugal the complete antithesis. I scarcely know any of my immediate neighbours (though Bill has just bought a house not far from mine, and Malcolm Smith also has a home there), and since I take someone to cook for me, I never have to leave the house. Guests, of course, want to see something of Portugal, so I very often take them into the little village of Guia which is famous for its chicken. The locals claim Guia is where piri-piri sauce was created, with which they baste the chicken as they grill it. They only use free range birds, and they serve the dish with chips and a fantastic tomato and onion salad. It's so basic but so delicious. You drink fairly cheap green wines and it's hard to spend more than £10 on a meal. Everyone who comes to stay says, 'What about chicken piri-piri? We've got to go and have it,' and I think, Here we go again – but as long as I don't have to do it more than once a week I can cope.

My housekeeper comes to clean the house every day. She used to have four jobs but she wanted to cut down to one and gave me first refusal. Maria's seventy-two this year and works like a Trojan, but she doesn't cook; and so I take Shamu, who works for Surinder Arora, to do the cooking and the pair of them get on like a house on fire. I don't know how. She doesn't speak a word of English and he doesn't speak a word of Portuguese, yet they rabbit away when they are working, and seem to love each other.

One person I did always go and visit on my trips to the Quinta was Peter Gormley's former fiancée Jean. She was Australian and highly independent; we had good times together, but she always resisted invitations to come and stay with me in England. A few years ago I knocked on her door as usual and heard a shuffling sound from the other side. I knocked again and the shuffling continued. Eventually the door opened and there she was, frighteningly thin and shrivelled. She could barely breathe. She said feebly, 'I'm not really very well.'

I helped her back to bed and said, 'Jean, I gave you a ticket and I said you could use it any time you liked and you never have. Now's the time. When I go home you have to come with me.'

She was so weak she couldn't even argue. So two weeks later when I went home I picked her up; she could barely walk. From Heathrow I took her home, where I installed her in my one of my spare bedrooms and instantly called Elizabeth, my doctor. She came round right away, examined Jean and said, 'You can't keep her here.'

I said, 'What do you mean?'

She said, 'The woman has tuberculosis

and is dying. She has to go to hospital.'

The next morning, Jean was taken by ambulance to a private hospital where she had a room to herself. She would only allow me and one other person to visit her. Ten days later she was dead. I had never realized how much air you need to breathe just to be able to drink. Try it; you can't breathe as you drink. She would merely wet her lips. She was so weak they didn't dare operate, but they gave her oxygen and before she died she was able to talk again. It was horrifying. I got a call at two in the morning and they said, 'I think you should come in,' and I just knew. They didn't say anything over the phone but when I arrived they said, 'I'm afraid your friend just passed away.' I hated it; I sat with her for a little while, and thought how silly it all was. She was so stubborn and independent, if only she had come back for a holiday two months before, she could have been treated and she might still be alive. I still miss her.

I don't think I am very good with death. I have never seen someone actually slip away and I don't know that I would like to. Peter Gormley had died by the time Jean passed on. He had cancer; his wife, Audrey, also died of cancer. My stage manager, John Seymour, was another one taken by cancer, in his mid-forties. Roger Bruce and I went to say goodbye to him in hospital just hours before he died – we were on our way to Bray Studios – and I found that very difficult. Peter Gormley's secretary, Diane, also died of cancer. She had been working for me since the age of seventeen when she left school. She became the office secretary, then went away to have children and returned as Malcolm's secretary. She was just forty-six when she died; her children were in their teens. I was on tour in Australia; Richard, her husband, rang Gill, who rang Roger Bruce, who broke the news to me while we were having dinner with Tim Rice. Breaking bad news seems to have been a large part of Roger's role in life with me. We couldn't make it back for the funeral so, as often happens, all I could do was send flowers.

I don't like to think of it but I will feel very sad when Billy Graham dies. He has been suffering from Parkinson's disease for some years. I appeared on his platform many times in Britain and Europe, and also in Tokyo, but I always turned down invitations to take part in crusades in America because I didn't feel I would have been of value there; far better for them to have some of those big country stars that everyone there knows. But if they came to me now and said he was doing one final crusade, I would go like a shot, wherever it was. He is an amazing man and I would love to be present the last time he evangelizes. I have such respect for people like him who have given their lives to something they believe, carried it through, remained above corruption and stayed true to their faith.

He was never a friend – as I would define the term – which is a pity: I would love to have known him better. Still, whenever he was passing through and I could make it, we would meet and we would talk. He once came to Charters, and to this day I still boast that I swam with Billy Graham in my pool. We swam up and down and talked and had a barbecue – it was a fantastic day. He's an unusually wonderful and honourable man. There are two things I remember vividly. When Billy and I first met, it was at Earl's Court – Bill Latham was with me. I introduced him to Billy and said, 'This is Bill Latham from Tearfund.' He said he knew Tearfund, how nice to meet us both. A couple of years later we met him in London and he remembered. 'You're Bill Latham from Tearfund,' he said, without prompting. I found that so impressive. The other memory is from many years later, when he was much older. He was doing a crusade in Birmingham, and I was going to join him on stage to spout my bit and sing a song. We went up to his hotel room beforehand to talk about what he wanted me to do. He was flexing his hand round a cudgel and I said, 'Are you having trouble with your wrists?'

He said, 'No; I'm toughening them up so that when I shake all those hands out there I don't give them a wimpish Christian handshake – I want my hands to be strong.'

Billy Graham was a very impressive orator. The last time I saw him was in Sheffield in midwinter. I felt sorry for him; it was freezing and he was controlling the Parkinson's with drugs but he was still able to speak authoritatively. At the end, he invited anyone who had reached a crossroads in their lives and felt they wanted to commit themselves to Christ to come forward. It was what he did at every crusade. He said, 'It's nothing to do with me or Cliff Richard – it's just you and Jesus – but there are people here who will help you.' I was thinking, No one will come up – but it always happens: the seats go click, click, click and suddenly there are hundreds of people coming forward.

Before I took part in that crusade at Earl's Court in 1966, Billy had been heavily criticized in the press for using music at the point where he invites people to come forward. The choir would sing 'Just As I Am' and it was very emotional. So in the '66 crusade he dropped the music – and it was even more emotional, because all you heard was the click of the seats going up and the sound of hundreds of feet walking. It brought tears to the eyes, and I thought, God really does work miracles.

I never imagined when I bought the Quinta that I would grow vines. I wanted to keep it looking tidy, and I wanted it to be productive. Many people in my world have bought farms with beautiful houses but the farm aspect dies; so, rather than lose the farm, I asked the farmer what we could grow. There were already a few vines, but they were old. 'The grapes are useless,' he said, 'but I could sell figs.' So as an experiment, we planted five acres of figs, which take three years to fruit. Each fig tree cost £30, and when I went out and looked at them I said, 'Where are they?' There were the tiniest green shoots peeping out of the ground. 'I paid thirty pounds for each of those?'

The year before the figs fruited, I met an Australian winemaker called David Baverstock, who told me that the situation was perfect for a vineyard. His credentials were good: he had studied in the Barossa Valley in Australia, then had come to Portugal to learn about port, and had taken over a defunct winery in the Alentejo region in the middle of the country, from which he was producing four million bottles a year. You're far enough away from the sea,' he said, 'and you've got a great climate, it gets cool in the winter and hot in the summer which grapes like: it's perfect.'

I said, 'But I've just planted all these figs

and I'll have my first crop next year.'

'Well,' he said, 'that's your choice – you can make syrup of figs, or you can have a nice bottle of wine.'

So I'm afraid there was no contest. The very next year we dug everything up and started the process of planting the grapes.

David had an ambition, which I wasn't aware of initially, to be the first winemaker in the Algarve to make decent wine. He showed me a book called *Wines of the World* which in one short sentence summed up the current situation. 'In the Algarve there are four co-operatives and basically, they bottle headaches for tourists.'

'That's because they don't know how to do it,' said David. 'You could get in first but the other producers will catch up – they're not stupid.' Sure enough, I planted my sixteen acres in 1998, and since then thousands of acres in the region have been given over to vines.

David took cuttings that were grafted in the Rhône Valley in France, where they lived in little pots for a year until they were big enough to be planted in the ground. We were lucky: they expect to lose between 10 and 15 per cent in the process of planting, but we only lost 5 per cent. That year David said, 'Please don't be disappointed in your first harvest because there won't be one. The vines need to grow up and mature.' That was

1999, and we picked seventeen tons of grapes. It was incredible. My farm became known as 'The Little Miracle'. David was completely taken by surprise and had to give them away to the local cooperative, which made more headaches with them.

By the next year, 2000, we were ready for the harvest and produced two or three hundred bottles. We found someone with a vineyard north of us and trucked our grapes to him, and he stored the wine there in a tank for us until it was ready for bottling. It was so good that David said, 'Do you want to call a press conference? Because next year we will be able to sell.' So all the wine writers came down; I gave them a buffet lunch and we all sat on the terrace and had a stupendous afternoon.

I called the wine 'Vida Nova', meaning 'New Life' – which I hoped I was bringing to my farm and possibly even to the wine-making industry in the Algarve. On the whole the reviews weren't bad. One major newspaper was very cynical: Please, a pop singer making wine? I'd warned David that we might come up against this attitude and that we'd just have to ignore it. Fortunately the publications that counted – *Harpers* and *Decanter* – were less scathing. One of them said, 'Cliff Richard's new wine, Vida Nova, is a deep, rich, red wine, full of chocolate overtones. There's blackberry and blackcurrant on the palate and tannins waiting patiently in the wings make their entrance and then discreetly retreat.' I thought it was the most wonderful way to describe a wine. David kept saying to me, 'I don't understand, it shouldn't be this good.' Over the years since then I've met people wandering in my vineyard, and I always go and say rather pointedly, 'Can I help you, please?' On two occasions they were horticulturalists; one was a professor, who said, 'I'm here to see the little miracle.' In 2005 our Vida Nova (2004) was awarded a Bronze Medal at the London Wine Fair. The following year we were awarded a Silver Medal at the International Spirit and Wine Fair. The whole process has been very exciting – and just the Gold still to get!

I confess I don't know a lot about wine, although I sometimes sound as if I do. It's like my Portuguese. I know very few words but I say them with a great accent, so locals are always surprised when I don't understand what they're saying. With wine I only know what I like. I'm not into any of the blackberry and chocolate overtones, but I do know that my wine tastes good and I can now drink a red wine and know whether it's complex or primitive. So I can't really claim to be anything other than the person who made it possible for David Baverstock to be the first man to make a good wine in the Algarve...

…Which brings me on to *The F-Word*, Gordon Ramsay's Channel 4 programme, on which I rubbished my own wine in a blind tasting. The irony is that I rather enjoyed the programme and I thought it was quite funny that I should have raved about Olivia's wine but been disparaging about mine. It was a trick, and I don't mind that: it was television, it was fun. What annoyed me were the things Gordon said to the press afterwards, along the lines that I knew F-all about wine or anything else for that matter. It was a terrible put-down, the like of which I don't think I would have expected from one professional to another. At first I was incensed; then I thought, Hold on, I'm doing what everyone else does – I'm believing what I read in the newspaper; so I did and said nothing, thinking that Gordon was bound to get in touch and say none of it was true. But he never did, so I have to assume that he did say what was reported. He also said I was so angry after the tasting that I'd beckoned him over and said, 'Young man, go f*** yourself.' I didn't. I didn't call him over and he's certainly not young. What I did do, when everyone was laughing, was lean into his ear as I was saying goodbye and say 'argwoff'. I didn't actually swear at all. Interestingly, the producers did bleep me, but in the wrong place. Oh, well – that's television!

CHAPTER SEVENTEEN

America

If I could make it in America, I would give up the pleasures of being anonymous there tomorrow. It's the one bugbear in my life that I have never been big in the fatherland of rock 'n' roll. When I've spoken to people like Elton John and Eric Clapton, who have had huge success in the States, they've said, 'I can't figure out why you didn't make it.' All I can say is, 'Tell me about it.' There can't be many other artists who were successful both before and after the Beatles, with number ones in England, who never made it across the pond. Back in the sixties the Americans were mad about anything English, particularly music, and anything that was number one here automatically made it into the Top Ten there. Even the Bachelors had a Top Five hit, and they weren't mainstream rock 'n' roll – but the Americans loved them because they were from our side of the pond. Rock 'n' roll was born in America, and rock 'n' roll has given me my life. Why did it never happen for me there? It is the one place in the world I would love to have had the same semblance of success that I've had everywhere else.

Over the years I used to think it was because I simply didn't appeal to enough of them. Then something happened on my thirtieth anniversary in 1988. EMI threw a big dinner for me in town to celebrate my three decades in show business – big-selling artist, still selling records – and they gave me a pure gold album, probably the only truly gold album there is. I keep it vacuum-packed in a beautiful gilt stand on display on one of my tables at home. It must be worth a fortune, but would be far too soft to play. That evening I heard the news that 'Stronger', the title song from an album I'd released that year, had come in at number sixteen in the Disco Dance Chart in America. This has nothing to do with sales. The disco dance people in America are huge and heavily influenced by radio; the DJs had chosen this song. Great, I thought.

The same week I heard that 'Some People', which I had released the year before, had gone into the charts on five adult contemporary stations in the United States.

So I said to Rupert Perry, who was EMI's managing director at the time, 'Rupert, look: without any of our help or even our knowledge, these two things have happened. Couldn't we try in America one more time? Let's capitalize on this. These are two good songs that I could sing on television.'

He said, 'Cliff, I don't know how to tell you this, but I'm going to have to say it anyway. EMI America are *not* excited by Cliff Richard material.' And he shrugged.

I said, 'What? You're kidding!'

In that one sentence was the entire explanation. No wonder I had never made it; what possible chance had I had if EMI America, my record company for most of that time, didn't like my music – and never had? Singles were released, but there was no follow-up. The only reason I'd had successes elsewhere was because I went there, at my own expense, and created some interest. And 'Devil Woman' did well because Elton took an interest. You can't do it by yourself in America; it's just too big. Not even the Beatles could do it on their own; when they finally made it in the States there was huge machinery behind them.

I console myself with that fact, but it was wrong of EMI to take that view. I went to the States nine times, and had nine Top Thirty hits; the cost was astronomical and I had to pay for it all myself. Nine times, I lost money. Each time I flew in my band and my crew; I had to pay for them, as well as for the venues, for the programmes and advertising – everything; and with up to fifteen people each time the expenditure was huge. I wasn't playing stadia, I was playing thousand-seaters, five-hundred-seaters and a couple of thousand-seaters here and there. As well as the concerts, I did all the television and radio shows. The *LA Times* gave me an unbelievable review and the next day I went into the American office of EMI – it is one of the last times I spoke to them – and threw the review on the table. I said, 'I can do no more than this.' The review was so good: it raved about everything – me, the show, the compositions; everything was glowing. It was so complimentary it was almost embarrassing. I got no response from EMI; and so I gave up on America. If they had said to me, 'We're not going to be supporting you with this album.' I wouldn't have gone. I recorded a country song called 'The Minute You're Gone', which was number one in the UK and should have been huge in America – it was a country song, for crying out loud – but was EMI America interested? They said, 'We don't think it's right for our market.'

American radio presenters are always shocked when I tell them how long I've been doing what I do for a living. They say, 'What did you do in the interim period between "Devil Woman" and "We Don't Talk Anymore"?' I say, 'Well, I've been touring Norway, Sweden, Denmark, Holland, Germany, France, Belgium, Hong Kong, Singapore, Bangkok, Australia, New Zealand–' and they go: 'Stop, stop, stop! We get the picture.'

I've come to terms with the fact that I may never make it in the States. Some Americans would recognize my music but the joy is they don't recognize me. When I go into a restaurant in New York, it's one of the nicest feelings to sit down, knowing that the waiter doesn't know who I am, but might notice a fellow diner spot me. We then come to the moment when he is giving me the check and he says, as only Americans can, 'Should I know you?' And I'll say, 'Well, did you spend any time in England or Europe?' He'll say 'No,' and I'll say, 'OK, well I'm a singer from Europe, so you shouldn't really know me.' And he'll say, 'What did you sing?' So I sing a couple of lines from 'Devil Woman', and the guy goes, 'You recorded that? Of course I know you!' But he doesn't know me, he doesn't know my name; he knows my record. So I still think there's an audience for my music in America, if only I could tap into it.

Not long after my year off I happened to mention to Stuart Ongley, a publisher friend, that I was looking for a new challenge in recording terms. I felt I wanted to get away from England, where everything was too comfortable, where I felt I'd done it all before. He said his publishing partner, Val Jannsen, lived in Nashville and was in touch with songwriters. 'Are you interested in meeting new writers?' I said, 'Of course,' so he arranged a writers' camp. Twenty-one songwriters came together and for two weeks they wrote songs specifically for me. Val thought this was the first time it had ever been done specifically for one singer. I loved the whole experience, because I knew that most of them didn't know who I was. One evening, when we were having our daily get-together, when we always had coffees and Krispy Kremes, I said to all the writers, 'I know you don't know what I've done but I've worked for a long time in Britain, I've sold a lot of records there, records like this – and I put on a tape of 'Devil Woman'.

Immediately, the same old thing happened: 'That's you? You did "Devil Woman"?'

'Yeah,' I said, 'I also did this one,' and sang a couple of bars of 'We Don't Talk Anymore'. They knew then that I was a serious pop star.

'Well, what do you want?' they said.

'The main thing I want,' I replied, 'is for every song to be a number one.'

They waited for a while – Americans don't always understand our humour – then said, 'Oh, of course, you're joking.'

So I said, 'Well, partly, but what I'm saying is that I need you to write the best songs that you can. I'd like some about love, of course, but do me a couple about cars.' Cars featured heavily in early rock 'n' roll.

346

So they wrote me 'What Car' and another called 'A Thousand Miles To Go'. They wrote twenty-one songs and I recorded seventeen of them. It was a real challenge in the studio because I worked with several different producers. I was a bit nervous, and then I found myself thinking, I'm going to show these guys what I can do, and I pulled out all the stops. Producers play a very important role; they have to draw the song out of you. Alan Tarney was brilliant to work with, never negative. If he asked me to sing something again it was always because something was wrong, and if I did a little twiddle with a line, I could see from his body language when he liked it: he'd punch the air – and I would think to myself, Yes!

People don't always realize how vulnerable you are as a singer. I've been doing it all these years, but I still don't know what's going to come out of a recording session or whether anybody's going to like it. So Nashville was a real confidence boost. The album that came out of that writers' camp was called *Something's Goin' On*, and I think it was the most exciting album I'd done in years. In some ways I think I reinvented myself. I hadn't gone to Nashville in order to do that, but when I listen to that album again I think – Wow. It's still pop rock, I can recognize me – but there is a different element to it. I thoroughly enjoyed making it, and it did exactly what it was supposed to do. Universal released it and it charted in the UK at number seven.

The tragedy for me is that it was never released in the States. The big chief of Universal in America came to England and Malcolm Smith mentioned in conversation that I had been recording in Nashville. He went over to the office and Malcolm played him the tracks. He was knocked out. 'Fantastic,' he said. 'I love it, I'd like to have it for Universal in America.' The only thing was, he would have to get the agreement of his sales team. Could he please have some copies to play to them? He telephoned some days later and said, 'I can't bear to tell you this; they loved the album, they absolutely loved it. Then they started asking questions about the artist – had he worked before, what had he done? And then they got to my age. Whoops – they were dumbfounded and said, "We don't know what to do with this." Basically, they reached the consensus that they couldn't work with someone of sixty-five. They didn't know how to present a rock 'n' roller who they assumed was new, but who'd been singing for nearly fifty years.

That was the first time ever that my age has seriously impeded me; it was a real body blow. I don't understand why they couldn't have just introduced me as a recording artist and confessed my age later. The music, apparently, wasn't enough; they had to have a youthful image, a face to show that was blemish-free and in its twenties. There was nothing I could do about that; but I can't believe there aren't enough people of my age in America who would enjoy what I do sufficiently to make it worthwhile releasing an album.

I am tempted to have another crack at it, but in a different way. I couldn't conquer the whole country – I am too old, and I'm not sure I'd be prepared to fight that hard for it any more – but I like the idea of going over to New York, for instance, where I have a small two-bedroom apartment, and offering my services in some little club or bar and sing with a small band I could put together locally. In the same block as my apartment is a hotel where a singer called Brian Feinstein has a dining club to which he invites guest singers. I don't know him personally but I recognize the names of some of the artists that do shows there, and maybe he could check me out and give me a go. Or Joe's Pub, where I played a couple of years ago – I would go back there any day of the week. It's very intimate and small-scale, with no more than eighty or a hundred people. There are any number of similar places. I'd love that – it would be fun, and I could probably make a mark for myself in New York.

The older I get, the more I like being in America where everything is so accessible. New York is unbelievable: I can walk for two minutes from my apartment and get my breakfast; within four minutes I can see cabaret; I can walk to Broadway in twenty minutes. I don't have to ask whether it is too late to watch a movie; it's fantastic, so buzzy, and New Yorkers seem to be really friendly. If you're eating an ice-cream a complete stranger will say, 'How's your ice-cream?' and the next minute they'll be telling you about their son at college. I like that, and I am trying to become a little more like that myself – more open. I try to do it when I go to the checkout counter in the supermarket, try to forget I am Cliff Richard and that they might know who I am, and it doesn't take much to say, 'You having a good day? You must be a bit frazzled.' Suddenly you have the makings of a conversation with someone.

I have friends I stay with in Fort Lauderdale, Florida, and it's the same there: I can walk straight out of the door on to Las Olas Boulevard, full of shops and restaurants; and it's just a five-minute drive to the Galleria Mall. I am beginning to think I am of an age (I don't feel a day over twenty-five, but I try to be sensible!) where I need to consider how I am going to live when I am really old. I would like to be able to walk everywhere, to be able to lock up and go and have everything I need close by. I would miss the garden – I do love gardens – but I have noticed in New York that you can look up and see dozens of roof terraces with trees and flowers growing. Maybe I could find an apartment with one of them and have a garden in the sky. I haven't made up my mind, but I'm looking at all the options and seeing what there is. I do recognize, of course, how lucky I am to have so many options to consider – I know that most people don't have the choices that are open to me.

This is a really difficult business to be in sometimes, and it's not always easy to keep one's confidence up. Everything is so personal. I am trading on my voice, my face, my physique, even my personality – and so it's hard not to take criticism or rejection as personal. When I've done something new, I use my friends and the office as sounding boards. Most of them are very positive and upfront. Bill Latham is always saying, 'I don't know what you're worrying about. You've done this before, you can walk through it in your sleep.' My family are also fantastic. If I feel down all I have to do is phone Joan – and she'll usually have to turn off one of my records to talk to me. She's a big fan and comes to all my concerts; she and Jacqui came with my nephews and nieces, who are in their twenties now, and they bring their mates, and when I meet them after the show, their friends seem impressed. 'Wow,' they say. 'Great show, Cliff, you're really good.' It's just wonderful when someone – especially someone in their twenties – says they enjoy what I do.

CHAPTER EIGHTEEN

Mum's Decline

I remember so often as a child saying to my mother, 'One day, Mum, I'm going to buy you a house.' Something I am sure all children say; but not all of them have the luck I've had to enable them to do it. I still choke up at the thought of that day when all six of us were living in our pokey little council house in Cheshunt, the day when I first said to her, 'I can afford to do this. I am going to buy you that house.'

The tragedy with Mum was that she developed dementia more than fifteen years before she died, so although it was only in 2007 that her body gave up the struggle, I lost the mother I knew and loved many years before. By the end, she didn't even recognize me; sometimes when I went to visit her, I would sit by the side of her bed for an hour or more and she would sleep throughout. Before she reached that stage, we used to take her out for tea and sandwiches, and she would sit and pull the sandwiches apart and pick at bits – this in a woman who was once so sophisticated and well-mannered, who knew exactly which knife should go where; the family and I were shocked. One day when I came in with the beard I'd grown for *Heathcliff* she completely ignored me. I said to Joan, 'I don't think she knows who I am.' So I took a napkin from the table and covered my beard.

She looked at me long and hard and said, 'You look just like Cliff Richard.' Funny; she called me Cliff Richard, not Cliff.

Dementia is the most horrific thing to have to come to terms with. Where I was so lucky was in being able to afford to buy the best possible care for our Mum so I knew that she was as happy as she could be. I feel so sorry for people who can't – I don't know how they cope.

I was lucky also in having sisters who were able to help with Mum. Jacqui was the first one to notice something was going on at the time when her son Phil was born, and she and her husband were staying with Mum. Looking back, they realized there were small indications that her mind wasn't as sharp as normal. Mum called Jacqui from Great Ormond Street one day, saying she must complain about one of the nurses in the high-dependency ward where Phil was being looked after. 'She's a complete learner,' Mum had said indignantly. She had evidently overheard one nurse going off shift, briefing the newcomer on the babies in the ward, and misunderstood the situation.

My mother once had an angina attack when she was staying with Jacqui and Peter. Everyone thought it was a heart attack – she went very limp and pale – and she was whisked into the Norfolk and Norwich Hospital; but fortunately it was not that serious. It did make us all think, though, that it might not be so sensible for Mum to be living on her own any more; the trouble was, like all mothers, she was loath to give up her independence.

Donna was not well herself and Jacqui was in Norfolk, so Joan, living in Hertfordshire, was the closest to Mum and therefore the one of us who was best able to keep an eye on her. One day she rang me and said, 'What am I going to do? David's got his car and my car is in the garage for a week, I can't get to Mum and she's not well.'

So I said, 'I'll tell you what: Mum likes living on her own, I'll design a bungalow just like the one she's living in now and we'll stick it onto your house.' We obviously had to get planning permission, so that's what we did. One door gave access to the bungalow from Joan and David's kitchen, in case of emergency; otherwise, my mother had her own front door and was independent. That worked for several years but gradually, as the disease progressed, she became more and more difficult to look after, until finally my sister was at breaking point. 'I can't do this any more,' she said. 'I do have my husband and I do have a family, and we've just found Mum – yet again – walking about on the High Street totally lost.' She'd forgotten where she had parked the car, and had no idea why she was there.

So Joan and Jacqui both went out looking for a nursing home where Mum would be safe. They found one in St Albans and I went with them to see it. It looked good to me – well-kept, clean, and full of people with varying degrees of Alzheimer's and other forms of dementia. By the time my mother moved in there, the disease had reached the point where she didn't appear to notice the woman who sat in the corner saying, 'ONE TWO THREE, FIVE SEVEN, TEN NINE EIGHT' – just counting all day long. My mother would step over this woman's feet, oblivious. Yet when the time came for us to go after each visit, she would cry and say, 'Don't leave me here, take me home.'

That was the worst bit. We'd have to lie and say, 'Just treat it like a holiday. If you don't like it then next time we come we'll take you home,' knowing that she'd forget very quickly – but it was horrible.

After this had happened two or three times, the nurses said, 'Look, never say goodbye to her face to face, give her a kiss, and we'll distract her attention while you slip away.' Thereafter, she'd never notice we'd gone; and the next week she'd quite forgotten we'd ever been there and would say, 'I haven't seen you for months and months. Why haven't you visited?'

She went downhill quite rapidly. I would phone her and she would hang up on me. I would say, 'Don't put the phone down, Mum,' but I knew she would, because she had already forgotten who she was talking to. The staff used to say, 'Oh, we love having Dorothy here, she's the most active person we have,' and I said, 'Well, that makes sense. She would never sit still at home, she was always busy cooking or washing up or ironing.' Ironing she loved, and I remember her ironing at home while we all watched TV. In the nursing home she used to go to the laundry room and say, 'Have you got any ironing for me?' They would say, 'Yes, Dorothy,' and they would put up a board for her, and she would iron sheets, towels, napkins and handkerchiefs. She would fold them all up neatly and they would say, 'Thank you, Dorothy,' and when she had gone they would shake the sheets and everything out again, and sure enough, an hour or two later she would come back and say, 'Any ironing for me?' So when the staff one day said, 'Your mother doesn't come round to iron any more,' it was a telling moment.

Then she fell and she broke her pelvis, and they said, 'Your mum won't walk after this.'

I didn't believe them. I said, 'Oh, please, my mum's been walking around the whole of her life, there was nothing wrong until she slipped.' But there is a pattern apparently and, sure enough, the minute she was put in a wheelchair, even when her hip was better, they could get her up to go to the bathroom, but afterwards she would sit right down again. She simply refused to walk. Then her muscles wasted away and she couldn't walk. So they would lift her into a wheelchair, where she'd sit for a while, looking at nothing in particular; and they'd find her sleeping, slumped, which was so uncomfortable. In the end they left her in her bed for most of the day, where she slept, just waking her up to feed her.

She was alive but she had no life. There was nothing there – no memory: she didn't know us – she didn't talk, she didn't walk, she was incontinent, and she slept a lot. The only consolation was that she had no pain. On the last few visits I made, she didn't wake up at all in an hour and a half. I went one of those last times with my nieces, one of whom had a new baby who was playing around and crying, but my mother was unaware even of this. Every time she turned over I gave her a gentle shake and said, 'We're here, Mum, how are you?' But she didn't bat an eyelid.

I said to my sisters that I felt as though I had already mourned our mother, and I think they rather agreed. They said, 'Well, our mother isn't there any more, is she?'

They were right, Mum was just the shell of the vibrant person she used to be.

Someone had said to me a few years before, 'Is there a photograph of your mother in her room?'

I said, 'No, but there are lots of little pictures of us with her and that kind of thing.'

'Find a really great picture of your mum,' he said, 'a big one and put it on the wall.'

I said, 'Why?'

'Because it's really important that these people who are looking after her should see the photograph and know that that was Dorothy. *That* is what this woman was. The woman in bed is just what she has become because of this terrible illness.'

So I found a wonderful picture of her – I think it was from one of my film premieres, but it was a shot of her by herself, with a fur on her shoulders, her hair just done, looking about twenty-two, and I was twenty-two at the time so she had to have been forty-two, but she looked fabulous. I had it framed and hung it right over the bed, so that anyone who went into the room to look after her would know that *that* was the real Dorothy.

It was an expensive home so it was never overcrowded, but often the staff were over worked. We did have to complain once, but not because of the staff; it was because one of the other patients hit my mother. This man should have been in a secure room, but someone had left the door open, Mum had wandered in and he had hit and kicked her. We were extremely unhappy. 'We leave her with you,' we said; 'we trust you, you can't let this happen.' They admitted this man was in the wrong place, and moved him into another home which dealt with people who were violent. But it was worrying, because all you can to do is trust that your loved one is being looked after. Every two or three weeks I used to send a postcard from wherever I was in the world. I would address it to Mrs Dorothy Bodkin, but I wrote it to the staff and said, 'Thanks for looking after Mum; I will see you soon. Big hugs to you all and a big kiss to my mum.' I wanted to keep them aware that they didn't just have a patient – I still had a mother.

I was in Florida with friends the day Mum died. It was 17 October 2007, three days after my birthday. I got a message to call my sister Joan urgently. I rang straight away, thinking there must be a problem with one of the kids. It never crossed my mind it might be my mother, so when Joan said, 'Mum just passed away,' I was completely unprepared. The doctors had told me that my mother could outlive us all – she could have lived to a hundred because her essential bodily functions were fine, it was just her brain, her memory that no longer worked. So the fact that she had died at eighty-seven was a shock; but my reaction to the news also came as a shock. I thought I had sorted it out long ago. Many times in my head I had been through the scenario of the phone ringing to say that my mother had died. I knew that a piece of me would be shattered, but I didn't think it would be as bad as if she had been compos mentis and we had been joking with her one day and she had gone the next. This had been a slow process of realizing that the brain is everything in terms of a person's personality, and I thought I had buried her, metaphorically speaking, and finished the grieving long ago.

Not so. It was the finality of it that got to me. It's that moment when the final pages of the book close and it's all over. It was tough. I didn't fly straight home; my sisters said there was no point, and the funeral couldn't have taken place before I was due back anyway, so I asked my office to make sure everything was dealt with financially and my sisters organized the ceremony. They didn't want a big shindig, they wanted it to be private – just family, two or three from my office, who were like family to her, and a couple of friends who knew her really well. There were thirty people at the most. Donna didn't make it. One of the consequences of her illness is that she finds it very difficult to be with large groups of people. Her husband Terry is very protective and in recent years I have seen very little of her. That day she wasn't well enough to make the journey.

My other two sisters did a lot of sobbing, and at the funeral itself, when I spoke about Mum, I found myself completely overwhelmed and had great difficulty getting through it. I broke down several times. But I thought I had to say something about her because she had been ill for so long that the kids – my nieces and nephews – didn't really know what she was like. They didn't know what my parents went through to get us going in Britain. We really had been on poverty street. None of my friends can relate to that because, luckily for them, they came from strong middle-class families. We had had a middle-class background – upper-class, even – in India, but when we came to Britain, we had zero, and my parents had to deal with that. They struggled, and their strength is really important to me now, even more important since my mother died. My father, of course, died a long time ago, but we always had Mum still alive, and very much kicking. Even in those years she was ill, we still had a parent; now, suddenly, it hit us that we didn't. I didn't realize until then that you are never too old to be an orphan.

Mum was buried in a plot I bought years ago at Bury Green in Cheshunt, where we used to live. There is a pretty little chapel there and a cemetery. She is there with my father and grandfather, and, as one of my nieces said, 'There's room for one more on top.' Trust kids to get you through a tough time with a laugh.

CHAPTER NINETEEN

The Perks Of Pop

If you come from the backwoods of Hertfordshire, it never crosses your mind that you might one day step through the front door of Buckingham Palace. It would just be out of the question. But I have found myself in places that fifty years ago I could never have dreamed of. Make it in the pop world – and probably any other world where your face is recognized – and all sorts of doors open up. You are treated differently, better. You get invitations from kings and queens, presidents and prime ministers; you go to galas and openings, to grand hotels and top restaurants; you are given memberships to exclusive clubs and tickets to opening nights and glittering parties, because everyone knows that a few luminaries in a room make an event extra-special. These are the perks of pop – but among them all, I still rank invitations to Buckingham Palace as the most exciting. I have been there many times now, not just to investitures, but also to a number of receptions, the nicest and most informal of which was many years ago when I was one of twelve people around the lunch table with the Queen, the Duke of Edinburgh and Princess Anne.

I can't now remember who all the other guests were – I know they included a horse-racing journalist and a lady in a wheelchair – but I do remember there were eight of us, and that upon arrival we were shown into a splendid room on the first floor and given a glass of sherry. We stood around awkwardly, none of us quite knowing what to do, or expect, when suddenly the doors opened and in flew four corgis. They stopped in the middle of the room and stood looking back at the doorway expectantly. We all put our sherries down, knowing that where the corgis went the Queen was bound to follow.

Sure enough, hot on their heels came the Queen, followed by Princess Anne and Prince Philip, accompanied by an equerry. We formed a line and they each shook our hands, then they mingled for a few minutes before we all went in to lunch. When I looked at the seating plan I was horrified. I was at the top of the table. I thought, There's got to be a mistake, surely the host must sit at the top; my heart was pumping, what to do? But they had been very clever. The Queen and Prince Philip sat opposite each other in the middle so they were closer to all their guests. The corgis sat under the table and I noticed the waiter more than once give one a little kick to try and get them out of the way.

The Queen's opening remarks to me were, 'I believe you've been doing some charity work. Where have you been recently?' I know someone had briefed her but it didn't matter; I was delighted that she should show an interest in what I had been doing.

Years before I had taken part in the *It's a Royal Knockout* fiasco, which brought so much criticism down on the royals. I remember getting the invitation and being told I was on Princess Anne's team, and wondering what on earth they were letting themselves in for. Prince Andrew, Prince Edward and the Duchess of York all had teams of showbiz celebrities and we did a whole lot of silly games, dressed up in mock Tudor costume. It was all for charity, but still I think they should never have done it – as I am sure they realized afterwards. It was in the eighties, at a time when they were being told they were out of touch with the world, and I suspect this was some ill-conceived way of trying to address that problem. At the end it dissolved into a royal bun-fight. I wish someone had said, 'Your Majesty, this is not a good idea.' Everything seems so simple with hindsight.

The Royal Family will never be like the rest of us and they shouldn't even attempt it. I love believing that they are special; I like being able to doff my hat and say, 'I'm meeting somebody really classy.' The Royal Family are a living part of our history, and they're always going to be different from us in every way; but by the simple expedient of asking over lunch where I'd been recently, the Queen immediately came down to my level without losing any of her dignity. The sight of Princess Anne during the pudding course, wrestling with her brandy snap, had the same effect. 'These are so annoying,' she said, taking it in her hand and tapping it on the side of the plate, 'I just don't know how to break the darn thing.' It immediately put the rest of us, also struggling with brandy snaps, at our ease. It's fantastic to have the royals – we're the only nation on earth that has castles and palaces that are not museum pieces, that have people living in them whose line can be traced back centuries; and we are the envy of the world for that. I can never understand why some people are so vehemently against them.

It seems to me that it's the politics of envy. When my friends and I stopped to look at that car and, of course, heard Elvis on that car radio all those years ago, what we were doing, effectively, was saying, 'One day I'm going to have a car like that,' not, 'Huh, let's scratch it.' The attitude today often tends towards, 'If I don't have it, why should somebody else have it?'

There is a lot about society today that I have difficulty accepting. Maybe it's an age thing, and maybe every older generation feels this about the one that follows, but people seem to have no respect for anything any more – for other people, for property, even for themselves. And there's no sense of responsibility. It's absurd that in schools a teacher is not allowed to discipline a child. I am completely in favour of banning the beating of children, but I come from a generation where punishment meant a smack. I knew that if I did something wrong my father would clout me. It did me no lasting harm at all, but it taught me where the boundaries were and it taught me right from wrong. Where are children learning that these days? When are they allowed to be children, even?

They all grow up so quickly; where is the naïveté that we all once had? When I read about young people in England shooting each other or knifing each other ... it just doesn't make sense to me – and I feel so frustrated, because I don't know how to help stop it. Maybe we have to go through a process of self-destruction; if we do, I hope the wheel eventually turns full circle.

The Bible says, 'Be in the world but not of it.' I am of Britain, and when I come home I like being here; but I refuse to follow the crowd. I refuse to swear just because someone else is swearing. You see people on television behaving in a way that is so revolting that if they were in your house, you'd never have them back – and yet they get given TV series of their own. I was on a programme with Terry Wogan once and George Best was a fellow guest. He was off the booze and we had a whole conversation about his alcoholism, and yet people during the show were egging him on, saying, 'Go on George, have a beer.' I couldn't believe they were saying it – it would have killed him; and in the end, alcohol did kill him. One of my nieces – Linzi – came rushing home to us one Christmas Eve; she had been in a pub and had been slashed in the face by a bottle. I don't know how to deal with that, and there seems to be more and more of it around – young people sitting around drunk in door-

367

ways and on kerbsides. Can they be the future of our country? They are not entirely why I spend so much of my time abroad, but they are one of the factors. I guess it's a way of protecting myself.

And if *I* feel that way, how, I wonder, must the generation who fought for the British way of life in the Second World War feel? Another unforgettable day I spent at the Palace, though rather less intimate than my lunch, was when I was invited to participate in the fiftieth anniversary celebrations of VE Day in 1995. It was the most intensely moving experience. On the Saturday there was a concert in Hyde Park attended by members of the Royal Family. The park was filled with hundreds of thousands of people and the atmosphere was quite unlike anything I had known before. I was there to represent the post-war era and was singing alongside the likes of Dame Vera Lynn, the 'Forces' Sweetheart', and Sir Harry Secombe, war veteran and star of the *Goon Show*. Because I prefer to speak off the cuff, I hadn't decided in advance what to say, but looking around, seeing faces, most of them old, and knowing that many of these people had been injured and had comrades who'd died for us, crystallized what I wanted to say, and out it came: 'I don't care what anyone thinks about war. There are many people here – and just as many people not here because they died –

who did something extraordinary for us. We would not be standing here doing this now, if it wasn't for those people, being brave and selfless in that particular war.' As I said it, I was choking up and thinking, 'It's true.' I hadn't really thought of it in those terms before.

On the following Monday, we three – Dame Vera, Sir Harry and I – and a few others, including Bob Holness as Master of Ceremonies, appeared on stage outside the gates of Buckingham Palace, where the celebrations continued. There must have been more than a million people in The Mall, hundreds of them swarming round the sides of our temporary stage facing the Winged Victory statue. As we made our way there, dozens were reaching out to Vera, touching her and holding her hand and saying, 'Vera, sweetheart, we love you and God bless you.' She was so much a part of their lives because of what she did during the war that I found myself, for the first time ever, wishing that I had been there. We – and I include anyone who cannot remember the war – are part of a generation that has lost unity; those people were united against a common enemy. I almost envied them. I would have liked to share that camaraderie. I was thrown by the whole thing, in a way I could not have imagined. I have always thought of myself as a pacifist, as most people do when they are young. I had always thought I would never fight or kill; but when I saw the faces of those brave people in the crowd and the emotion the celebrations wrung from them, knowing the pain and the loss they had endured on our behalf, I wasn't so sure any more.

I say I would like to have been there, but I would probably have been a coward. In my heart of hearts, I wouldn't have wanted to fight in case I was killed. I wouldn't want my family to fight for the same reason. In the end, though, most of us survived because other people were prepared to sacrifice themselves for us.

When I was young I saw everything in black and white. Now just about everything is in shades of grey. There's no way war will ever be right, but sometimes it may be the lesser of two evils. Do you say to the aggressor, 'OK, take over, we're yours,' or do you say, 'You can't get away with killing six million Jews, you have to pay'? Do you let terrorists kill innocent people or tyrants commit genocide? I am just glad I am not the one who has to make those decisions.

Ideally, all humankind should be against war, but clearly that is not the way it is. We can be against starting war, which is where we fall short right now – we've recently started one, and only time will tell whether George Bush and Tony Blair genuinely made a mistake over those weapons of mass destruction in Iraq – because they were given the wrong intelligence – or whether they were both warmongers. And now, if the troops withdraw, there could well be slaughter. Now it really *is* choosing between two evils. It's so easy in *Star Trek*, where the prime directive is, You can go anywhere you like, to any planet, but you mustn't interfere. The problem is that we *have* interfered, and now we have to face the consequences.

There's a story in the Old Testament about David sending a man to his death in battle so he could marry the man's wife. David was a special being and most of the time he did exactly what God wanted. Just this once he didn't. So what is the message? I believe that almost everything I read in the Bible has a truth in it for me. I guess the truth in this story is that David must have felt remorse at some point and begged for forgiveness, from which we can conclude that no matter how badly any of us behaves, provided we repent – and remember, God knows if we mean it – everything is forgivable. I find the Bible a fantastic guide. In the end there will be one judge and it's not going to be any of us. We are just given guidelines about how to recognize goodness and love in people; we're not qualified to judge them.

That day while we were singing outside the Palace, the Royal Family were on the balcony behind us, and our task was to lead the crowd. Dame Vera, aged seventy-eight, sang 'We'll Meet Again' and 'The White Cliffs of Dover', and a few more of the songs that she was so famous for singing to the troops; Harry's material was somewhere in between Vera's and mine; and I led the crowd in 'Congratulations'. On the balcony the Royal Family had their song sheets and were singing along with everyone else. It was the last time Dame Vera sang in public, and I felt privileged and humbled to be sharing a platform with such a marvellous and distinguished old lady.

I don't know how they orchestrated it, but the timing was perfect. As we finished our singing, we heard the rumble of distant aircraft and a moment later a fleet of bombers and Spitfires flew over our heads and for ten minutes, maybe more, there was a constant stream of aircraft passing overhead. It was quite heart-stopping, and I felt an incredible sensation of togetherness. Everyone around me was waving their Union Jacks, and I thought, At last, we've got our Union Jack back. It doesn't belong to the far right or anyone else; it's our nation's flag once more.

Afterwards, Bob Holness, Sir Harry, Dame Vera and I were all invited to have tea with the Royal Family. I asked the Queen Mother whether she had enjoyed it and she said, 'Ohhh, we loved it,' and it was quite clear she had – they all had: it was their world, they had lived through it.

'And you probably knew all those songs better than I did,' I said, referring to the wartime favourites.

She said, 'My dear, we've been rehearsing for a month!'

Not all the doors that my fame has opened in the last fifty years have been as gilded as those of Buckingham Palace. Some have been at the opposite end of the spectrum – and, while sitting down to lunch with the Queen thrilled me beyond belief, I wouldn't have missed all those times when I have sat on the bare earth with a young child who's been orphaned by AIDS, or with a grief-stricken mother whose baby has just died of hunger. Sometimes I come home from these trips and I am so disturbed it takes me days to recover. Until you have seen it, smelt it and heard it, you can't begin to know the horror. I come back home, where we want for nothing, and sometimes find workers are striking. Where I have been the people have no work, no food and no life: it's as basic as that. We are so eaten up in the West with the desire to have everything that we can't seem to be grateful for what we do have – and we have so much more to be grateful for than many, many millions of people on the planet.

I don't think anywhere has shocked me as much as Bulgaria. I went there about ten years ago with Tearfund. It is not a Third World country (in 2007 it joined the European Union) and it has a thriving tourist industry; yet behind the gloss there was homelessness on a massive scale. Whole communities of children – orphans and kids who had been abandoned by impoverished parents – were living on the streets, and there were thousands more, the 'lucky' ones, living in shocking conditions in institutions. The winters are bitter in the Balkans, and the street children would congregate around the sewer openings and the vents, where hot air came up from the underground. Yet these kids still had a capacity for fun; we had a good time with them. One little girl had had a baby – she was so young herself – and when she'd been pregnant the other kids made sure she was closest to the warmth, and now they were helping look after the new-born child. On the other hand, the older children made the younger ones beg, and the money was used to buy glue to sniff to kill the cold and the hunger – and of course sometimes it killed them too. Several had been killed by marauding gangs – just one of the many other dangers. Some of the children hid down holes in the ground, and we were told that sometimes the police would pour boiling water down the holes to flush them out. Whether this was true or not I was unable to confirm.

I found the whole experience so shocking that I said to Bill, 'This is ridiculous. We could probably get all of those kids off the street in one fell swoop. Let's give them a big lump of money and sort it out.' It is so hard not to get emotionally involved and always so tempting to pay the money – whatever it takes – to make the horror go away; but I can't single-handedly solve all the problems of the world. There are just too many. What I can do, and *do* do through my Charitable Trust, is give to a wide range of causes, in the hope that my giving will encourage others to give also and thereby help ordinary people to do something extra-ordinary. I used to have a gardener called Mick, and he asked me if I would take my guitar round to the local branch of the British Legion because the village was try-ing to raise a couple of hundred pounds to buy a child a wheelchair. I went round and sang for twenty minutes in a smoky atmos-phere, everyone paid a bit to come in, and they raised their £200. It would have been easier for me to write them a cheque, but that's almost too easy. No single one of us can solve all the problems, but we can all be part of the process.

Whenever I am on tour, people in every venue I go to write to the promoter when they know I am coming and ask whether I will visit some charitable project or another.

In Sri Lanka last year I went to see a woman from England, a nice ordinary woman, who had felt compelled to go there after the tsunami to help build houses for some of the families who'd lost their homes. What she was doing was so marvellous, and I felt as though I did absolutely nothing except breeze in and out and have my photograph taken with her and a whole bunch of children. I always feel I am doing zero, but I'm assured it encourages people like her and makes them feel they are not quite so alone in their struggle; that someone appreciates the sacrifices they are making.

Bulgaria shocked me, but was that any worse than my visit to Uganda, where I knelt in a mud-hut and prayed with a woman who was dying of AIDS? Her husband was a truck driver who had dallied with an infected prostitute across the border, and he had come home and infected his wife. By now they are almost certainly both dead.

We have to get rid of the stigma attached to AIDS. It's just another deadly disease that's killing people, and we need to be free to come alongside them to help alleviate their pain and sorrow. There is a moral issue that shouldn't be lost sight of – if the guy hadn't cheated on his wife he wouldn't have caught AIDS and passed it on to her – but it's not our place to judge. It was encouraging to see churches running AIDS projects in Brazil, because many churches refuse to have anything to do with the problem, and that's something I feel strongly the Church needs to address. We have to become more compassionate and less judgemental.

I have felt very humbled by my experiences with Tearfund and the other charities I've come into contact with over the years. I've met some of the most amazing people, ordinary people who have given up the comforts of home and taken their skills to help in disaster areas. I have known, ever since I was set straight by those nurses in Bangladesh in the early seventies, that my skills were better used on the stage, but it has been very gratifying to have played some tiny part in raising awareness of what's going on around the world and raising funds for relief. And to see, as I did on this year's trip to Brazil, the effect that people's giving has had.

This trip was like none I had ever made before. It wasn't the smells, the flies or the lack of sanitation, all of which had turned my stomach in those early visits. It wasn't even the grinding poverty, the disease, the emaciated animals shackled by the side of the road or the damaged, sickly children that normally make the tears well up, unbidden. I couldn't immediately put my finger on what was different about this year's trip, but for the first couple of days I felt distinctly uneasy. I woke up on the second morning feeling lethargic and depressed. I couldn't understand why.

The previous day had been a good one. We had spent it with Diaconia, a local Christian charity that Tearfund partners – today's equivalent of the Christian working on the ground in the disaster area who George had said must receive the money. We were looking at where that money had been spent. We went to the *favelas*, the shanty towns, where people exist crammed in cheek by jowl, where HIV/AIDS and crime are rife and where many of the children are forced into prostitution as the only means of survival. Families of five, six or more live in one- or two-room hovels, constructed from any kind of scavenged material like driftwood and packing cases. The area is so dangerous, the government had insisted that four armed plain-clothes policemen accompany us. But in the midst of this warren of poverty some kids had started a community radio station; others were belting out percussion music; a couple of women were making multi-coloured candles to sell; and the local talent for graffiti was being harnessed and sold on T-shirts. Diaconia, using money raised by Tearfund, had injected a modicum of hope into this community – and that hope was infectious.

We went to a centre for people living with

HIV/AIDS. Many of them were wasted and wraithlike, but they performed for us the raunchy little play that they take into schools to promote the use of condoms, and we were all helpless with laughter. A mothers' group in another desperately poor hillside community danced for us in bright colourful costumes; again the children played percussion, and we all took to the floor at their insistence and tried to follow the complicated dance steps. Someone produced a guitar and I sang 'Summer Holiday' and a few other oldies. None of them really knew who I was, but they all went mad and started clapping in rhythm and screaming excitedly. I played football with ten-year-olds on a concrete pitch and scored three goals – a fix, if ever I saw one – and everyone cheered and gave me high-fives.

And then I realized what it was that was so different; what it was that was making me feel so uneasy and unnerved. I was enjoying myself. The people in the communities we were meeting were living in desperate situations, but they knew that help was at hand. However small, however subtle the change, they had been given hope – and it showed.

On all my other trips I had been looking at desperate situations where help was yet to come. The mothers cradling dying babies in their arms, babies too weak to brush away the flies, had not yet felt the benefit of Tearfund's help. It had taken me days to recover from those trips. I would go home to my clean and comfortable life, with running water, three square meals and medical help at the press of a button, and feel weighed down by a slough of despond. People often used to ask me if I felt guilty that I had so much when some people had so little. Yes, is the answer, I probably did feel guilt – but guilt is a great spur to action. What I felt more than guilt though was gratitude. I thanked God for everything I had – family, friendships, food and the riches of fame – and I believe that gratitude is an equally potent spur.

Realizing that I was enjoying myself, I began to wonder what I was doing in Brazil. What *good* was I doing? My task had always been to open people's eyes to the horror; I didn't travel to the Third World to have fun. These communities, it seemed, didn't need me.

After our terminally long bus journey and the dubious stop for lunch that day among the flies, when I'd eaten my granola bar, we arrived at a town called Afogados de Inga-zeira, in a semi-arid region, where Diaconia has been tackling rural poverty. Subsistence farmers in this region are so poor that many have to send their older children to the cities in the hope of finding work; but they have barely any education, unemployment is high and most of them end up in the *favelas*, never to return and sometimes never to be heard of again. It seldom rains in this region: the soil is poor, the diet is poor, and the nearest water supply for drinking, washing and irrigation is often up to a mile away, sometimes much further. They have no transport – if a family has a bullock or a donkey they are rich.

One family we visited had lived in this way until eight years ago, when they began receiving help from Diaconia. The charity had shown them how to collect rainwater if and when it fell, and provided the money for a tank to store it in. It had helped the family dam an underground stream, build a well, and install solar panels to pump the water to irrigate their twenty-five acres. It had taught them about beekeeping and shown them how to build a wormery for making compost to improve the soil. After five years these people were self-sufficient and growing enough produce to sell at market, and Diaconia had felt able to stop funding them. They had planted mangoes, papayas, lemons and oranges, guavas and avocados and other fruit trees that seemed untranslatable; they grew vegetables, kept goats, cows, chickens and sheep, and made cheese and honey. They had bought a motorbike to get to market and they were even in the process of building a fine new house.

This family showed us round the farm with such pride, and gave us lunch – a huge spread, and almost all of it home-produced. The women of the family had been cooking all morning with grandchildren running round their feet. Everyone was smiling – even the matriarch of the family, who confided that all the years of hardship had taken their toll on her health and she was dying, but she would die happy knowing that her children and grandchildren would now have a future.

That was the point at which it all became clear. What I was seeing in Brazil in all the smiling, happy faces and the dancing, the singing and the laughter – when by most Western standards what they had was still zero – was George Hoffman's vision. His great saying was, 'One man can't change the world; but you can change the world for one man.' The Third World may seem like a bottomless pit to most of us, devouring hundreds of millions of pounds' worth of aid and growing ever more needy and more demanding; but what this last trip taught me is that there are people out there, maybe miles from anywhere, people whose names and circumstances will never be recorded, but who, thanks to even the smallest coin tossed into a collection tin, have regained some hope, some dignity and a future.

By our standards, the family on whose farm we were given such a feast for lunch – grown, prepared and cooked by three generations – were living on the breadline. They had an outside loo that didn't flush, no hot water and no bathroom, and the entire extended family lived in three rooms, some with curtains in place of walls. Their only means of transport was one small motorcycle and they must have been about ten miles from the nearest town. Yet they were visibly in seventh heaven: they were eating well for the first time in more than twenty-five years of living on the farm; they had water on tap outside the door, chickens in the yard and a television – next to the Bible, I couldn't help noticing – in the living room. One of them told us they were very content, yet we, who have so much, can't seem to find satisfaction.

My mum once said to me, 'It's ridiculous; my few shillings aren't going to help anybody,' and I said, 'Mum, you can't think that way,' and I introduced her to a Tearfund initiative. You could sponsor a child for £10 a month, which would feed, clothe and educate that child. So she did, and on the refrigerator in her house she had a series of photographs, of this little girl and was able to watch her growing up. My mum changed that child's life. If everyone does a little, as much as they can manage, all those little drops in the bucket make it less empty. We must just not let the drops stop coming.

There's a great story about Tearfund, about an engineer from Edgware in London who went out to some part of Africa that hadn't seen rain in years, where the local population was starving. He drilled for water and installed a pump for a well. The whole process took a few weeks, and when he was done he said farewell and went back to base camp. A couple of days later, a runner from the village appeared breathless at the Tearfund base and said, 'The chief has said that he would like you to come back, because we want to know why you did this for us.'

Generations back, that village would have been in no doubt: missionaries would have made sure that they had Bibles before anyone felt a drop of water on their tongue. The likes of Tearfund helped to change all that. The Bible says, 'If someone is hungry, feed them, if they need clothes, clothe them.' After that, goes the argument, they will be strong enough and warm enough to understand, if and when you start speaking about your faith.

Tearfund's philosophy is just this: 'We go into places which have needs. And when we go in we fulfil the needs of the people.' That's it. This was what appealed to me so much about the charity when I first joined George

Hoffman in the late sixties. They didn't just fly in tons of food, they made sure the food or the money or the equipment went directly to the place it was needed; they gave it unconditionally, and they bypassed the corruption that was endemic in so many of these countries. When the runner came from that village to ask why, the engineer went back in and said, 'We did it because our God tells us to love everybody,' and *then* – only then – the Tearfund team talked about Christianity. I don't know if the village became Christian after that; probably some of them would have done; but they would almost certainly have been hearing the story of Christ for the first time.

I can't say that Christianity is the sole provider of truth. It would be arrogant to claim that; there are clearly all sorts of good and truthful things that come from other philosophies. Anyone who genuinely seeks God will find the path. It happens to be the one that works for me and has worked for millions before me. It is very simple – the path is Jesus – and maybe it is the simple logic of Christianity that I, being not very well educated, find so appealing.

It hasn't always been easy being a Christian with my profile. About fifteen years ago some newspaper ran a poll to find out who was the most famous Christian. To my embarrassment, I came number one. I beat

Mother Teresa. The Pope, I think, was number three. I quipped, 'Well, the Pope hasn't had a record in years, has he?' I can joke about it, but the truth is it's been a difficult mantle to wear, and it is certainly not what I intended when I lay on that bed in Finchley all those years ago and invited Jesus into my life. But I have come to believe that God chooses people to fulfil different functions, and for whatever reason, he chose me to do what I do.

I have never been much of a songwriter because I've always been too happy, too much of an optimist, but there are three songs I've written of which I am really proud. I wrote them during Tearfund trips when my emotions were heightened – usually towards feelings of complete helplessness. I think it's difficult for contented souls to create meaningful music. Paul Simon says he's the most neurotic person he knows, which is probably why he is such a great songwriter. My three songs sprang from the horrors I had witnessed. One was 'Bulange Downpour'. We had just come out of a hut in Uganda, where so many people were dying from AIDS. It was swelteringly hot and the heavens suddenly opened. Within forty-five seconds the dusty red earth had turned into what looked like rivers of blood running between the rondavels, and I couldn't get the sight of it out of my mind. Another was called '(There's) No

Power In Pity', which summed up my feelings of desperation and total impotence. The third, and possibly the best, is 'La Gonave', which is the name of a little island off Haiti, one of the most impoverished nations on earth. I wrote it on a little boat, with a big mast but no sail, churning its way towards the island. I could just discern land through the mist. I used the rhythm of the engine as a tempo and wrote the song in my head. As soon as we moored, I rushed off the boat, found my guitar and discovered the song was in E minor. I played it every night until it was firmly in my head. With 'Bulange Downpour' I had no guitar. I was on the plane in the dark, so I found a piece of paper and drew five lines and wrote down the notes in a way I would understand them. When I arrived home I got out my guitar and followed the marks; so, in a way, I wrote my own music.

I have never learnt to read music – or write it – and I can't get excited at this stage of my life about learning anything new. I would love to have been taught the piano but my parents didn't have the financial wherewithal to contemplate it. But I learnt the guitar and I did all right. I would rather be what I am today than the most gifted piano player in the world. I like the life I have made for myself, I like being Cliff Richard, and I like the thought that I have been able to give something back. I still have to pinch myself to make sure it's all true, that this really did happen to me; but if I were to die tomorrow, I don't think I would leave this world regretting much, and I know I would go feeling grateful for all the love, the friendships and the opportunities that have come my way. I also know that I would die happy, knowing that I had not followed the herd, I had not compromised my principles. That I'd lived my life my way.

But if I die before I'm a hundred and don't get that final game of tennis, I shall be having words above.

50 THINGS YOU DIDN'T KNOW ABOUT CLIFF

1. Who is your favourite author? *Wilbur Smith*

2. What is the best/strangest present you've ever been given? *A fan who delivered herself in a box – she just wanted an autograph!*

3. When did you stop believing in Father Christmas? *When we were living in Cheshunt – I was probably about 12!*

4. Where/when did you learn to ride a bicycle? *In India by doing 'wheelies' on my tricycle!*

5. Who taught you to drive? *Tom Tucker*

6. What is your favourite pudding? *Treacle pudding and custard (with skin)*

7. How many scars do you have on your body? *One small one on forehead*

8. What is your favourite flower? *Frangipani*

9. What was the most dangerous thing you've ever done? *Swimming in the sea in Durban – it was full of sharks!*

10. Where did you learn to swim/at what

age? *At Cheshunt Baths, probably when about 12.*

11. **What luxury would you take to a desert island?** *A desalination plant!*

12. **What is your favourite song?** *'I Honestly Love You' (by Olivia Newton-John)*

13. **What is your favourite movie?** *Gladiator*

14. **What do you drink first thing in the morning?** *Coffee*

15. **Do you prefer baths or showers?** *Baths*

16. **What was the most embarrassing thing you've ever done?** *At a function once, when Peter Kay wasn't as well-known as he is now, I was being introduced to a number of people and, as I approached him, I said, 'Who am I being introduced to now?' Peter overheard and was a little affronted that I didn't recognise him!*

17. **What's your favourite animal?** *Dog*

18. **Did you have a favourite toy as a child?** *3-wheeler bike (tricycle)*

19. **What age did you enjoy being best?** *Between 30 and 40.*

20. **Who would you most like to meet?** *Oprah Winfrey (but 'live' on TV!)*

21. **If you knew you were dying tomorrow what would you choose for your last meal?** *Curry and rice*

22. **How do you like your tea?** *Black with honey*

23. What was your favourite holiday? *Any and every time in Portugal – loads of sun and tennis!*

24. What is your first memory? *Seeing monkeys jumping into a pond in India and coming out the other side.*

25. What is your shoe size? *8½*

26. What do you think is your best stroke at tennis? *Forehand ground stroke*

27. Which famous person in history would you most like to have dinner with? *Jesus!*

28. Do you put your left sock or your right sock on first? *Right*

29. What was the first single you ever bought? *'In A Persian Market-place' by Sammy Davis Jr*

30. What do you sing in the shower? *Whatever I'm currently learning for a show or recording*

31. Have you ever driven a double decker bus? *Only in 'Summer Holiday'*

32. What is your favourite drink? *Absolut Ruby Red vodka and tonic water*

33. Do you like Marmite? *Yes, but I prefer Vegemite*

34. What time do you go to bed? *Rarely after midnight, except when I'm on tour*

35. What do you eat for breakfast? *It varies – yoghurt, eggs, non-wheat cereal and soya milk*

36. Have you ever ridden a horse? *Yes*

37. **Have you ever been in a fight?** *Not since school-days!*

38. **What was the last time you cried?** *At Mum's funeral*

39. **What song would get you on the dance floor?** *If I'm at a club, I'll dance to anything*

40. **What music would you like to have played first at your funeral?** *'When I Survey The Wondrous Cross'*

41. **What is the best dish you cook?** *My gravy is second to none*

42. **Who would you like to sing a duet with?** *Olivia – any time*

43. **What is the strangest food you've ever eaten?** *Camel's foot*

44. **What do you do with your old spectacles?** *Often donate them to charity*

45. **Who is your favourite comedian?** *Tony Hancock*

46. **What makes you laugh?** *A good joke*

47. **Who is your favourite film star or actor?** *Russell Crowe, Meryl Streep*

48. **What sportsman or woman do you most admire?** *André Agassi*

49. **Do you use a brush or comb on your hair?** *Brush*

50. **What would your rap artist name be?** *C-rap!*

51. **What would be the 51st question you would ask yourself?** *When will you retire? (Answer: Mind your own business)*

50 YEARS – HOW THEY THINK HE DID IT

Cliff has got to be the most consistent hit-maker in the history of the British charts; he has never repeated himself or become slapdash. He is still that smouldering firework we want to see ignite again.
Brian May (Reproduced with permission from Brian May Soapbox at www.brian-may.com)

He is very driven, motivated. A perfectionist – he will give 100 per cent and expects the same. He is so energetic, so positive and he cares about the end result – he cares about what he delivers – about the concerts – and that's why he has been so successful.
Keith Hayman, current musical director and keyboards player, worked with Cliff since the mid-nineties

He has survived all these years because he is bloody good. Good voice – he puts a song over well – and he does look good. He hasn't got any kids or grandchildren and doesn't do the garb-

age on a Thursday morning – he looks after himself and keeps himself fit. He looks in good shape.
Brian Bennett, The Shadows' drummer

How has he endured so long? Tim Rice put his finger on part of it when he said the amazing thing about Cliff is that he has managed to remain interested in his own career. Many people when they have had a number of hit records, and especially when they have earned a significant amount of money, think they have done it and they try less hard Perhaps they are no longer consumed by ambition – perhaps they think they have achieved their goal – but Cliff has treated every release as if it were the first one. He has tried to make a good record and do a good promotion job to get it to the top. He has never lost interest and even now is still trying to extend his list of achievements.
Paul Gambaccini

He is always in what's happening music and for me that is the key ingredient for his continued success.
Elton John

Cliff has survived and become an artist who cuts across all boundaries making great pop records.
Pete Townshend, The Who

He's ambitious to a fault. When he's on stage he

*gives 150 per cent to entertaining his audience.
He puts his heart and soul into everything he
does. If an album doesn't do well, other bands I
work with will say, 'What's the point in putting
out another one?' Cliff goes, 'How can I make
that better?' That's what you want. He has an
uphill struggle with radio stations banning his
music and he's been angry about it for years, but
he doesn't give up. That explains why he's still
here. He's like a dog with a bone.*
Peter Howarth, current backing vocalist,
worked with Cliff since 1987

*I always tend to view him in the same context as
myself in a way. The longer you cling to the
wreckage the better – the British have always
confused longevity with merit and if you can
just hang on for long enough, irrespective of
talent, you become impervious to criticism or
beyond comment!*

  *But seriously, you go to a Cliff Richard concert
and an hour after it's finished, he is still out
there signing autographs. That's the essence of
his success: he doesn't forget his fan base. He has
utter dedication. He's also a very good performer, a really good singer and everybody who
knows him likes him. He's been very clever. He's
moved with each passing trend but he's always
been clean living and he's tapped into a middle-
class respectability that people who don't want
the world to change adhere to.*
Terry Wogan

He is one of the great British vocalists and as an interpreter of songs he's right up there. He endures so well because he doesn't tend to make enemies. He is very, very likeable and goes out of his way to be kind, polite, charming and grateful to the people who work with him – as his promoter, we always get more out of him than we expect to. He doesn't mind hard work and he is a great professional.
Steve Davis, EMI records

One of the reasons Cliff's still here is he has maintained an interest in his own career. Many people get to the top and think, now what? He hasn't done that. He has very few external distractions. But the main reason for his success over all these years is that he's very good at his job. He's very talented, very polite, very well-behaved and very likeable – and that counts for a lot in this business. Also, he puts himself out for people as much as he dedicates himself to his career.
Sir Tim Rice

Cliff Richard is an unusual and endangered species – there is only one of them left on this planet that I know of. Perennially handsome, this rare singer never seems to age and even his voice gets better with time! The warmth in his singing and the joy that he exudes touches everyone.

The reason why Cliff is still as popular as he has ever been, or maybe even more so, is because he is so talented and timeless – likeable and genuine – with great songs.
Olivia Newton-John

The publishers hope that this book has given you enjoyable reading. Large Print Books are especially designed to be as easy to see and hold as possible. If you wish a complete list of our books please ask at your local library or write directly to:

Magna Large Print Books
Magna House, Long Preston,
Skipton, North Yorkshire.
BD23 4ND